COLONIALISM AND RESISTANCE

Part of the Transition in Northeastern India series, this volume critically explores how Northeast India, especially Manipuri society, responded to colonial rule. It studies the interplay between colonialism and resistance to provide an alternative understanding of colonialism on the one hand and society and state formation on the other. Challenging dominant histories of the area, the chapters provide significant insights into understanding colonialism and its multiple effects on economy, polity, culture, and faith systems. It examines hitherto untouched areas in the study of Northeast India and discusses how social movements are augmented, constituted, or sustained.

This book will be of great interest to researchers and scholars of modern history, sociology, and social anthropology, particularly those concerned with Northeast India.

Arambam Noni is Assistant Professor in the Department of Political Science, Moirang College, Manipur, India, and Executive Editor of *Alternative Perspectives*.

Kangujam Sanatomba is a Post-Doctoral Fellow with the Indian Council of Social Science Research (ICSSR), New Delhi, and Research Associate at the Centre for South East Asian Studies, Manipur University, India.

TRANSITION IN NORTHEASTERN INDIA
Series Editor: Sumi Krishna,
Independent Scholar, Bangalore

The uniquely diverse landscapes, societies and cultures of northeastern India, forged through complex bio-geographic and socio-political forces, are now facing rapid transition. This series focuses on the processes and practices that have shaped, and are shaping, the peoples' identities, outlook, institutions and economy. Eschewing the homogenising term 'North East', which was imposed on the region in a particular political context half a century ago, the series title refers to the 'northeastern' region to more accurately reflect its heterogeneity.

Seeking to explore how the 'mainstream' and the 'margins' impact each other, the series will foreground both historical and contemporary research on the region including the Eastern Himalaya, the adjoining hills and valleys, the states of Arunachal Pradesh, Assam, Manipur, Meghalaya, Mizoram, Nagaland, Sikkim and Tripura. It will publish original, reflective studies that draw upon different disciplines and approaches, and combine empirical and theoretical insights to make scholarship accessible for general readers and to help deepen the understanding of academics, policy-makers and practitioners.

Also in this series

EDUCATION AND SOCIETY IN A CHANGING MIZORAM
The practice of pedagogy
Lakshmi Bhatia
978–0–415–58920–8

BECOMING A BORDERLAND
The politics of space and identity in colonial northeastern india
Sanghamitra Misra
HB 978–0–415–61253–1
PB 978–1–138–84745–3

UNFOLDING CRISIS IN ASSAM'S TEA PLANTATIONS
Employment and occupational mobility
Deepak K. Mishra, Vandana Upadhyay and Atul Sarma
978–0–415–52308–0

AGRICULTURE AND A CHANGING ENVIRONMENT IN NORTHEASTERN INDIA
Edited by Sumi Krishna
978–0–415–63289–8

CONFLICT AND RECONCILIATION
The politics of ethnicity in assam
Uddipana Goswami
978–0–415–71113–5

NORTHEASTERN INDIA AND ITS BORDERS
Negotiating security and development
Rakhee Bhattacharya
978–1–13–879533–4

EVANGELISING THE NATION
Religion and the formation of naga political identity
John Thomas
978–1–138–92203–7

COLONIALISM AND RESISTANCE

Society and state in Manipur

Edited by Arambam Noni and Kangujam Sanatomba

NEW DELHI LONDON NEW YORK

First published 2016
by Routledge
2 Park Square, Milton Park, Abingdon, Oxon OX14 4RN

and by Routledge
711 Third Avenue, New York, NY 10017

Routledge is an imprint of the Taylor & Francis Group, an informa business

© 2016 Centre for Alternative Discourse, Manipur (CADM), a division of Research Foundation

The right of Arambam Noni and Kangujam Sanatomba to be identified as the authors of the editorial material, and of the authors for their individual chapters, has been asserted in accordance with sections 77 and 78 of the Copyright, Designs and Patents Act 1988.

All rights reserved. No part of this book may be reprinted or reproduced or utilised in any form or by any electronic, mechanical, or other means, now known or hereafter invented, including photocopying and recording, or in any information storage or retrieval system, without permission in writing from the publishers.

Trademark notice: Product or corporate names may be trademarks or registered trademarks, and are used only for identification and explanation without intent to infringe.

British Library Cataloguing in Publication Data
A catalogue record for this book is available from the British Library

Library of Congress Cataloging-in-Publication Data
A catalog record has been requested for this book

ISBN: 978-1-138-79553-2 (hbk)
ISBN: 978-1-315-63831-7 (ebk)

Typeset in Bembo
by Apex CoVantage, LLC

CONTENTS

Acknowledgements	ix
List of abbreviations	xi
Notes on contributors	xiii

Introduction	**1**

PART I
Framework, administration, and democratisation

1 **Cast of colonialism: constructing the peculiar
North East India** — 15
ARAMBAM NONI

2 **Colonial administration, knowledge and intervention:
colonial project of ethnicisation in Manipur** — 28
HOMEN THANGJAM

3 **Revisiting the Kuki Rebellion and *Nupi Lan*** — 42
LISHAM HENTHOIBA

4 **Colonialism and movement for democracy in Manipur** — 56
KONTHOUJAM INDRAKUMAR

v

CONTENTS

PART II
Literature, popular culture, and religion

5 Religious revivalism and colonial rule: origin
   of the Sanamahi Movement   75
   KHURAIJAM BIJOYKUMAR SINGH

6 Politics, society and literature in modern Manipur   91
   ARAMBAM NONI

7 Desire, disgrace and colonialism: a reading of
   Bor Saheb Ongbi Sanatombi   104
   RAJKUMARI SMEJITA

8 Jesters of popular genres as agents of resistance
   through reflexivity   115
   KSH. IMOKANTA SINGH

PART III
Imperial strategies and distinct political histories

9 Situating Manipur in the geopolitics of
   imperial powers   133
   LAISHRAM CHURCHIL

10 Consolidation of British 'indirect rule' in Manipur   147
   NAOREM MALEMSANBA MEETEI

11 Interrogating into the political status of Manipur   159
   KANGUJAM SANATOMBA

12 Christian missionaries and colonialism in the hills
   of Manipur   181
   LIANBOI VAIPHEI

CONTENTS

PART IV
Post-Empire Manipur, organisational politics, and frontier

13 **Organisational politics in 20th-century Manipur: trajectories and footprints**   193
ARAMBAM NONI

14 **Polemics of the Manipur Merger Agreement, 1949**   206
KANGUJAM SANATOMBA

15 **Centrality of body politics in Thokachanba's script and cultural revivalism in Manipur**   218
NAOREM MALEMSANBA MEETEI

16 **Recasting space: politics of frontier-making**   238
THINGNAM SANJEEV

Glossary   249
Index   255

ACKNOWLEDGEMENTS

Writing an acknowledgement for the book would have been irrelevant if there was no social collective involvement. This book is a product of the team work of the members and researchers who are deeply involved with activities at the Centre for Alternative Discourse, Manipur (CADM). The ever-ready attitude of the members to extend all kinds of help and trenchant comments made the book's birth plausible. It would not be wrong to say that the idea of the book itself is a product of our collective engagements with the what and why of things, be it historiography, knowledge, politics, economy, culture, faith systems and colonialism and resistance. The debating culture of CADM has enormously enriched the focus of the book. The stiff challenge to knit together a variety of articles from different contributors into a volume was not an easy task. The realisation of this work has been made possible with the academic inputs provided by the members of the centre.

The book would have been merely imaginary without the great support and commitment of the article contributors who hail from different universities in India. We thank all the well-wishers who took pains to go through the manuscript, which led to the improvement of the book. Hidam Praem deserves special mention for going through the manuscript and identifying moot points in the book. We also thank Chongtham Gunnamani for his passionate conceptual feedback, and Thingnam Sanjeev for providing technical inputs and keeping the authors in touch with the publisher particularly in the initial times. The much-needed teamwork to improve the manuscript was provided by well-wishers and great friends like Naorem Homeshwor, eche Benimala, Laishram Churchil, Dr Konthoujam Indrakumar, Rajkumari Smejita, Dr Hanjabam Isworchandra, Laishram Malem Mangal, Krishnachandra, Moirangthem Prakash, Lisham Henthoiba, Laishram Nandalal, P. Rebecca, Hanjabam Gyanendro and Pukhrambam Rakesh.

ACKNOWLEDGEMENTS

We also thank Dr Manindra N. Thakur, Associate Professor, Centre for Political Studies, Jawaharlal Nehru University, New Delhi, for his interest in the book. Regular exchanges of ideas and debates with the faculty members at Moirang College deserve a special mention. We thank Dr K. Anand, Dr Anil K Sharma, Dr Oinam Gobin and Dr Naorem Kishorchand for keeping the editors alert and active. We thank R.K. Reresana for volunteering to help us in collecting the photographs for the book.

Last but not the least, we appreciate the exemplary support and encouragement received from Sumi Krishna, the series editor. The support and encouragement that we received from the officials of Routledge kept us all focused to complete the book.

Arambam Noni
Kangujam Sanatomba

ABBREVIATIONS

AFSPA	The Armed Forces (Special Powers) Act, 1958
CMC	Constitution Making Committee
INC	Indian National Congress
GoI	Government of India
KNA	Kuki National Assembly
LEP	Look East Policy
MKS	Manipur Krishak Sabha
MPS	Manipur Praja Sangha
MSC	Manipur State Congress
MSCA	Manipur State Constitution Act, 1947
MSD	Manipur State Durbar
NEIGM	North East India General Mission
NHMM	Nikhil Hindu Manipuri Mahasabha
NIPFP	National Institute of Public Finance and Policy
NMM	Nikhil Manipuri Mahasabha
PMSD	President of the Manipur State Durbar
PSP	Praja Shanti Party
NEIGM	Northeast India General Mission
RPF	Revolutionary People's Front
UNLF	United National Liberation Front

CONTRIBUTORS

Arambam Noni is an assistant professor at the Department of Political Science, Moirang College, Manipur. He is a participant observer and commentator on contemporary social and political movements. He has published a number of articles in edited books and journals. Formerly he has worked and was associated with Developing Countries Research Centre, University of Delhi, Vidyajyoti College of Theology, Delhi, and G. B. Pant Institute for Social Sciences, Allahabad. Currently, he is the executive editor of *Alternative Perspectives*, a quarterly journal.

Homen Thangjam is an assistant professor at the Department of Political Science, MB College, Manipur. He has edited and co-authored many books and published several articles in academic journals. His co-authored books include *Location, Space & Development* and *Quest for Development in Manipur: Continuity, Constraint and Contradictions.*

Kangujam Sanatomba is a post-doctoral fellow with the Indian Council of Social Science Research (ICSSR) New Delhi. He received his PhD in political science from Manipur University. He has written a working paper titled 'Conflict Transformation in Manipur: The Four-Point Proposal for Plebiscite' under the sponsorship of Centre for Social Development (CSD), Imphal. Besides presenting papers at various National Seminars, he has also contributed articles in three edited books. Dr Kangujam is a regular contributor to *The Sangai Express*, a leading English daily based in Imphal. Currently he is Research Associate at the Centre for South East Asian Studies, Manipur University.

Khuraijam Bijoykumar Singh was formerly an assistant professor at the North East Institute of Education, NCERT, Shillong. He received his doctoral degree from the Centre for Study of Social Systems, Jawaharlal Nehru University, Delhi. His doctoral thesis is titled 'Sanamahi

CONTRIBUTORS

Movement amongst the Meiteis in Manipur'. Currently he is assistant professor at the North East India Study Programme, Jawaharlal Nehru University, New Delhi.

Konthoujam Indrakumar is an assistant professor at the Department of Political Science, GP Women's College, Imphal. Indrakumar received his PhD from Manipur University. He has co-authored an edited book titled *Location, Space & Development*. He is the editor of *Alternative Perspectives*, a quarterly journal. The author is currently working on development and security issues in India and South East Asia.

Ksh. Imokanta Singh received his doctoral degree from the Centre for Study of Social Systems, Jawaharlal Nehru University, Delhi. His doctoral thesis is titled 'The Social Dynamism of Shumang Lila of Manipur: A Sociological Analysis of Some of Its Contemporary Manifestations'. He is member of Manipur Finance Service and is presently special officer at the Directorate of MIS, Government of Manipur.

Laishram Churchil is a journalist by profession. He takes keen interest on the issues of environment, military history and armed conflict. He is the director of the Centre for Alternative Discourse Manipur. He is a co-author of the forthcoming book *Identity and Culture*.

Lianboi Vaiphei teaches political science in Indraprastha College for Women, Delhi University. She has written a great number of articles on various issues from Christianity to identity politics among ethnicity in Northeast India to Indian Diaspora in Canada. Her articles have been published in many edited books and journals such as Ajay Dubey (ed), *Indian Diaspora Contributions to Their New Home, Tribes in Today's India: Challenges and Prospects,* and Sharma, Neeta; Borkataki, Arindam (eds) *Women Issues and Perspectives and Counter Insurgency and Issues of Human Rights.* She has also authored a book on politics in Northeast India as a study curriculum for the postgraduate political science students of Tripura University, India.

Lisham Henthoiba is a doctoral scholar at the Department of Political Science, Manipur University. He is currently working on popular movement in Northeast India for his doctoral thesis. He is co-authoring a forthcoming book titled. Currently, Henthoiba is an associate editor of *Alternative Perspectives*.

xiv

CONTRIBUTORS

Naorem Malemsanba Meetei is an assistant professor, History Department, Tamenglong College, Manipur. He earlier taught history in SGND Khalsa College, University of Delhi, Delhi. He specialises in colonial historiography.

Rajkumari Smejita is assistant professor, Department of English, Gargi College, University of Delhi. Her areas of interest include issues of history and violence in contemporary fiction. Currently, she is an associate editor of *Alternative Perspectives*.

Thingnam Sanjeev is an assistant archivist at the National Archives of India, Ministry of Culture, New Delhi. He received his PhD on military history at the Jamia Milia Islamia University, Delhi.

INTRODUCTION

To speak of decolonisation as passé in the contemporary world would mean something like talking about the infamous thesis of Francis Fukuyama's the 'end of history'. This collection of chapters seeks to delve into some contemporary questions about colonialism and its continuing implications. A fresh look into an otherwise old issue can perhaps offer significant insights in understanding the forms and multiple effects of colonialism in the present. The book is about possible ways of re-engaging the questions of colonialism and resistance in North East India, more particularly with reference to the events in and references to Manipur. Colonialism, here, refers to the British colonialism and subsequent socio-political developments in North East India. The chapters in this volume attempt to explore colonialism with ample references to various important sites of the lived world such as economy, polity, culture, religion, literature, etc. The compilation is expected to contribute to and fill in the critical shortages in existing studies and narrations on colonialism in North East India by not entirely restricting it to a British colonial timeline but by extending beyond it, mainly through practical and theoretical grounding.

One of the primary areas of the study is to reveal how colonialism came to array in an intertwined structure of capitalist market expansionism and its associated cultural logic to overlay the imperial fulfilment over the region under study. Colonialism in this manner produced administrative arrangements and knowledge that was imposed upon to appear either 'modern' or 'superior'. Nonetheless, the colonial construction of the colonised hardly made a substantial stoppage to the ways in which indigenous societies were inherently finding their own ways of resisting the oppressions. Put simply, the chapters in the book try mainly to explore how resistances to colonialism do not come as a bare act of copying and extension of the modular forms of what has already happened in the West. Most of the chapters give ample insights into how the indigenous

INTRODUCTION

subjects themselves evolved their own ways of coping with colonialism. This is where the second aspect of the book is located, which studies the interplay between colonialism and resistance. An attempt to historicise this relation may help one to understand the nature of the political project of re-narration of the autonomy of the colonised in the form of resurrection as well as internalisation of cultural and administrative elements that came along with colonialism. While certain values and practices under colonialism, it may be noted, were absorbed, many others were simultaneously rejected in the process of resistance. Equally revealing is the fact that resistance was the massive action of contesting the colonial state or power. And yet, inability to reject the colonial power in totality also led to a lingering compliance to the project of colonialism, which served as the site of colonial validation of its power and rule. For instance, colonisation began to have deeper impacts on the faith systems, language and culture.

The notoriety of a colonial operation is such that it entails converting the specific regions into a strategic frontier while continuously advancing the economic, territorial and cultural control at the same time. Colonialism comes both as a mixed package of appropriation and negation of what is 'local' or 'indigenous'. The appropriation and negation is done through a crafty induction of hefty civilisational argumentation ensuring hegemony over the subjects. Recent scholarship on this aspect of colonialism have already argued that we may see colonialism not only through the ways in which it was associated with military campaigns, occupation of a territory and usurpation of political power, but also how colonial power was constituted through incorporation of indigenous culture and knowledge as legitimising sites of colonial rule. Resistance to colonial rule may be regarded as efforts by the colonised to dismantle and reclaim what had been lost to colonialism. Resistance points to a material critique of colonial rule and its allied structures that directly or indirectly strengthen oppressions.

Colonial and anti-colonial politics can be further discussed through the events that unfolded in Manipur with the expansion of British rule. One can analyse the nature of various forms of resistance to colonialism immediately after Manipur was defeated by the British in the Anglo-Manipuri War of 1891. Although the British pursued an indirect rule in Manipur giving the status of suzerainty, the then king was subservient to colonial designs with ever increasing administrative rearrangements that gradually segmented the communities into habitational untouchables in the long run. The resistance movements in Manipur, during the period from the early part to the second half of the 20th century, may be discussed by taking into account the various forms that began to question the combined

INTRODUCTION

oppression under feudal social stratification and colonialism. During the period, resistance to the king and other high-ranking officials was also displayed in theatrical performances like the famous parody known as Kabul Leela. Besides, the period also revealed efforts to resist colonial rule by attempting to recover traditional 'heritage' and identity through publication of journals, newspapers and literature, especially through poetry and novels. In the political sphere, resistance was visible in the form of anti-monarchy movements and quest for socialistic politico-economic and cultural arrangements. The movement that led to a peasant revolution in the region under the leadership of Hijam Irabot is a case in point.

Underscoring the history of colonialism, the book deals with some of the important events and developments associated with British rule in Manipur. The arrival of the British in the region did not immediately alter the political status of Manipur. In the initial phases, the relationship between the British and Manipur was strategic in nature, characterised by mutual engagement against a common enemy and support for each other. However, the relationship on an equal footing and co-operation gradually transformed into one in which the colonial British manipulated the relationship for their own gain. The geo-strategic location of Manipur was recognised by the British right from the beginning of Anglo-Manipuri relations in the 18th century. For example, the British needed help from the king of Manipur to counter the expansion of resource-rich Burma, which was actually a part of the larger struggle for the division of the world's markets among the European capitalist powers. The geo-strategic location of the North East in the larger imperial interest in South and South East Asia had become an integral part of colonial expansion and a market for the ever-increasing demand for raw materials, cheap labour and military recruitments. Such an imagery of colonial North East India is being generally perceived to be operational till date in experiential discourses of resistances, which have largely influenced the title of the compilation. Discussions on the duping of Manipur and Nagaland into becoming a part of India, only to be followed by strong armed struggles, reflect the thematic continuity, interplay and significance of colonialism and resistance.

The end of British colonial rule in Manipur presented newer forms of adapting to institutional arrangements that is either dominant or coercively integrationist. These conditions had framed crucial shifts in the ways in which the economic and political capacity of the people produced a sense of resilience and consolidation of nationality questions. The question of nationalities in the North East abruptly became both a remarkable construct and a reality – a construct because there was a

INTRODUCTION

dominion of this historiography of nationalism that was on popular circulation, whereas the real question of nationality based on class issues was oppressively relegated to the margins of possibility. The chapters elaborately touch upon three important political junctures that occasioned in quick succession: first is the departure of British rule from Manipur; second is the newly acquired status of being a politically independent state with a constitution of its own; and the third juncture is a swift change from that of an independent kingdom state to the experience of being forcefully merged with India in 1949. The project of making India in the case of the North East had been rather unnatural and somewhat dubious. Present-day political movements, economy questions and ethnicity hover around the causal significance of the third juncture. Analysis of the third juncture can lead to capturing the intricate roots and nuances of the nationalist revolutionary movements and locate the historicity of the modern state in North East India. Chapters in the compendium engage with issues specific to Manipur using a broad theoretical framework, yet quite substantially explicating the trends in North East India. One of the important contributions of the chapters is their attempt to locate the imageries of people and the ways in which the imagery converges into an experiential becoming which gets shaped through the oppressive lived worlds. The three constitutive political moments mentioned earlier, albeit of the contemporary history of Manipur, cannot be separated from one another despite the inherent and critical limitations. One can understand the politics of why we cannot completely deny the impossibility of separating the three most significant junctures into distinct possible locations with recognisable character of their own. In the reckoning of the history and context of the three constitutive political junctures, the theme of the chapters in this volume may have sometimes switched to the colonial period too. However, it does not entirely elude the current theme that seeks to attend to the intrinsic reality of territoriality, ethnicity and resistance.

The book is a compendium of 16 chapters that are thematically arranged under four units, each unit consisting of four chapters. The units are rendered with a view to club together the chapters that fall under similar subject matter, yet distinctively contribute towards enriching the overall concern of the compendium. The units are organised under the following themes:

I. Colonial Framework, Administration and Democratic Movements
II. Literature, Popular Culture and Religion
III. Imperial Strategies and Distinct Political Histories
IV. Post-Suzerainty Manipur: Issues and Trajectories

4

INTRODUCTION

The units thematically deal with the founding parameters of colonialism while contextually discussing the emergence of today's North East India. The chapters in the first unit, titled 'Framework, administration and democratic', probe into how multiple colonial apparatuses cast deeper control over economy and politics. The control is further consolidated through the capillaries of imperial imposition of civilisational claims and also equally through the invention of new values and belief systems. The wholesome design of colonisation involved ethnicisation of the subjects under control, which later came to be popularised as the proverbial imperial divide and rule. Seeding the communal electoral arrangement in India and subsequent separate hill – valley administrative set-up in Manipur by the British are significant cases in point. Quite substantially, engaging with the issues of colonialism and its apparatuses, the chapters in the first unit interrogate the complex epistemic status of the subject and coloniser, which, ultimately, is about relations of actual contestation and resistance movements. Differing from the school of thought that emphasises colonialism determinism of the imageries and identities of the colonised, the chapter by Arambam Noni argues that colonialism is waged as a higher ideological product with an incessant use of spiritual and religious sources as a pre-emptive negation of resistance (Chapter 1). The process of colonialisation can be considered to have acquired a higher stage when it appropriates and reworks the existing bodies of knowledge and align with several classes to a higher efficacy of imperial control. The chapter by Homen Thangjam, 'Colonial administration, knowledge and intervention: colonial project of ethnicisation in Manipur' (Chapter 2), argues that politics of control and subjugation, and defining the people with a neat boundary, became an actual instrument to pre-empt and derail any possible consolidation and tangible consciousness amongst the indigenous people that could overthrow British rule. Thangjam argues how, consequent upon such an approach, there began an anthropological categorisation of the people that perfectly fitted in a cartographic landscaping and, above all, a humanist and civilisational defence of colonialism itself. The chapter shows how imperial control employed instruments of appropriation and negation of local knowledge as far as colonial ethnicisation was concerned. 'Revisiting the Kuki rebellion and *Nupi Lan*' (Chapter 3) by Lisham Henthoiba discusses the Kuki Rebellion of 1917 and the *Nupi Lan* (women's war) of 1939, as two significant referral points for analysing the resisting site of the colonised. Instead of simplifying resistance movements of the colonised as an outcome of the policies of the colonial rule, the chapter explores the internal capacity of the colonised to conceive and deal with the

5

INTRODUCTION

externality of power that is alien to them which Henthoiba calls questioning consciousness ability. The resistances of 1917 and 1939 are the two events in the modern history of Manipur that can be read as having acquired a long-term conjecture of anti-colonial articulation among the communities and masses of Manipur. Supplementing well the theme initiated by Henthoiba, the chapter titled 'Colonialism and movement for democracy in Manipur' (Chapter 4) by Konthoujam Indrakumar studies the socio-political history of Manipur having undergone British colonisation. The chapter locates the democratic movement in Manipur within the broader socio-economic background beginning from the late 19th century to the 1940s, and shows how British colonialism was simultaneously facing a site of resistance. A combined interplay of feudalism and colonialism had begun to taste of gradual and abrupt contestation, which ultimately resulted in the emergence of organised political movements.

The chapters in the first unit provide a theoretical contour and framework to move beyond monolithic representations of the anti-colonial movement as mere incidences of the past. They abundantly use archival, colonial reports and writings, and a range of primary sources to understand and interrogate the imperial apparatuses and their designs. One crucial aspect of the chapters is their thoroughness in locating the historicity of the resistance and movements, which provide an interesting clue to the presentness of the past, particularly of Manipur and the North East in general.

The second unit, titled 'Literature, popular culture and religion', also consists of four chapters that deal with revivalist movements, literature and popular culture. The unit examines how during colonial rule the common people of Manipur were subjected to the dual regime of the British and indigenous Suzerain. The dual authority produced harsh taxation regimes that hardly left out any sphere of political economy which became a growing arena of tussle. As a result of this stringent control, educational and literary products of the period were restricted. The first two chapters deal with the issues of religious revivalism and modern literary genre in Manipur. The third chapter constitutes a very significant part for it picks up a particular text to explore the constitution of the subject and territory under the conditions of colonial rule as a site of colonial objectification. The fourth chapter in the unit highlights how actual resistance was coming from the jesters of the popular theatrical works, which are today known as the Shumang Lila.

In brief, the chapter by Khuraijam Bijoy (Chapter 5) studies the Sanamahi Movement (a religious movement) not only as a religious revivalist movement but also as a form of resistance directed against the combined forces of

6

INTRODUCTION

colonialism and feudalism. In the author's argumentation, understanding Sanamahi revivalism is essential in order to understand the establishment of the modern worldviews and the energy of the modern world. This is a proposition that appears very intricate if one refers to the modern scientific explications, for religious revivalist movements have inherent characteristics of the dominant and its belief systems. The chapter is expected to ignite interesting debates. The chapter by Arambam Noni titled 'Politics, society and literature in modern Manipur' (Chapter 6) discusses the history of modern Manipuri literature under the imperial socio-political milieu of British imperialism. An important observation of the author is that the early 20th-century literary works in Manipur indirectly dealt with the then-existing oppressive social order and political systems. The author argues that the pioneering literary generations of the 20th century were more or less compelled to work within a limited norm stipulated by the Empire and monarchy, which he describes as the 'official opening' of literary thinking. Nevertheless, the chapter traces the gradual evolution of radical literature in Manipur. The chapter by Rajkumari Smejita, 'Desire, disgrace and colonialism: a reading of Bor Saheb Ongbi Sanatombi' (Chapter 7), is located within the perspective of recent post-colonial theorising on the site, object of desire, sexuality and colonial power and knowledge. Her chapter (a) explores how the notions of desire and disgrace are circulated in M. K. Binodini's novel Bor Saheb Ongbi Sanatombi; (b) locates the love affair between a 'White' colonial officer and the protagonist within the colonial fantasies, which is imbued with a desire for the 'native' and 'exotic' beauties; and (c) explores the constitution of the body (Sanatombi's) and territory (Manipur, in this context) under the conditions of colonial rule as the site and object of colonial desire. Quite aptly addressing the theme of the book, the chapter studies how the categories are socially organised within the notion of the colonised otherness and colonial racialisation. In 'Jesters of popular genres as agents of resistance through reflexivity' (Chaper 8), Kshetrimayum Imokanta Singh discerns the various courses of the performing art forms in colonised Manipur. The chapter considers these popular genres of theatrical spaces as a mouthpiece to voice the dissension of the powerless majority against the powerful minority. Such expression of resistance, both passive and active, was comparatively more open in popular genres than in a proscenium theatre, commonly categorised as 'elite theatre', because the latter was more meticulously screened and attended by the ruling minority. So, the popular genres were cloistered to the peripheries of the power structures.

Each unit of the book is designed to build up to engage with a specific theme, yet has a broader intersection with the issues across all units. The

INTRODUCTION

third unit, titled 'Imperial strategies and distinct political histories', consists of four chapters with a thematic focus on geopolitics and colonialism while exploring the intricate blending of geographical factors, imperial strategy (missionary politics), statecraft and state-making processes. The first chapter in the unit by Laishram Churchil, titled 'Situating Manipur in the geopolitics of imperial powers' (Chapter 9), argues how knowledge about certain areas or regions can foreground necessities and ground for control. It tells us how maps, charts, surveys, reports and ethnographies are significant instruments for executing power and control. The author refers to the political histories of both South East Asia and the Northeastern region of present-day India to illustrate regions that were trapped into the geopolitical ruptures of contemporary world politics. The chapter is illustrative as it gives a theoretical attempt to explicate the process of how the Northeastern region acted as an interface among the imperial quest for conquest. The author cites the case of Manipur, which, although never a geopolitical player by itself, occupied a crucial site in the geopolitics of the colonial powers such as Japan and Great Britain. The Battle of Imphal, which formed one of the bloodiest episodes in the history of World War II, is analysed to augment his point and illustrate the geostrategic significance of the region.

Naorem Malemsanba Meetei's 'Consolidation of British "indirect rule" in Manipur' (Chapter 10) examines the events and processes that went into the formation of the 'modern' princely state of Manipur. While referring to the events and trajectories that developed during the period between the signing of the Anglo-Manipuri Mutual Defence Treaty in 1762 and the departure of the British in 1947, the chapter studies the treaties and agreements that went on to make the British Empire. The chapter argues that the actual beginning of British occupation goes back to the Treaty of Yandaboo, 1826. The treaty was responsible for not only driving out the Burmese from the soil of Manipur but also was the instance when the British began to interfere and manipulate political proceedings in Manipur, which ultimately led to Manipur becoming a 'protected or dependent state'. The chapter problematises how the British paramount developed the notion of 'indirect rule' on the one hand, while creating the unclear domain of 'independence' on the other hand.

'Interrogating into the political status of Manipur' (Chapter 11) by Kangujam Sanatomba critically examines the political status of Manipur from 1762 to 1947, adopting a politico-legal approach. Refuting the conception that Manipur was not a truly independent state in 1947 by virtue of signing the Standstill Agreement and the Instrument of Accession signed on 11 August 1947, the author argues that Manipur sustained its

INTRODUCTION

independent sovereign status notwithstanding the execution of the Instrument and the Agreement. To explicate his thesis, he brings to attention the necessity of moving beyond the fading days of British imperialism and analysing the nature of relationship between Manipur and the British in the formative years and consequent developments which ultimately led to Manipur losing its sovereign status. The chapter explores the legalities of the Instrument of Accession in order to examine the nature of Manipur's political status towards the impending departure of the British Empire. To substantiate his argument, the author analyses various treaties, acts, policies, administrative arrangements, etc. The chapter provides an insightful reading into one of the highly complex issues of state-making and unmaking in India.

The fourth chapter titled 'Christian missionaries and colonialism in the hills of Manipur' (Chapter 12) by Lianboi Vaiphei discusses the experiences of the hill communities in Manipur particularly in the light of conversions to Christianity. Vaiphei's central argument is that the hill population could differentiate between the 'political' mission of colonial power and the evangelistic efforts of the Christian missionaries. While the former was treated with distrust and hostility, the latter found a hospitable place among the hill people. Thus, contrary to popular perceptions that Christianisation would make the natives more hospitable and susceptible to colonial rule, the opposite happened as evidenced by the Kuki Rebellion of 1917 against the introduction of taxation system in the hills. The chapter believes that Christian missionaries were indeed agents of colonial powers and worked within the ambit of imperial interests. Not only did the missionaries invoke spiritual and religious elements to deal with the hill people of Manipur, but they also branded them as 'savage' and 'barbaric'. Interestingly, the possible realms of contestations and resistance to the colonial project were weakened with the introduction of modern education and schemes. The author argues that the notion of religion as something related to the private domain of the self has often been seen converging into a collective political identity. However, it would be a 'fallacy', according to Vaiphei, to credit Christianity as the sole harbinger of all the post-Christianity (modern) awareness and struggles.

The fourth unit in the book, titled 'Post-Empire Manipur, organisational politics and frontier', consists of four chapters on different themes. The end of British rule in Manipur was filled with new political ambience of state-making and movements with various ideological trajectories. The unit attempts to capture the nuances of democratic movements, nationality and the edges of identity and revivalism in the wake of departing British Empire and coercive, integrationist Indian nationalists

9

INTRODUCTION

polity, which harped more on an expansionist framework that resembled the contents of the fallen Empire's frontier-making. The chapters explore the dominant nationalists' onslaught and the features of indigenous determining institutional experiments.

'Organisational politics in 20th-century Manipur: trajectories and footprints' (Chapter 13) by Arambam Noni discusses the colonial history and movement for democratisation in Manipur, particularly with reference to the first half of the 20th century. Noni argues that the alienation of people was heightened with the ever-increasing economic exploitation. While discussing the history and form of British rule, he extensively explores the emergence of organisational politics, unfolding the trajectories of anti-colonial assertions and complexes in 20th-century Manipur. The chapter argues that the years of 1947 and 1948 signify the making of a new democratic Manipur whereas the 'annexation' of Manipur with India in 1949 marked the beginning of a new era of complexity. Prior to the 1949 political incident, the political relationship between Manipur and India was marked by newer arrangements, which the author discusses in the context of the Instrument of Accession and Standstill Agreement of August 1947. The author argues that history is important mainly for the numerous events and dates it produces, but also for the potential implications, legacies and materials of interpretative sources that it leaves behind.

The second chapter in Unit IV addresses some important issues that are not sufficiently taken up in the first chapter of the same unit. 'Polemics of the Manipur Merger Agreement, 1949' (Chapter 14) by Kangujam Sanatomba revisits the historical events surrounding post-1947 Manipur, which the author feels is 'increasingly indispensable for identification of the core issue of the prevailing conflict in Manipur'. The author analyses the events and the circumstances surrounding the signing of the Manipur Merger Agreement in Shillong between the Maharaja of Manipur and the Indian authorities on 21 September 1949 in order to discern the finer nuances underlying the politics of resistance. In the chapter, an attempt has been made to describe the 'historical trajectories' leading to the signing of the agreement. The author is of the view that the legality and validity of the Merger Agreement is highly questionable, and that the Agreement violated the Manipur State Constitution Act, 1947, since the Maharaja of Manipur was no longer a de facto sovereign. In the words of the author, the Government of India had committed serious procedural lapses in the process of integrating the state of Manipur.

The third chapter, 'Centrality of body politics in Thokachanba's script and cultural revivalism in Manipur' (Chapter 15), by Naorem Malemsanba Meetei, introduces a different terrain of nationalist revivalism. The

INTRODUCTION

chapter traces the movement that emerged around reviving the traditional socio-cultural religious practices of the Sanamahism to reconstruct a new Manipuri identity, which the author describes as the Laininghanba Eehou (revivalist movement), aimed at reconstructing or reshaping the Manipuri identity (a) through reviving the traditional cultural heritage of the people; (b) to do research in the ancient history of Manipur, language, script, and other literature and (c) to worship and chant religious hymns in the mother tongue. The author argues that such rediscovering and reproduction of materials to revive the traditional socio-cultural practices could be what Eric Hobsbawm described as invention of tradition. Similarly, in the second half of the 20th century, post-merger Manipur experienced transformation in various spheres. The chapter understands the revivalist movement was an integral part of the people's response to the changing situation that started with the establishment of British colonial rule. However, capturing the revivalist movement as a people's movement invites critical scrutiny. Therefore, the concept of 'people' being used here by the author seems to refer to one segment of Manipuri society, not what one can generally call 'the masses'. The chapter locates the emergence of the revivalist against the backdrop of Brahminical hegemony, Hindu proselytism and Christian missionary activities. In the author's argument, the consciousness of language and script becomes an identity issue symbolising the project of uniting ethnic communities in Manipur, as it was first started by Thokachanba Meetei – also regarded as the Kanglei eeyek lamyanba (pioneer of the Manipuri script). The author brings out the whole philosophical interpretation of the origin, styles of the scripts and its phoneme, while analysing the works of Thokachanba Meetei. He argues for an organic relation or link between the Kanglei (Manipuri) script and the human body. The main contention of the author's chapter is to show the centrality of the 'human body' in Thokachanba's argument that provides a better and more complex understanding of the human body in the history of socio-cultural, language and script revivalism in Manipur. The author is of the view that Thokachanba's argument for the organic relation or link between the Kanglei scripts and its allied writing system to the human body essentialised the significance and importance of the human body – the body, that is to say, of the colonised – as a site of conflict and contest between colonial power and Manipuri identity politics.

The final chapter 'Recasting space: politics of frontier making' (Chapter 16) by Thingnam Sanjeev is an attempt to trace the trajectory of the consolidation of the British Empire in the North East Frontier and thereby show how a series of treaties and alliances and the production of 'accurate' maps in the 19th century constantly recast the boundaries of the frontier region and

INTRODUCTION

transformed what the author calls 'amorphous frontiers' into modern boundaries. The chapter argues that at the advent of the British Empire, indigenous spatial imagination was competed and superseded by a new system of modern geographical measurement based on mathematical accuracy and scientific objectivity. Since then, the process of practising frontier in the region has never been smooth. Thingnam argues that after independence, the Indian State retains the region within the logic of strengthening the core and creating a sphere of influence in the Northeastern region. The resistance against such geographical restructuring, from the earlier democratic movement to the present-day armed insurgency movement, indicates the possibility of an alternative geographical/regional imagining.

In lieu of a conclusion

The chapters in the volume are organised into four separate units, yet carry a chronological and thematic unity. Most of the chapters are derivative of incidents and events from the annals of contemporary Manipur, yet some of these quite capably address the trajectories of colonialism and socio-political questions in the entire North East India. The strength of the volume lies in its ability to come out with a thorough discussion of some of the critical issues of colonialism and resistance of our times. Another contribution of the volume is its theoretical argumentation that enables us to understand the contemporary history and politics of North East India. From a colonial administrative arrangement to its cartography, and from civilisational trappings to administrative ethnicisation on the one hand and class and mass on the other, these constitute the key themes of this compendium. The editors of this compilation acknowledge the difficulty in simplifying several strands of chapters into a continuum of flawless argumentation, but are hopeful that the volume will interest academicians, researchers and students. This, probably, is going to be one of the main limitations of the volume, which for sure will make the readers less intriguing.

12

Part I

FRAMEWORK, ADMINISTRATION, AND DEMOCRATISATION

1

CAST OF COLONIALISM

Constructing the peculiar North East India

Arambam Noni

Pre-modern societies are considered to be marked by a barbarous fight for conquest and de facto domination. Such characteristics are considered to be the yardsticks that distinguish between pre-modern and modern. If modernity is to be understood in terms of a new-found rationalism of the Western world, the way this rationalism was experienced by the non-Western societies continues to contradict the foundations on which modernity was based. The evidence of the contradiction could be seen in the context of exploitative explorations of Western rationalism and continued construction of recipient inferiors against whom the project of hegemony was to materialise. The need for such project was heightened along with the occurrence of the Enlightenment movement in Europe, which ultimately brought Europe to a stage of economic concentration and stagnation in terms of technological benefits as well. Modernity became a stage of the world's history when the European hegemony had begun to abundantly affect and cast the socio-economic and political lives of several peoples who were to be ultimately called as subjects. In other words, it can be said that the early modern history of non-European societies had been sweepingly marked by a vertical form of a sophisticated political and power relationship called colonialism. Consequently, colonisation became an inescapable condition with manifest self-proclaimed projects and justifications to sustain over time.

The chapter is aimed at exploring the way colonialism was unleashed on the non-Western societies so as to understand the larger cast of colonialism on economy, politics, culture, belief-systems, etc. Colonialism here is understood as subjugation of a society or country by a foreign entity having deeper objectives of economic and political control backed by military and cultural foundations. The chapter broadly employs both colonialism and imperialism interchangeably to mean politics and economy. The author is aware of the problems in treating both the concepts similarly. Put simply, colonialism came as a mixed package which brought into play self-proclaimed ideological values, civilisational claims and employed spiritual and religious sources in a strategic manner in order to realise its wholesome commercial inroads. Such a mix can be read as a strategic element of the colonial project to trim down the possibilities of rejection and resistance from the ones who were to be finally dominated. Such a packaging is regarded as a product of the early 'frenzy of liberalism' (Singh 1996: 89), which unleashed an unparalleled and unilaterally defined 'superior' West. Predominance of a similar kind of frenzy was found within several strands of liberalism, which, nevertheless, rarely questioned the characterisation or hierarchisation of races and inherent forms of exploitation. The intentions and perspective of the debates within Europe was to justify the then-existing relations of difference, that of superior and inferior, as it was considered to be rather natural.

The debates generated during the middle of the 19th century can be mentioned in this regard. James Mill (1820), while speaking on the question of wages of the plantation labour in Africa and India, argued that European hierarchy was a product of different rates of development, and not immutable laws, and thus Africans and Asians could be improved if exposed to European civilisation. What followed then was the indiscriminate conquest and manipulation of all varieties, leading several scholars to construct a popular term known as the 'despotism of Orientalism', which matures into a long-term hegemony. Antonio Gramsci (1992) views colonial hegemony as the cohesion spiritual and cultural supremacy as it exercises through the manipulation of civil society. Hegemonisation harps on new methods of socialisation mechanisms; it invents and coerces new institutions of hegemony such as the church, schools, press, values, culture and beliefs systems. Such a deliberate attempt to enforce new cultural directions is integral to hegemony, and in this sense it is made to become a rule by consent and ground for claiming habitual legitimacy (Parsons 1964: 33–70).

In this regard, Edward Said argues that the construction of knowledge of the 'other' must be seen as a crucial site for the operation of colonialism. Said argues, 'without examining Orientalism as a discourse one cannot possibly understand the enormously systematic discipline by which European culture was able to manage – and even produce – the Orient, politically, sociologically, militarily, ideologically, scientifically, and imaginatively during the post-Enlightenment period'

(Said 1973: 3). Said's critique is one of the most considered theses on Eurocentrism. Nevertheless, his formulation has been criticised for having failed to shed enough light on the complexities within Europe. For instance, the argument of Said is reworked, rather challenged, by Aijaz Ahmad when he rejects the essentialisation of Europe as a unified historical entity.

> The plain fact is that whatever Homer or Aeschylus might have had to say about the Persians or Asia, it simply is not a reflection of a 'West' or of 'Europe' as a civilizational entity, in a recognizably modern sense, and no modern discourse can be traced back to that origin, because the civilizational map and geographical imagination of antiquity were fundamentally different from those that came to be fabricated in post-Renaissance Europe.
>
> (Ahmad 2001: 275)

Ahmad further explains by suggesting that there have historically been of all sorts of processes – connected with class and gender, ethnicity and religion, xenophobia and bigotry – which have unfortunately been at work in all human societies, both European and non-European. Therefore, the ideologically full-blown racism and other forms of devastations of Eurocentrism came into eminent existence in the wake of colonial capitalism (ibid.: 276). To be precise, the debate is the need to locate Eurocentrism and colonialism as a consequence of post-Renaissance fabrication. The failure of locating a resisting subject is missing in Said, and consideration of a heterogeneous Europe as put forth by Ahmad is significant as long as it questions colonialism.

Contextualising the North East

The idea of North East began to first appear in the European colonial map of the 19th century. To recall, the initial journey of the European empire into non-European societies began as trading commercial enterprises. The case of North East India is not an exception. The two most evident reasons that heightened the British expansion in the region were its mercantile interests and strategic necessity to mobilise areas in the North East to restrict Burmese expansion and threats and misgivings caused by the French presence in Burma. Towards the first quarter of the 19th century, the British mercantile interest began to make inroads into the North East, where the prospect of tea cultivation was confirmed, a highly coveted and capital-spinning article of international commerce. On the other hand, there was a prolonged military tussle between the Burmese and the native kingdoms, with logistic backup extended by the British, which was only to be replaced by a new apparatus of British imperialism. With the signing of the Treaty of Yandaboo, 1826, the British fully consolidated their domination over the North East. Once the region was brought under British control, it was only a matter of time before the subordination of the turbulent hill people. Subsequently, by 1833, industrial capital gained ascendancy over mercantile capital, which resulted in the absolute colonisation of Assam (Guha 1969: 569–622). By 1871, the wastelands in Assam were settled with tea planters. In addition, the Empire took full advantage of the political unrest to consolidate its sway in the region such as the then-existing inter-kingdom wars, faction-ridden nobility, internal insurrections, dynastic feuds, frequent Burmese raids, etc.

Typical of capitalism, the wholesome economic impact was that, like in Europe, the subsistence farming in the North East was discouraged and no substantial attempt was made towards industrialisation as the thrust was given to tea plantation aimed at surplus and exploitation of cheap labour. Similar perspectives were maintained in other aspects of colonial policies as it was manifested in the case of construction of roads and transportation. The colonial power was prepared to make it 'to be simple, cost effective and only to the extent it was required' (*The Calcutta Gazette* 1866: 1965). In other words, a restrained and pre-determined policy outlook was the main hallmark of colonial exploitation.

Consolidation of political hegemony

The dissolution of the East India Company can be said to have marked a beginning of a newer economic and political subordination of the people in the North East. Thus, the political history of the North East witnessed maturing of a mercantile enterprise into a permanent political subjection. The subjection was to rather rigorously pursue capitalist exploitation of the region's cotton, minerals, wild rubber, petroleum and wild tea (Chaube 1973: 6). Transformation of mercantilism to total political hegemony was seeded through the region mainly on two grounds. The initial mercantile journey spread all over and made crucial inroads as apolitical business groups. And, second, it was complemented by rigorous pursuit of 'institutionalising' of a colonial administration, through military expeditions, proselytisation, conquests and treatises. Hence, it became imminent in the practice of the Empire to emphasise the need for a moderate display of physical force to bring the hill tracts and the plains into order. For obvious reasons, the conciliatory approach of the Empire was in fact corrupt in its perspective as the local leaders were bribed to make them comply with the colonial interests. If in case bribery was to prove ineffective in expanding the colonial outreach, 'punitive measures' were officially carried out.

The thriving framework of the imperialist was dependent on 'conciliation, backed by display of force when it could be effectively applied' (Bhuyan 1949: 33–34). As a result, buffer zones and semi-independent states were created or uprooted as imperial strategic necessity dictated. The core of imperial response to peoples' resistance ranged from moderate display of force to severe punishment, and from bribing to luring of local chiefs, which consequently led to the formulation of a forward policy, the idea of the North East region as a strategic, wild and savage frontier came into being. The spread of the tea gardens from the middle of the 19th century strengthened the case for a 'forward policy' in the North East (Chaube 1999: 7) thereby inducing not only a policy of coercion and contemptuous devastation from the beginning, as it has sometimes been erroneously described, but also a firm and policy of defence and conciliation (Mackenzie 1999: 55).

The following statement is reflexive of the political drive of the imperialists to hasten their hegemony over the region, 'Fate seems determined to prove that there shall be no rest for the English in India till they stand forth as governors or advisors of each tribe and people in the land' (ibid.: 369).

> What is of the utmost importance in dealing with uncivilized tribes is patience. No one supposes that their civilization is to be effected in a few years, and no one expects that in endeavouring to conciliate them the Government will not meet with occasional disappointment, but the policy is none the less on this account sound and intelligible.
>
> (ibid.: 54–55)

The cunningness of the imperialists embarked on a combined policy of direct and distanced interference. The invoking of the Inner Line Regulation system in 1873 reflects the distanced interference as manifested in the following quote:

> The active control of the district officer need not necessarily extend up to the boundary, but it must, under no circumstances, be carried further. Beyond this line the tribes are left to manage their own affairs with only such interference on the part of the

frontier officers in their political capacity as may be considered advisable with the view to establishing a personal influence for good among the chiefs and the tribes.

(*The Calcutta Gazette* 1871: 89–90)

The proclaimed rationale of the regulation was that there was a pressing necessity of bringing the region under more stringent control for a smoother commercial jurisdiction. In the words of Mackenzie: 'There was a pressing necessity of bringing under more stringent control the commercial relations of our subjects with the frontier tribes living on the borders of our jurisdiction' (Mackenzie 1999: 55). The Inner Line Permit system was to consolidate and sustain the spreading revenue areas that had enormous resources such as rubber forests, tea gardens, etc. The regulation gave power to the lieutenant governor to prescribe a line in each and every district affected beyond which no British subject of certain classes or foreign resident could pass without a licence. Moreover, the ever-spreading tea cultivation had faced strong resistance from the hitherto unoccupied tribes. According to Mackenzie, while the policy of permanent occupation and direct management had been successfully carried out in the Naga, Garo, Khasi, Jaintia and Chittagong Hill Tracts, annexation of the Abor Hills in the same way was not possible as it would 'bring us into contact with tribes still wilder and less known, nor should we find a resting place for the foot of annexation till we planted it on the plateau of High Asia; perhaps not even them' (Mackenzie 1999: 5).

The varying circumstances in which the British authority was extended over eastern India may explain different forms of the same (authority) over different areas. To start with, Sikkim and Bhutan were never annexed to the British Raj, presumably because of their international significance, nor were they reduced to the status of native states. Technically speaking, the native states were vassals of the British Indian Government which exercised considerable authority in the internal affairs of the principalities (Chaube 1973: 24). The other trajectory of the colonial administration was that it opted for the politics of engagement and disengagement as and when the situation demanded. For example, engagement and conciliation was opted for when it came to territoriality and administration, which was linked to imperial political economy. There was disengagement when it came to social customs in order to avoid immediate reactions and unnecessary backlashes. The Empire was always clear in this regard as it felt

a main principle to be adopted in dealing with these people when they have been made to understand and feel the power of the government through a simple plan of government suitable to their present condition and circumstance, and interfering as little as possible with existing institutions' through the extension of intercourse with them and endeavour to introduce among them civilization and order.

(Mackenzie 1999: 242)

The gesture of 'direct' and 'distanced' engagement was a strategic policy to ensure an unprovoked consolidation of the Empire as it was to prove cost-effective. Put simply, effective norms were set up to encompass a wide range of differences, based on the assumption that Europeans were superior to the rest. This assumption became a crucial basis for marking cultural and racial classification of societies all over the world. The Asians and Africans remain at the bottom of this hierarchised relationship. In the words of Frantz Fanon:

Colonialism . . . has never ceased to maintain that the Negro is a savage; and for the colonist, the Negro was neither an Angolan nor a Nigerian, for he simply spoke of "the Negro". For colonialism, this vast continent was the haunt of savages, a country riddled with superstitions and fanaticism, destined for contempt, weighed down by the curse of God, a country of cannibals – in short, the Negro's country.

(Fanon 1963: 170)

The colonies underwent a hegemonic deployment of cultural supremacy in order to validate the subsequent consolidation of the Empire that inevitably promoted racial and military oppression. Though the policy of conciliation and not a policy of repression or devastation was emphasised, on the contrary the actions of the local authorities were empowered not to have been in full accordance with what was emphasised. One of the most commonly cited reasons against this stringent, but loose, packing of administrative arrangement with regard to the 'wild' people of the North East, according to the Empire, was to restrict intimidation to *coolies* employed in the tea estates and specific cultivators (Reid 1942:104). The idea of producing a restrictive administrative regime of the Empire entailed a strategic approach to effectively deal with hostile forest residents. The concern to introduce a line of demarcation came from the Empire's interest to deal with any further outrages on British subjects, violation of 'Inner Line' and danger to the interests of people dwelling inside the British borders by reason of the proximity of disturbance outside (ibid.: 157). Colonial consolidation was not only about direct brutalisation

ARAMBAM NONI

of administration but it also had ample features of restrained brutality and selective administrative arrangement and cultural stupidity. The Inner Line Permit system is illustrative, used to check the entry of 'outsiders' to the frontier. The following passage reflects the strategy and conspiring attitudes of the colonial design while characterising its civilising claims:

> What is of the utmost importance in dealing with uncivilized tribes is patience. No one supposes that their civilization is to be effected in a few years, and no one expects that in endeavouring to conciliate them the government will not meet with occasional disappointment, but the policy is nonetheless on this account sound and intelligible.
>
> (Mackenzie 1999: 54–55)

The Empire's civilisation project, therefore, had a conscious pursuit of twin deployment: administrative, political and economic consolidation, and proselytisation. Initially, it was projected as if administration and Church were entirely separate entities. Gradually, the missionaries and their education were brought in to play a crucial role in affirming what was politically required. Under a similar framework, direct administrative attempts were distinctively ventured, where the imperialist faced difficulties, only to be followed by Christian missionaries. There are many instances to show that although the administration and the Church were functioning in the hills with the same objective, namely, the consolidation of British rule, the results of their operations were not complementary in all respects. The strategy of the administration was least interference with the existing order, while the activities of the Church tended to provide the new elites with intellectual ammunition. Having accepted the need for an indifferent policy, 'dealing with patience', on the previously existing exploitative socio-economic system, the coming of the British rather encouraged the feudal rights of the kings over land, territory and people, which was to remain intact even when the imperialist proceeded to direct political control. British rule was the chief external factor to weaken the community control on land. The colonial encouragement of the exploitative systems and its impossibility to sow substantial democratic governance had simultaneous anti-colonial currents. The inevitable result was social imbalance in the lives of the peoples in the region as there was no commitment towards self-government.

Critiquing the colonial perception about teaching British self-governance, John Atkinson Hobson observes that 'the theory that Britons are a race endowed, like the Romans, with a genius for government, that our colonial and imperial policy is animated by a resolve to spread throughout the world the arts of free self-government' is nothing more than a hypocritical claim (Hobson 1902: 120). The colonised, therefore, no more remained 'as an undifferentiated mass but as situated social agents impelled by our own conflicts, contradictions, distinct social and political locations, of class, gender, region, and so on' (Ahmad 2001: 267). Such a proposition hints to the point that the Orient was hardly to be seen as a permanently silenced subject, which is a departure from what is commonly considered in theses such as Edward Said's *Orientalism.*

Colonialism and resistance

The question of establishing a comparative chronology of colonialism and resistance has been often made to appear complex, in many cases deliberated as a derivative of the former. In simple parlance, are resistances detrimental to the ways and norms laid out by the exploiters? Or can resistance be an autonomous consciousness to a given material reality? These two are the main questions that have dominantly figured in the debate on which came first. This work is not to treat resistance question in the colonies simply as consequent artefacts of the imperialist. Rather, it broadly examines how simultaneous resistances against the Empire came from the peoples. An important indicator to this fact is the way people from the North East region began to consciously respond to the colonial questions, be it in terms of native kings who sought alliances with the Empire or of tribes who had been hostile to the alien encroachments upon their habitations. Towards the final stage of domination, colonial intervention was like a last resort for the power-seeking native princes despite fair apprehension of its temporariness. On the other hand, the people from the region had confronted the colonial policies and forces on a regular basis. The expansion of tea plantation projects had severely shrunk tribal economic spaces, which became a source of formidable outrage. The subjects in the region started to resist what was meant to be imposed.

The reported refraining of Jaintias from eating potato as a mark of protest against colonialism is remarkable in this regard. For instance, the Khamptis, Singpho, Miri, Muttock, Nagas and Manipuris posed serious resistance to the alien power. While the secondary sector of economy failed to come up, large-scale immigration of labour took place in connection with tea plantation. By 1871, Assam had become a deficit area in food grains (Burman 1999: 7). The continued mercantilism and industrial capitalism of the Empire necessitated a 'forward policy' from the middle of the 19th century having extensive and direct political implications.

The Empire's policy towards North East India had to become more stringent due to the French presence in Burma and Russophobia in the Himalayas.

Although the Empire was clever enough to maintain a policy of restricted interference, it was during this phase that the Kukis were settled in North Cachar with arms and rent-free land only to internalise the hostility in the long term. It is often said that the British Empire continued to struggle to bring the region under effective control till the last moments of their presence in the region. Much later, in 1914, the McMahon Line was drawn to consolidate the frontier areas of the Eastern Frontier called North East India. Politically corrupt practices and extensive tax systems faced strong resistance as in the case of the Khasi Jaintia Hills. The Empire's apprehension to spread its administration into the Naga Hills and Himalayan borders was due to the expected deficit of administrative cost. The Nagas were demanding their exclusion from the political reformation of British India. Resistance and preparation for a distinctive political representation began in North East India when the Britishers were set to leave the region. This was seen in the formation of the Khasi Jaintia Political Association, the Naga Club and the movement for a responsible government in Manipur.

Thus, the dispute between hillmen and the government regarding possession of the land at the foot of the hills north of the Brahmaputra remained a chronic problem. Nevertheless, the writings of colonial ethnographers such as Mackenzie and Jenkins attempting to throw an altruistic image did not find a universal acceptance. As a part of neutralising discontentment, various projects were introduced. One of these was to engage the youths through distinctive employment. It became very desirable that the young men of the tribes be induced, if possible, to take service in the police force, and the hill tribes be provided training and education. Not only were they, by their physique, better qualified than the people of the plains for most of the duties required of the police in frontier districts, but their employment set free the labour of others accustomed to industrial occupations (Mackenzie 1999: 54) as well. Imperialism set its ground amidst hostility and incessant political resistance.

Ghost of colonialism!

According to critics, post-colonial India's dispensation remains imitative of imperial notions as suspicion and prejudices mark the parameters of mainstream politics. For example, the Manipuri and Naga nationality questions have mainly reasoned against the alleged retention of the colonial 'frontier framework' in the political imagination of India's dominant nationalist discourse. The framework appears to have become so imminent that one generally encounters the 'idea' and appears to cause enormous deadlock(s) in contemporary North East. A case in point is the nature of integration of politics pursued by India in the North East as it had thwarted the newly attained representative democracy in the region. For example, by 1947, Manipur had enacted its independent State constitution and, in 1948, became the first state in the region to hold an independent election based on adult franchise. Responding to Manipur's reluctance to join the Union of India, the then home minister asked 'whether the Governor did not have a Brigadier in Shillong' (Rustomji 1973: 109). In the words of Sanjib Baruah, the process of Indian 'integration' began with an 'authoritarian accent', (Baruah 2001) thereby producing grounds for lingering dissents. The actual birth of India in Manipur in particular and North East in general was done through invoking a substantial amount of militarism, which India was capable of showcasing during the construction of nation in India. The dubious nationalist paradigm of making the nation in India did not consider the need to acquire a compatible legitimacy for its project of actualising the nation in India. From this standpoint the Indian nationalists view the post-British India as something existed for millennia and any voices that questioned this were of necessity 'anti-national' (Kaviraj 1994: 330). Today, a myriad unresolved political questions trouble the region. From politics to economics, the North East continues to be seen and projected as a peculiar, strategic and insecure region. At present, more than 30 major armed groups operate and a variety of conflicts over political rights, largely in the form of extra-constitutional movements and development projects, exude in India's North Eastern states. According to some studies, a low-level equilibrium of poverty, non-development, civil conflict and lack of faith in political establishments mark the condition in the region. With a poor human rights record, controversial development projects and sluggish economic state of affairs, it appears that the North East has become a contradictory geo-body to the much celebrative imageries of India's democracy and pluralism. A pertinent question that arises is what makes the North East such a difficult terrain of politics and governance. One significant reason for this prolonged deficit in democracy, development and peace seems to be rooted in the retention of a specific framework of politics, which sees the North East as a frontier, thereby resulting in all kinds of arrested practices of politics.

There is a close connection between the historicity of modern North East India's emergence as a frontier in the British colonial project and the subsequent post-colonial India's dispensations. From the British regime's framework to dominant Indian nationalists' imagination, as discussed earlier, the idea of the North East has been largely a construct, confined and particularised. The implication of the particularisation is the retention of colonial legislation such as Armed Forces (Special Powers) Act, 1958, that gives immunity to military officials. India's rampant violation of consensual state making process in the region has systematically harped on policy paradigms that potentially implicate the region into a military geo-body. India's neo-liberal economic policy, called the Look East Policy (LEP), which is to open the 'Eastern Gate' (*sic*; the North East region) to East Asian countries is largely played out to achieve economic expansion while at the core ensuring in its frontier geo-military needs. The idea of geo-militarism is put into praxis through India's obsession with border rationalisation and security with Myanmar and China, which is simultaneously pushed through inventing harsher diplomatic military technologies mainly to contain armed resistance in the North East.

Beyond arrested politics!

Inherent tendencies and practices of dominance and fixation of people and region into specificities are natural to invoke grounds for politics of resistance, capable of evolving collective questions and movements. The collective in the process consolidates itself with the identification of a common 'experiential antagonist' or 'the other', to be fought against, and carry on its claims for liberation as genuine aspirants. The claimants of this 'liberating' resistance might be a loose aggregation of certain claims – real and romantic – that are capable of acquiring moral, social and political legitimacy.

As a result, there is an 'image trap' in which the North East is caught and is sustained over time by an extensive capillary of power configuration, which resists and oppresses alternative and revolutionary political ideas and movements. Understanding such a complex interface between 'fixation' and 'resistance' would require unfolding of the mediations that sustains the 'state of exception' in the region called North East India. The pertinent question that keeps (re)-surfacing is whether there is a possibility of rescuing the region from the colonial fixations and externalities of images, which is a reality not exclusively in the context of past but also of contemporary lived experiences.

References

Ahmad, Aijaz. 2001. 'Orientalism and After: Ambivalence and Metropolitan Location in the Work of Edward Said', in Peter J. Cain and Mark Harrison (eds), *Imperialism: Critical Concepts in Historical Studies, Volume III*. London: Routledge.

Baruah, Sanjib. 2001. "Generals as Governors: The Parallel Political Systems of North East India" in *Himal South Asia* (June), Himal Publications: Kathmandu.

Bhuyan, S. K. 1949. *Anglo-Assamese Relations, 1771–1826: A History of the Relations of Assam with the East India Company from 1771 to 1826*. Guwahati.

Burman, B. K. Roy. 1999 [1884]. 'Prefatory Introduction', in Alexander Mackenzie, *The North-East Frontier of India*. New Delhi: Mittal Publications.

Chaube, S. K. 1973. *Hill Politics in North East India*. Patna: Orient Longman.

Fanon, Frantz. 1963. *The Wretched of the Earth*, trans. Constance Farrington. Harmondsworth: Penguin.

Gramsci, Antonio. 1992. *Prison Notebooks*, ed. and trans. Joseph A. Buttigieg. Columbia: Columbia University Press. *The Calcutta Gazette*, 2 March 1870, part II and I; November 1871, Part II.

Guha, Amalendu. 1969. 'Socio-economic Changes in Agrarian Assam', in M. K. Chaudhuri (ed.), *Trends of Socio-economic Change in India, 1871–1961*. Shimla: Indian Institute of Advanced Study.

Hobson, J. A. 1902. *Imperialism: A Study*. London: James Nisbet & Co.

Mackenzie, Alexander. 1999 [1884]. *The North-East Frontier of India*. New Delhi: Mittal Publications.

Mill, James. 1820. *History of India*. London: Baldwin, Cradock & Joy.

Parsons, Talcott. 1964. Some Reflections on the Place of Force in Social Processes, in Harry Eckstein, ed., *Internal War*. New York, Free Press of Glencoe.

Reid, Robert. 1942. *History of the Frontier Areas Bordering on Assam from 1883–1941*. Shillong: Assam Government Press.

Rustomji, Nari. 1973. *The Enchanted Frontiers*. New Delhi: Oxford University Press.

Said, Edward W. 1995 [1978]. *Orientalism: Western Conceptions of the Orient*. London: Penguin.

Singh, J. 1996. *Colonial Narratives/Cultural Dialogues: 'Discoveries' of India in the Language of Colonialism*. London: Routledge. *The Calcutta Gazette*, November 14, 1866. Calcutta.

2

COLONIAL ADMINISTRATION, KNOWLEDGE AND INTERVENTION

Colonial project of ethnicisation in Manipur

Homen Thangjam

In contemporary discourse of political identity, especially of the various cultural communities in Manipur, we witness what Benedict Anderson understands as conscious invention of 'national identities and process of imagining a nation' (1983: 20). Invention, Anderson notes, implies a conscious construction. Intellectuals and those involved in this project of inventing and imagining a community as a nation have largely moved to activate ethniccentred organisations that are actually working at various levels in contemporary Manipur. These tendencies lead to fragmentation among the people of Manipur to the extent of posing a threat to its political territorial entity.

However, one needs to see the history of how such practices of identity discourse actually have now rendered something as an uncritically accepted truth of identity of ethnos. Seen from this perspective, an examination of the process where natives were ethnicised during the British colonial rule in Manipur would reveal a discourse that brought into reality the conditions of such truths of identities that were invented and imagined. Ethnicisation in the case of Manipur – particularly regarding natives of the hills – was a conscious effort undertaken by the British to serve colonial interest. Invention (defined as devising, contriving or fabricating) of identities, such as Naga and Kuki, was built upon a previous body of knowledge. They were not created anew, but rather manufactured, or assembled, from an existing body of knowledge that, consciously or unconsciously, included myths and symbols. Such an ordering facilitated a new form of conquest (power) – for example, politics of control and subjugation, defining the groups with a neat boundary – and became

28

COLONIAL ADMINISTRATION

an actual instrument that was something like a pre-emptive bid to prevent consolidation by the native power of its people to overthrow British rule. This involved anthropological categorisation of the natives that perfectly fitted in a cartographic landscaping and, above all, a humanist defence of colonialism itself. This chapter attempts to focus on the material basis for the assembling of different natives under particular identities, ordered and bounded in respective administrative territories (physical immobilisation) during British rule in Manipur. At the same time, it proposes a discursive move from understanding the colonial policies regarding fluid native groups merely as 'administrative convenience' to thinking in terms of the effects of which was solely responsible for creating dichotomy among people irrespective of one's habitat, be it the hills or the valley. This is not to deny the importance of 'convenience' which did form the immediate condition of formalising a policy related to administration, but to see the need to understand a priori framing of the natives, which was what happened during the British rule and which actually was the way in which the colonial governmentality was practised. Therefore, understanding the colonial project of ethnicisation can provide an entry point to understanding the ongoing politics of ethnic identity assertions in Manipur.

Knowledge production: appropriation and negation of local knowledge

Understanding implicit in the foregoing argument presupposes prevalence of the interplay of certain forces underpinning the 'nativist' integrationist rule, which can also be understood as statecraft. In addition, there is another element, which nevertheless forms a body of knowledge (along with the aforementioned) regarding the natives of the hills, and this was used by the British in order to classify them. Fundamentally, this relates to naming the natives in terms of belonging to a particular ethnicity. Ethnicisation involved discerning this body of knowledge by the British, for power was inherent within this knowledge and it was a matter of choosing the ones expedient – and reproduction of the knowledge in a new form – in subjugating the natives. Thus, we find the dialectics of appropriation and negation of local knowledge primarily informing ethnicisation during the colonial period. This proposition lays bare essential contradictions in colonial rhetoric between preserving the past and promoting economic development on the one hand, and protecting natives from the traumas of modernity on the other.

29

The negation

Statecraft, or, more precisely, integrationist rule followed by kings of Manipur can best be understood in the words of Clifford Geertz as ceremonial forms by which kings take symbolic possession of their realm. He says:

> In particular, royal progresses (of which, where it exists, coronation is but the first) locate the society's center and affirm its connection with transcendent things by stamping a territory with ritual signs of dominance. When kings journey around the countryside, making appearances, attending fêtes, conferring honors, exchanging gifts, or defying rivals, they mark it, like some wolf or tiger spreading his scent through his territory, as almost physically part of them.
>
> (1983:125)

Thus, drawing authority from folklore and myth, for example, a belief in a common ancestor of the inhabitants, and that the Meetei was the youngest of three brothers (nowadays known as Kuki and Naga, these names were hitherto unknown and unused in Manipur until the British made the terms functional.[1] It was mandatory for the king to wear the costume of the hill brother (the Tangkhuls) at the time of coronation. Inclusive policy is extended in worship of deities and celebrations, wherein a *Kanglei Lai Haraoba* (ritual observed by Meeteis implicating the creation of mankind) is incomplete without the character of a Tangkhul (*Tangkhul shaba*). Here, Tangkhul, a large group of natives of the hills, can be taken as a representative of the hill natives. Tradition based on legends and myths, which form a basis of state formation as well as sense of brotherhood among the people, are nullified in ethnographies compiled by the British as lacking 'veracity' and 'unscientific'.

Further, the festival of *Mera Haochongba*, encapsulated a world of Manipur in which hill natives of Manipur in genial amity 'freely participated in events (of history) as lived experiences, free showmanship in events (of history) as collective memory'; and, thereby, 'helped in re-exalting the idea of nationhood and rekindling a heightened sense of patriotism in the unlettered, uninformed and un-imaginative public mindset of yore' (Kamson 2009: 131). Thus, the festival symbolises a productive forum of producing a semblance of stability in the kingdom among its populace. According to Kamson, *Mera Haochongba* implies two things:

COLONIAL ADMINISTRATION

1 First, it was resorted to as an administrative-cum-ritualistic practice quite regularly on a fixed day of the year in the two-millennium long history of Manipur except during the British regime . . . In the process it has helped bring to effervescence the cultural achievements shared by both the brethrens of the hills and the plains . . . a kind of reciprocal love and an ultimate mutual respect for each other.

2 Second, it also means that both have suffered together 'the birth pangs of the past and many an ordeal of survival sharing a common destiny against heavy odds' . . . In that moment of bliss, ecstasy, togetherness and semi-divine happiness participants hardly find their different languages or any other antecedent a barrier.

(ibid.: 140)

Moreover, it relates to the notion of innate and symbiotic cultural ties among various natives invariably expressed through the medium of festival and characterised by secularism. However, subsequently, the British negated the festival in it being primitive and as wasteful expenditure. Banning the festival could serve the purpose of delinking the organic ties people in the two geographies shared, all the more sever allegiance to the Manipur sovereign power, nullify native hegemony, and, finally, forge loyalty towards them. For obvious reasons, the British were keen to keep the hill administration under the exclusive charge of the president of the Manipur State Durbar, i.e. away from the control of the Manipur administration represented by the King in Durbar (ibid.: 141). In 1892, at the time of the British takeover of Manipur, Major Maxwell proclaimed that the hill tribes were henceforth to be 'treated as on a footing as distinct from His Highness' subjects, being only "dependent on" the Manipur State' (cited in Kamson 2009: 173). This hastened the process of ethnicisation and widened the gap between natives of the hills and of the valley in Manipur.

The appropriation

If the cultural and traditional aspect of statecraft were negated, then we find the opposite happening as far as 'negative' use of power to quell centrifugal stresses by natives to political authority is concerned. In case of the former, it was through anthropological study, travelogues surveys, and official reports of the customs, practices and institutions of the communities that knowledge was gained; the latter was marked by practical acquaintances. The Britishers' knowledge of Manipur's statecraft, such as espionage system and technique of warfare, or that which had played a prominent part in the politics of the North East Frontier, were reasons for its being 'noticed' by them as early as 1762 (Mackenzie 2001: 149). For example, the Manipur Levy was formed in 1825 as a force to fight against the expanding Burmese Empire. The first 'practical' acquaintance of the British with the Nagas in the Naga Hills was in 1832 (popularly known as the Manipuri Expeditions of 1832 and 1833), when Captain Jenkins and Lieutenant Pemberton escorted by Ghumbeer Singh's troops forced a passage through the hills with a view of ascertaining if there was a practicable route into Assam. Manipur was invited by the British to occupy the Naga Hills in 1835. 'The Government was not prepared itself to take over the Naga country, and still inclined to regard the Manipuris as the *de facto* master of the hills' (Mackenzie 2001: 103). Subsequently, this led Sir James Johnstone to observe:

> Ghumbeer Singh reduced several villages to submission, including the largest of all, Kohima . . . Even up to the Naga Hills campaign of 1879–80, the Nagas regarded Manipur as the greater power of the two, because her conduct was consistent; if she threatened, she acted. One British subject after another might be murdered with impunity, but woe betide the village that murdered a subject of Manipur. A force of Manipuris was instantly despatched, the village was attacked, destroyed, and ample compensation exacted. The system answered well for Manipur; many of the Nagas began to speak Manipuri, and several villages paid an annual tribute. Still, up to 1851, *we considered that we had some shadowy claim to the hills, though we never openly asserted it.*
>
> (Johnstone 2002: 41–42, emphasis added)

Subsequently, various other expeditions were taken up together with Manipur, such as the Lushai, Kambows, Chassad, and others, primarily to stop raids and plunder, and to allow free movement of traders in both the British and Manipuri territory. In addition, we find in later phases of colonialism, after the repression of the Kuki Rebellion of 1917, planting of Kukis as fronts against other tribes, a practice earlier undertaken by Manipuri kings. As early as 1853, before the establishment of the Naga Hills District, proposals were made to utilise the 'Kookies as a buffer or screen between our more timid subjects and the Angamis. In 1856–57 lands were assigned rent-free for 10 and afterwards for 25 years

COLONIAL ADMINISTRATION

to any Kookies who would settle to the east of North Cachar . . . Firearms and ammunitions were given to them by Government' (Mackenzie 2001: 147). Thus, the Kuki militia was formed primarily to prevent raids by other tribes such as the Angamis. Other pre-existing structures were the appointment of *lambus*, making chiefs the centre of authority who reported to the British and others whom the British appropriated into their own structures of power. Thus, we find colonial authorities incorporating pre-existing body of knowledge and structures, with their own structures of authority and political processes, into colonial structures, themselves in the process of being developed in response to local conditions (Spear 2003: 4).

Finally, we witness neither nullification nor negation of the negative use of force. Rather, we find the transformation of the same into what Weber understood as legitimate power of the modern State. In so far as order is continuously safeguarded within a territorial area by use of threat and application of physical force, the colonial administrative staff presented British rule as benevolent to the natives of the hills.

In this regard, mention can be made of the directives concerning the Lushais and the Naga Hills. The Government of India, in a letter in 1870, directed the political agent in Manipur to impress on the Raja, in an emphatic manner possible, that while he should take all necessary measures for the protection of his frontier, no unprovoked aggression on his part would be permitted, and that he must take effective steps to make his subject Kookies understand this, and to punish rigorously any disobedience (Mackenzie 2001: 161). The political agent in Manipur was referred to this letter as a policy to be pursued by Manipur towards the Kukis and Lushais in 1872. Regarding the Naga Hills, as Alexander Mackenzie puts it,

> Manipur, whose only system of control consisted in raids as savages as those of the Nagas ([*sic*] Angamis) themselves, did occupy Semkhor for a time and harass the Nagas in a desultory way, the only effect of which was to bring down the hill men upon our villages in raids as soon as the Manipuris had withdrawn.
> (Mackenzie 2001: 161)

It was precisely on account of the hardship faced by the British in such 'raids' that the British cancelled the aide from Manipur, and instead a European officer was ordered to occupy a post near the Naga country. These instances highlight a process in which the 'Manipuris' were utilised, in the way in which knowledge about them was produced in

33

the colonial discourse as well as in the manner in which power was exercised. To add to this was the policy of abandonment of the idea that was sought to represent Manipur once colonial goals were achieved, such as once a semblance of understanding had been achieved with the natives of the hills.

The construction of this type of knowledge about the natives by the British was used to rule over the natives of the hills. This knowledge, which was inscribed in the reports, was recorded in the form of memories and later on became the productive sites of collective memories of the natives in order to constitute the notion of 'brethrens' of hills, in which to symbolise the Manipuris ([sic] Meeteis) as the oppressor and common enemy. The British were successful in sowing the seeds of ethnicity in this way through their 'superior' administrative interventions and procedures. Ways of controlling the natives had to carry a moral compulsion with which to justify the control by forwarding the claim of colonial superiority to the natives. For example, the control was closely associated with a 'civilizing mission' with which to practice the colonial rule and its forms of justification. As Edward Said remarked, the West according to the colonisers was synonymous of the modern, rational and civilised. The non-West, meaning the Orient, was the opposite of all the attributes that characterised the West. Cultures, which were different from the coloniser, according to Said, were treated as inferior and, therefore, savage. At the same time, the coloniser asserted their culture as advanced as well as superior (Said 1995: 3, 7). Thus, the coloniser posited control and domination as a civilising parameter of culture.

In this context, we find the interpolation of anthropological knowledge and appropriation of a local body of knowledge to serve colonial economic interest. As mentioned earlier in this chapter, this relates to naming of the natives in terms of belonging to a particular ethnic group. As a matter of fact, the term 'Kuki' is of Assamese or Bengali origin and of some antiquity. Moreover, they are considered as migratory in habit. As Thomas Callan Hodson reportedly quotes Kukis defining themselves as, 'We are like birds of the air. We made our nests here this year, and who knows where we shall build next year' (Hodson 1996: 2). Likewise, the term 'Naga' is said to be derived from the Assamese *Noga* – applied by them to the hill tribes in the hinterland of Lakhimpur and Sibsagar districts (Grierson 1903: 1, 194). These local names became important to the British to classify and 'order' the natives in a logical or comprehensible arrangement so as to exploit optimal economic benefits. Once classified, the next step involved immobilising them into politico-administrative units. This is the genesis of ethnicisation of the hill natives of Manipur to

COLONIAL ADMINISTRATION

generic ethnic terms such as Naga and Kuki. However, at the same time, such extrapolations were against the local knowledge of Manipur; for example, the names did not find a place in Manipuri vocabulary. The hill natives were known by their respective root names, such as the Tangkhul, Kabui, Mao, Khongjai, Khoibu, Maring, Anal, and so on, or, in derogatory terms, as 'Hao'. William McCulloch admitted this when he said:

> Inhabitants of the hills surrounding the valley of Manipur are known in the *west* under the general appellations of Nagas and Kukis, that in Manipur, the Manipuris use the term *Hao*, to embrace them all, and that the term "Khongjai" is used to denote the Kukis.
>
> (1857: 56–7, emphasis added)

The Meeteis occupied an ambiguous and problematic position in the colonial civilisational hierarchisation (Jilangamba 2008: 20). They were, in the colonial understanding, oscillating 'between the wild paganism, unsophisticated manners, and savage customs of their hill cousins, and a desire to be esteemed worthy of the beautiful visionary history which the Indian epics have been so kind as to assign them' (Dalton 1872: 48). Thus, British ethnicisation involved use of local knowledge, negation of another and the ultimate transformation of the knowledge into the colonial discourse with which to represent natives as savages that needed constant guardianship and intervention.

In spite of contradictions in defining the terms on the basis of language and culture, British anthropologists pushed ahead the agenda of crafting the two terms over other fluid groups of the hills in Manipur, the Naga Hills and other places. To cite an example, in his work on the Kuki-Lushai tribes, Soppitt emphatically said, 'The word "Kuki" was too well established to be given up. It has to be thus retained so that a large race of people be properly classified for *ethnological purposes*' (1893: 1, emphasis added).

Similarly, the difficulty to accurately ascertain the extent and nature of 'tribal divisions' was not peculiar to one particular case but was common to all. As J. P. Mills pointed out, the term 'Konyak' was used to cover a large number of people who could probably be classified as separate tribes. The basis on which it has been used as a generic term is based on the observations that 'all sections of the tribe, however, possess certain characteristics which distinguish them from other Nagas' (Mills 1926: 30). The use of language, dialect, customs and manners as indicators of classification was a complex issue. Similarities in language or dialect do not necessarily mean

35

similarities in customs and manners. It was observed that the Mao and Maram Naga, though very similar in dress and customs, spoke very different dialects. The language of the Lotha Naga differed from its neighbours, whereas in dress and customs resembled each other closely (Godden 1897: 166). Moreover, similitude in ecology and material culture, which is regarded to form a common substratum, does not necessarily mean a similarity in social structure. In other words, 'virtually identical economic systems can be associated with diametrically opposed types of social organisation' (von Fürer-Haimendorf 1971: 339).

In addition, it must be added that colonialism also produced the concept of the 'other' even among the natives. It is common in the colonial accounts to point out the differences amongst the 'hill-tribes' despite being lumped in the same category. However, the commonality ascribed to them is in contradistinction to the 'plains people', as Robert Reid puts it, '[The peoples of the Excluded Areas of Assam] differ markedly among themselves, but they have this one characteristic in common, that neither racially, historically, culturally, nor linguistically have they any affinity with the people of the plains' (1944: 19). The customs, language and religion of the hill tribes are projected as being quite different from those of the plains. Most colonial accounts insist that the inhabitants of the state of Manipur included both 'civilised Hindus and barbarous tribes' since the topography of the land 'consists of both tangled forest-covered hills and of open cultivated plain' (Dun 1975: 17). Moreover, it was asserted that the term 'Manipuri' was applicable only to the Hindu dwellers of the plains. As opposed to them, it was argued, the 'Hillmen, though divided into numerous clans and sections, may be grouped generally into the two great divisions of Naga and Kuki' (Royal Geographical Society 1891: 292). Subjective observations like cleanliness and dwellings, as a result, become important points of classification. These *observed* differences, between the people of the hill and valley, were productively used as a basis of colonial rule.

Colonial administration of ethnicisation vis-à-vis united resistance

The period subsequent to the Anglo-Burmese War of 1885–86 and finally the Anglo-Manipuri War of 1891 marked the hardening of ethnicisation. Deployment of the knowledge about various natives into administrative policies had two purposes. On the one hand, it was to exact efficient revenue and labour and exploit natural resources. On the other hand, drawing up of different administrative units based on ethnic lines in

COLONIAL ADMINISTRATION

the hills was primarily to negate a united resistance against colonial rule, which was represented through a proxy king and a few local aristocrats. Of these two purposes, the latter can be discussed in some detail.

The British were always apprehensive of a united resistance against them. They were aware of the Manipuri 'national manner of showing ill-feelings' (Maxwell 1904a), and they obviously suspected a militant form of resistance from disbanded officers and soldiers of the Manipur army, defeated in the Anglo-Manipuri War of 1891 (Maxwell 1904b). One way of reining in opposition and united resistance was to divide the territorial area of Manipur into manageable administrative divisions. British officials, on behalf of the King of Manipur, through the Manipur State Durbar were made responsible for administration of the hill village communities. The scheme of divide and rule continued with the spread of British hegemony despite the fact that Manipur was theoretically restored to a nominated king. British reinterpretation of the Rule, revised from time to time after consultation with the king and the political agent, as a policy meant for better management of the Manipur hills only reflected colonial intention to directly rule more than 90 per cent of Manipur's territory (*Administration Report of the Manipur Political Agency* 1919–20, hereafter *AR*). The British rejected the demand by the Nikhil Manipuri Mahasabha and the Durbar members for amalgamation of the hill and valley administration in 1938 and 1939, respectively, on the grounds that the valley should be properly governed first (*AR* 1931–32).

Thus, till 1947, the administration of the hill and 'plain' areas were kept divided from each other. The scheme for division was similarly extended among the natives in the hill areas. These were neither natural division nor did they correspond to any community border. By 1893, the hills were divided into five divisions. When a new scheme of hill administration was proclaimed on 16 October 1919 subsequently after the Kuki Rebellion, three new subdivisions were formed. The new subdivisions were:

Southern west Division with head quarters at Churachandpur, which had been named after His Highness, the Maharaja; the North-western Division with new headquarters at Tamenglong, inhabited mainly by Kukis, Kabui and Kacha Nagas; the Northeast Division with headquarter at Ukhrul, which was inhabited by Tangkhul and Kukis. Apart from these three subdivisions a large area in the north of the state, including the Mao and the Maram, the whole of the Mombi area in the Southeast, and the various hill villages bordering the valley were administered directly from Imphal under the President of the Durbar.

(*AR* 1919–20)

In December 1929, it was decided, as an experimental measure for three years in the first instance, to withdraw the subdivisions from the hills, and the two assistants made their headquarters at Imphal and took control of the whole hill area, one taking the north and another the south (*AR* 1931–32).

Administrative acts that divided Manipur into several divisions and subdivisions helped in the development of the psychology of disparity and disunity (Ningthouja 2004: 20). The suspicion that was born in the minds of the hill village communities vis-à-vis the Meeteis is self-illustrative in this context. Whenever British repression or oppression of the hill villagers took place, the oppressive mechanisms employed in most cases were dominantly recruited from amongst the Meeteis (for instance, take the case of Manipur Military Police as repressive mercenaries). As early as 1893, three Meetei officers and 144 men, all newly recruited by the British, were deployed on the Cachar, Naga Hills and Tammu roads, Nungbi, and Powi (in present-day Ukhrul district) (*AR* 1893–94).

Moreover, the British had made use of the Manipur State Durbar as a means of oppression, on behalf of the King who was shown as representing the numerically dominant community among the Manipuris, i.e. Meetei interest. Though different administrative rules were enforced for the hill areas and cases involving hill villagers were tried by the British courts, all forms of oppression and subjection of the hill villagers were done on behalf of His Highness by the president (a European officer) of the Durbar. Distrust and hatred against the king and his court, dominantly composed by men from the valley communities and classed as non-tribal, were constantly reproduced and popularised among the subjected hill village communities of Manipur. This factor interplayed or reinforced with other factors in the construction of communal stereotypes that subsequently became a threat to the territorial integrity of Manipur.

British law courts and churches also helped in the construction of an image of the king and the Meeteis as oppressor of the hill natives; primarily achieved through British projection of their own role as defender, protector and 'moderniser' of those who were portrayed as the oppressed or subjugated, or denied social justice by the Meeteis. Moreover, messianic announcement to grant tax holidays helped in projecting themselves as emancipator and, thereby, enhanced the consolidation of British control over the hills. Thus, the British were able to construct their image as saviour from the oppression of *lam-subedars*, a revenue official, and Manipuri soldiers and retainers. Finally, the British policy of forbidding the state Durbar and any Manipuri law court to interfere in cases in which members of the hill villages were involved (*AR* 1915–16) acted as surrogate to the construction of the psychology of otherness among the Manipuris, particularly between the Meeteis and natives. The king lost not only a large part of his jurisdictional area but also his symbolic importance as the source of justice in Manipur.

A divided administration throughout the century was aimed at obliterating any form of resistance against colonialism. It was informed by a knowledge produced by the British and aimed at weakening the power of the king. The administrative area of the Manipuri King was restricted to less than 10 per cent of the recognised territorial area of Manipur. It went on decreasing as the British kept on expanding their reserves and *mahals* (*AR* 1895–96, 1936–37). This policy enabled the British to freely exploit resources available and thus enrich their coffers. The divided administration helped in the development of distrust among the people, who were more or less grouped under different administrative zones. This created a psychology of disparity and disunity among the people.

Conclusion

The particular instance of incursion of the British into Manipur could be understood in a way that provides a more authentic reading of the reference point of the notion of 'primordiality' and to also see the practice of imagining a nation that is largely founded on the colonial administrative construction of distinctive ethnic lines and characters. Perhaps it would not be an overstatement to emphasise that ethnic groups began to assert their identity only during the post-Independence period of India. One can say that the colonial project in Manipur involved production of a knowledge which finally resulted in the creation of what came to be known as 'tribalism' by a colonial authority, and at the same time supplanting earlier social groups with patronage into ethnically and territorially defined political – administrative units and identities. Such enterprises were given substance by standardised written languages, published ethnographies and collections of folklore (Geertz 1983: 5) and the reorganisation of local polity.

Terms such as Naga and Kuki, which were crafted by the British along with the stereotypical representation of them as wild savages and tribal, have now become the very basis of identity and contestation over it in the political and social terrain. However, internalisation of the very basis of defining 'otherness', which was constituted by a series of political practices of these nomenclatures, needs to be further interrogated in order to understand the very nature of the 'situatedness' of claims such as the notion of 'uniqueness' and 'sovereign territories' upon which the former is firmly built.

Note

1 T.C. Hudson renders 'tribes' such as Tangkhul, Mao or Maring or Khongjai into Nagas and Kukis, and Meetei is equated with Manipuri (see Hodson 1996: 9–17). Here, it is noteworthy to mention about the framing of the natives (as a caricature) in the eyes of the coloniser. The colonial difficulty in civilising the 'tribals' can be drawn out from an account by Ethel St Clair Grimwood. She narrates:

> The Nagas never burden themselves with too many clothes, and these in particular wore little beside a necklace or two. I mentioned this fact to a spinster lady friend of mine on one occasion, and she was so horrified that she sent me shortly afterwards nine pairs of bathing-drawers to be given to them. They were very beautiful garments; some had red and white stripes, and some blue, and they were all very clean. I presented them gravely one morning to my nine Malis, and a few days after I went into the garden one evening and found two of the men at work. One had made a hole in his bathing apparatus and had put his head through it, while his arms went into the places for the legs, and he was wearing it with great pride as a jacket; and the other had arranged his with an eye for the artistic on his head as a turban. After this I gave up trying to inculcate decency into the mind of the untutored savage.

(1891: 24)

References

Administration Report of the Manipur Political Agency (AR), 1893–94, 1895–96, 1915–16, 1919–20, 1931–32, 1936–37. Imphal: Manipur State Archives.

Anderson, Benedict. 1983. *Imagined Communities: Reflections on the Origin and Spread of Nationalism.* London: Verso.

Dalton, Edward Tuite. 1872. *Descriptive Ethnology of Bengal.* Calcutta: Office of the Superintendent of Government Printing.

Dun, E. W. 1975. *Gazetteer of Manipur.* Delhi: Vivek Publishing.

Geertz, Clifford. 1983. *Local Knowledge: Further Essays in Interpretive Anthropology.* New York: Basic Books.

Godden, Gertrude M. 1897. 'Naga and Other Frontier Tribes of North-East India', *The Journal of the Anthropological Institute of Great Britain and Ireland*, 26: 161–201.

Grierson, G. A. 1903. Director of the Linguistic Survey of India, *Report of the Linguistic Survey of India* III, ii & iii: 1–250.

COLONIAL ADMINISTRATION

Grimwood, Ethel St Clair. 1891. *My Three Years in Manipur: And Escape from the Recent Mutiny*. London: Richard Bentley and Son.

Hodson, T.C. 1996 [first published in 1911] *The Nāga Tribes of Manipur*. Delhi: Low Price Publications.

Jilangamba, Yengkhom. 2008. 'A People without History: Colonialism and the Historical Legacy of Ethnic Classifications', *Biblio*, 13(5–6): 19–20.

Johnstone, James, Sir. 2002. *Manipur and the Naga Hills*. Delhi: Manas Publications.

Kamson, A. 2009. 'The Mera Haochongba Festival: The Traditional Hill – Valley Interface: The "Carnival" of Manipur', in H. Dwijasekhar Sharma (ed.), *New Insights into the Glorious Heritage of Manipur, Vol. 1*. New Delhi: Akansha Publishing House.

Mackenzie, Alexander. 2001 [1884]. *The North-East Frontier of India*. New Delhi: Mittal Publications.Maxwell, Colonel H. St. P. 1904a. Letter No. 373, 1 October 1904 from Colonel H. St. P. Maxwell, P.A. in Manipur and the Superintendent of the state, to the Secretary to the Chief Commissioner of Assam. In *Disturbance in Manipur 1904 (Women Agitation) 1904*. R-1 / S-A. Imphal: Manipur State Archives.

———. 1904b. T/N No. 73-p, 15 October 1904 from Colonel H. St. P. Maxwell, PA in Manipur and Superintendent of the state in *Disturbance at Imphal*, Manipur, R-1/ S-A, Imphal: Manipur State Archives.

McCulloch, William. 1857. 'Account of the Valley of Munnipore and of the Hill Tribes with a Comparative Vocabulary of the Munnipore and Other Languages', Selections from the Records of the Government of India (Foreign Department), Issue 27. Calcutta: Bengal Printing Company.

Mills, J. P. 1926. 'Certain Aspects of Naga Culture', *The Journal of the Royal Anthropological Institute of Great Britain and Ireland*, 56: 27–35.

Ningthouja, Malem. 2004. 'Meetei Resurgence and Nationalism (1900–2000): A Study of the Role of the Meetei in the Formation of 20th-century Manipur', M.Phil. dissertation, University of Delhi.

Royal Geographical Society. 1891. 'Manipur', *Proceedings of the Royal Geographical Society and Monthly Record of Geography: New Monthly Series*, 13(5): 292.

Reid, Robert. 1944. 'The Excluded Areas of Assam', *The Geographical Journal*, 103(1–2): 18–29.

Said, Edward W. 1995. *Orientalism: Western Conceptions of the Orient*. London: Penguin.

Soppitt, C. A. 1893. *A Short Account of the Kuki-Lushai Tribes on the North-East Frontier*. Aizawl: Tribal Research Institute.

Spear, Thomas. 2003. 'Neo-traditionalism and the Limits of Invention in British Colonial Africa', *The Journal of African History*, 44(1): 3–27.

Von Fürer-Haimendorf, Christoph. 1971. 'Comparisons between the Mountain Peoples of the Philippines and some Tribes of North-East India', *The Geographical Journal*, 137(3): 339–48.

41

3

REVISITING THE KUKI REBELLION AND *NUPI LAN*

Lisham Henthoiba

Colonialism and its operation

There are debates regarding the forms of colonialism that have been evolving in a variety of ways. The precise nature and period in which colonialism and imperialism had occurred, and for that matter has been occurring, are being questioned and disputed. There is no question that the evolution of capitalism to its other forms and the way it is operating has been changing in the last few decades and has transformed the world to the effect that there are no forms of domination and subjugation that existed in the times of colonialism and imperialism (Amin 2005: 2). There are other views that argue that the scientific and technological revolution will produce forms of economic and political management of the planet and surpass those associated with the defence of national interest, and that this evolution has led to a world where issues and questions about colonialism and imperialism are anachronistic (ibid.: 3). However, such views cannot deny the relevance of a study on colonialism and imperialism if seen in the context of causality ensuing from imperialism.

Imperialism is generally understood and identified with the rise of great powers that began to rule the world. For example, Britain, which by the late 1800s was competing with emerging great powers such as Germany and the United States, began to control major part of the globe. The rise of powerful States, which began during the 1870s and consequently became colonial powers, is known as 'new imperialism'. The result was the imposition of colonial rule by European countries. European imperial powers felt the obligation to import their 'superior' culture to respective colonies. One way of comprehending Christian missionaries of different denominations travelling across Africa and Asia to spread Christian religious beliefs was in this context of the civilising mission that was strongly promoted.

Many writers construed imperialism in terms of their understanding of the motivating forces behind imperialism. Among these, John Hobson, Nikolai Bukharin, Rosa Luxemberg, and especially Vladimir Ilyich Lenin focused on economic factors, the rational pursuit of new markets and sources of raw materials (Griffiths and O'Callaghan 2002: 152). Lenin argued in *Imperialism: The Highest Stage of Capitalism* (1917) that imperialism was an economic necessity of the industrialised capitalist economies seeking to offset the declining tendency of the rate of profit, by exporting capital. It was the monopoly stage of capitalism. Coming to the nature of the imposition and its forms, another term was widely shared in the recent past on the study of imperialism, i.e. informal imperialism. Informal imperialism is said to render direct political control unnecessary in the presence of other ways of exercising domination, for example, through technological superiority or the free trade imperialism of a leading economic power and cultural imperialism (Griffiths and O'Callaghan 2002: 154).

There are views that advance the idea that colonialism, latent or manifest, has affected and continues to affect in one way or the other the whole human population at one point of time or the other. Colonialism is responsible for the making, unmaking and remaking of the world order, political, territorial alignments, misalignments and realignments, and the mapping and remapping of the globe. Colonialism 'reveals itself a stark and blatant form of exploitation in every sense of the term' (Singh 2006: 2).

Such views have pointed out a problematic understanding of colonialism which is what studies of colonialism overlook the local population that inhabited the regions before they were 'discovered' by the coloniser. Questions regarding the status of these natives have been largely and conveniently ignored. Two contrasting and paradoxical views of history underline a serious debate on the status of the natives. The first view is that of cultural difference and points out that there exists a culture wholly different from that of European perception. The second view holds that historical status grows only through relations in terms of trade or colonialism (ibid.: 7).

The latter of the two views has its origin in the classical articulation on imperialism, as discussed earlier, that focused on economic factors, the rational pursuit of new markets and sources of raw materials and finally on a trading relationship that results in the exploitation of the natives. However, in its emphasis upon class and larger economic forces, the questions of natives are ignored, for example, in economically backward regions. The former view on cultural differences thus far has not been completely captured in literatures on colonialism. However, nascent deliberations on the issues can be garnered from a few writings as in the case of Bernard Cohn and Edward Said. Nevertheless, Cohn's writings focus on the ways of power of the colonisers that reside in the control of the knowledge and power without touching upon resistance as a way of countering colonial hegemony. For example, Cohn, in one of his most celebrated works *Colonialism and Its Form of Knowledge*, forwards an argument that the British during their colonial expansion unknowingly and unwittingly invaded and conquered not only a territory but an 'epistemological' space as well. The 'facts' of this space did not exactly correspond to those of the invader. The British believed they could explore and conquer this space through translation to make the unknown and the strange world of the colonised as something that was to become 'knowable'. There was a conscious effort on the part of the coloniser to explore the colonised and present its rule as legitimate and justified. Colonialism, according to Cohn, was exercised and sustained in this way to the effect of actual control of the natives (Cohn 2002: 3, 8).

The way of controlling of the natives by the coloniser was embedded in the claim of their being superior to the natives. The control itself was closely associated with a civilizing mission with which colonial rule was justified. This view was studied, albeit in a different way, by Edward Said in his classic work *Orientalism*. Said elaborated it by focusing on the relation between the colonisers and the colonised with his employment of two entities, the 'West' and the 'Orient'. The West, according to the colonisers, was a synonym for the modern, rational and civilised. The non-West, meaning the Orient, was the opposite of all the attributes that characterised the West. Cultures that were different from that of the coloniser, according to Said, were treated as inferior and, therefore, savage. At the same time, the coloniser asserted their culture as advanced as well as superior (Said 1995: 3, 7). Thus, the coloniser posited control and domination as a civilising parameter of culture.

Thus, one finds that in the above-mentioned formulations, theories on imperialism and colonialism impinge on causes, operational aspects and means to sustain hegemony. Exploitative relationships ensuing from economic extraction and justification based on control of knowledge – thereby legitimising colonial rule – form the main currents of thought. The limitation of these theories, as pointed out, suffers from inadequate attention given to the natives.

The study

To capture the centrality of the natives, this chapter suggests that there could be an alternative intervention in addition to the above-mentioned debates on colonialism. Forms of colonial rule and its operation can be understood by focusing on how the natives actually came to counter it. In other words, an attempt to understand colonialism in the light of anti-colonial movements may be more productive. In this exercise, an inescapable aspect that needs to be taken into account is how anti-colonial movement was articulated in the encounter between the coloniser and the colonised. Such an understanding is suggestive of moving beyond the monolithic representation of anti-colonial movement as things of the past. This is also to suggest that understanding of anti-colonial resistance, which is always occasioned in anti-colonial consciousness, is essential to linking the past to the contemporary resistance and movement. Equally important is the possibility to counter the understanding of the events of resistances to the colonial rule only in the ways in which they have been understood as anti-colonial resistance to a certain type of colonialism of the past. Thus, rather than considering anti-colonial resistance as a thing of the past, the chapter intends to investigate two possibilities: first, to see that resistance offered by anti-colonial movement (during the period under study), at least in terms of the way in which resistance was practised, provides ways of looking at the very relevance of (contemporary) 'presentness' of the resistances; and second, to find ways in which to locate the very relevance of forms of colonialism that is currently in operation. Thus, the framework of the chapter includes investigation into the general features of colonialism so as to discern a possibility of revisiting the occurrences of events of resistance against colonial rule in the context of Manipur.

Colonialism, without any doubt, is domination and exploitation. Rather than understanding the resistance movement as an outcome of the policies of colonial rule, it can be understood from the perspective of the consciousness of the people, in the ways in which they came to know how they were being dominated and exploited. Through this consciousness, colonial rule, its form and power, is being questioned. Two specific forms of anti-colonial resistance to the British, such as the Kuki Rebellion of 1917 and the *Nupi Lan* of 1939, are taken up as referral points for the study. What is being attempted in this chapter is to see how the two historical events were articulated as anti-colonial resistances to British rule in Manipur. Anti-colonial movement in Manipur in this way can give light to understanding colonialism as a form of domination. Put differently, these two events of resistance in the modern history of Manipur can be read historically as events that put into operation anti-colonial consciousness among the masses. This could be further extended to seeing the operation of colonial rule in the manner it was articulated in the very encounter between the coloniser and the colonised. There are two ways of looking at this issue. One way of doing this is to abolish the idea that anti-colonial movement was a reaction to the colonial rule. The other is to consider the possibility of changing coloniser as the central figure in the discourse of anti-colonialism. Finally, the issues raised by these two forms of resistance have relevance in the context of contemporary Manipur.

The Kuki Rebellion and the *Nupi Lan* can be understood as conscientious forms of resistance challenging colonial rule and exploitation. The challenge was not reactionary or instantaneous in the sense that accumulated grievances of the people finally found an outlet in the historical events. Here, consciousness is understood as an alert cognitive state in which one is aware of oneself and one's situation. It is not the consciousness of men that determines their existence, but their social existence that determines their consciousness. Thus, anti-colonial consciousness among the natives was determined, in short, by the emerging new forms of social relations and material conditions engendered by colonialism itself.

The Kuki Rebellion, 1917–19

Particularly in the case of the Kuki Rebellion, the nature of articulation was not 'civilised' or 'modern' in Western parlance; they relied upon the Kuki ways of knowing the world and carried out in a language that carried meaning to themselves; perhaps, it might not be the case to a Westerner. The key characteristic features of the Kuki include 'respect of birth and knowledge of pedigrees, clannish feelings' (Carey and Tuck 1983: 165.) In addition, Kukis took pride in being a warrior. For example, the Thado clan of the Kukis is understood to be bellicose in nature since it is derived from the words 'Tha', meaning 'to kill', and 'Doh', meaning 'to resist' or 'to make war' (Paokai 1995: 235) The Kukis were head-hunters, like its neighbours the pre-Hinduised Meeteis or the pre-Christianised Nagas, and collected heads of slain men and animals as offerings to their dead ancestors. In general, Kukis were martial people who considered war and hunting to be the first and second best pursuits for a man. The Rebellion followed the traditional course of Thado warfare, involving the *Shajam Iha* rite, where a *mithun* (a wild animal considered to be the most prized possession by the Kukis) was slaughtered and its meat shared in a communal meal by the willing chiefs. A fascinating feature of *Sajam Ihah*

> is the taking of the liver and heart of the animal. The liver symbolizes the "heart of the matter" or "the core" of the issue at hand. The eating of the heart and the liver attributes to the associated event, a significance of great moral accountability. It is used as a "seal" to a commitment of particular cause.
>
> (Haokip 1998: 78)

Then a smouldering piece of wood from the cooking fire wrapped in red chillies was circulated around the villages to signal war. Twenty-three Kuki villages rebelled. This is against the popular understanding that the Kukis were nomadic and warring tribes who did not have an idea of unity and solidarity. The modern idea of a State as the gathering spot of people for political action was rendered meaningless in the nature that Kukis articulated their sense of 'cause' against colonial rule. They did rebel in the language of war, a worldview permitted by its belief and the only means they knew to deal with a situation.

Causes of the rebellion

After the 1891 Anglo-Manipuri war, the subsequent administration that was carried out by the British in Manipur produced a negotiable space for administration where the position of the native king had been protected while a new system of administration was gradually promoted. The arrangement served the interest of the British Empire in a way that ensured colonial control of administration using the king as the nominal ruler. British political control and its impact on Manipur's political economy and social strata were of less importance to the native aristocrats as they were preoccupied with the struggle for acquiring the throne among themselves. Moreover, the British, without using much force, had control over the overall political affairs with appropriated accommodation of natives.

The immediate cause for the revolt was the British demand for labourers to be part of the Manipur Labour Corps that was to be sent from the state. By May 1917, 'the First Labour Corps (No. 22) consisting of 2,000 Nagas and Kukis from the hills was completed and sent away' (Reid 1884: 79). After the first batch of labourers, a second corps was demanded from the state but the idea was dropped. Instead, the War Office asked for drafts for the existing corps. In September 1917, when the political agent met the chiefs, they flatly refused to accept the effort of drafting labourers. During World War I, the State authority was to donate a sum of Rs 1,34,000 as war loan. Apart from this, the men from the Naga and Kuki communities were recruited to raise the Manipur Labour Corps and they were sent 'much against their will' to France in May 1917 (Dena 1991: 126). They were used as labourers for digging trenches, carrying loads and building base camps. The question of recruitment came up with the urgency of sending more labour to war fronts in Europe. To discuss the matter, Higgins, the then political agent of Manipur, proceeded to the Hills in September 1917 to meet a deputation of chiefs. The chiefs, however, were reluctant to send youths to France as labour forces and they even gave money to the British officers not to call for such recruitment again for France service. They paid to the political agent a sum of Rs 1,500, three gongs and one *mithun* as *salam*, adding that 'it was the custom of the Kukis to bring the head of the dead man wherever they died' (Dena 1991: 126–27). However, Higgins was insisting on either giving to him a supply of recruits that he proposed within a fixed period or submitting to punishment. Following the disagreement between him and the Kuki chiefs, Higgins burned down a village and that laid the foundation of the Rebellion (Dena 1991: 127). This is reminiscent of Edward Said's description of 'general European effort to rule distant lands and peoples' or of their description about the Orientals:

> What are striking in these discourses are the rhetorical figures one keeps encountering in their descriptions of "the mysterious East" as well as the stereotypes about "the African [or Indian, or Irish or Jamaican or Chinese] minds," the notion about bringing civilization to primitive or barbaric peoples, the disturbingly familiar ideas about death or extended punishment being required when "they" misbehaved or became rebellious, because "they" mainly understood force or violence best; "they" were not like "us," and for that reason deserved to be ruled.
>
> (Said 1994: xi)

The recruitment was suspended in November 1917, and in December 1917 the Thadou Kukis broke into open revolt and raided the Manipur valley. The revolt was widespread affecting even some of the villages in the Somra Tract. The 'Thadou Kukis had responded', in the words of Sir Robert Reid, 'poorly to the calls for labor Corps sent to France early in the year' (Reid 1884: 80).

REVISITING THE KUKI REBELLION AND *NUPI LAN*

Causes for the revolt from the colonial administrators' viewpoint is found in a letter of June 1919 submitted for orders of the Governor-General. The following are enumerated as causes of the Rebellion in the letter (Reid 1884: 80):

1 Rules did not make adequate provision for the administration of the hills, and it was general defect in administration of Manipur. And for a single officer, (meaning the President of the Manipur State Durbar, an Indian Civil Service Officer) to tour in the huge area under his control was impossible
2 The "unsatisfactory intermediary" between the British Officers and the hill men in the shape of the *lambus* were responsible in small measure
3 Because the President of the Durbar remained tied to Imphal as a result of the changes of rules in 1916, he was thus prevented from making long tours in the hills
4 The President of the Durbar could not devote the proper amount of time to the hill tribes because of the war (First World War) and other local troubles

Colonial explanation for the outbreak of the Rebellion was dictated by the perception of the failure to physically control the tribes. The implied reasoning was that if the President was not tied to Imphal, he would have taken measures to subjugate the tribes purely on the basis of force. Colonial understanding negated accumulated grievances as the source of the Rebellion. They implied, in the above-mentioned reasons, that if the rules had made provisions for many officers (as against a single officer) with a massive force to go to the hills, probably the outbreak of the Rebellion may not have taken place. Ironically, it was the Britishers who made the rules. On account of the changes in 1916, a power vacuum existed in the hills. This was especially true when Manipur Durbar had no jurisdiction in the hill affairs. Lokendra Singh observes, 'Throughout the period of colonial rule, the administration of the hill tribes was always under the direct supervision of the Vice President/President and after 1916 the Durbar as a whole had no jurisdiction over the affairs of the hills' (Singh 1998: 39). Thus, the British had prevented the exercise of Manipur Durbar authority over the affairs of the hills. Moreover, the President, yet again because of the changes in 1916, could not take long tours in the hills. This policy had freed the tribes, to an extent, from direct external hold.

Apart from the Britishers, many writers accrue the enforcement of house tax and forced labour (*pothang*) as cause for the Rebellion. A house tax of Rs 3 per household (annual) was levied from the hill areas as against Rs 2 per household (annual) in the valley areas. Moreover, although *pothang* (including *senkhai*) was abolished from the valley areas in 1913, it remained in operation in the hill areas. Under this system, villagers were under obligation to provide free labour for construction works or carry baggage and goods of the touring government officials, as well as pay monetary levies for feeding the officials. Naorem Joykumar and Lal Dena, among others, share the view that house tax and *pothang* were major sources of discontent among the hill people and crucial factors for the outbreak of the Rebellion.

One important factor that none of the authors (including the British) have given thought to is the worldview of the Kukis. This factor – for example, manual labour which they consider below their esteem – in my opinion, is the basic premise on which the Kukis built up their resistance to colonial domination and oppression. Prim Vaiphei observes this trait in his discussion of the Kuki ethnoses, although he did not discuss the Rebellion:

> During the reign of Chandrakirty . . . the ancestors of the writer (Prim Vaiphei) lived at Mahabali in Imphal. The ancestors left Imphal because the King not only used them as warrior, but he wanted to use them also to carry palanquin. They wanted to serve the King as warrior but not as servants.
>
> (Vaiphei 1995: 127)

Perhaps, the British – as well as scholars who have analysed the Kuki Rebellion – were unaware of the power and autonomy of the culture and ideas of the natives. Precisely by drawing strength from their culture and worldview, the Kukis raged their Rebellion for around three years. This factor, in Vaiphei's opinion, is also one of the most important causes (for example, against recruitment for the labour corps) for the Kuki Rebellion.

The Rebellion, thus, was an expression of outrage incited by a cumulative military power and indignation felt at various stages since the beginning of colonial rule. And they asserted themselves in the form of a powerful uprising. The General Officer Commanding of the Burma Division, Sir H. D. U. Kerry, wrote at the time: 'I . . . decided to put an end to the Kuki revolt by force of arms, break the Kuki spirit, disarm the Kukis, exact reparation and pave the way for an effective administration of their country' (quoted in Shakespeare 1980: 237). The 'Punitive Expedition' was summarily undertaken, involving a systematic sweeping

REVISITING THE KUKI REBELLION AND *NUPI LAN*

back and forth across Kuki villages by Shakespeare's 3,000 men and the sacking of many villages. The suppression of the Rebellion cost the government Rs 28 lakh (Phanjoubam 2005: 147). Colonel L. W. Shakespeare observed, 'It [the Kuki Rebellion] therefore grew into the largest series of military operations conducted on this side of India since the old (full-scale) expeditionary days of Generals Penn Symonds and Tregear in the late (eighteen) eighties, or the futile Abor Expedition of the 1911–12, eclipsing them all in casualties and arduousness of active service' (Shakespeare 1980: 200). J. H. Hutton observed, 'Before the Kuki Rising of 1918–1919, the administration of the hill areas of Manipur State was not very close' (quoted in Reid 1884: 79). It was only after the Rebellion of 1917–19 that the hill areas were put under intense administrative control.

Towards the close of the year, in 1919, following the Kuki Rebellion, the hill people were for the first time brought under the intensified political and administrative control of an imperial power. Under a new scheme that year, three new sub-divisions were formed, namely, the southwest area with headquarters at Churachandpur, the northwest area with temporary headquarters at Tamenglong and the northeast area with headquarters at Ukhrul. Each sub-division was placed under the charge of a British Sub-Divisional Officer who was directly accountable to the President of the Manipur State Durbar (Dena 1991: 134). Shakespeare wrote, 'The Kukis were now made to open up their country by constructing fair bridle paths through their hills connecting with points in the Manipur and Chindwin Valley (Burma), and also connecting with the various posts with each other' (Shakespeare 1980: 237).

As Reid (1942: 78–82) later acknowledged, there were genuine grievances and genuine abuses behind the revolt, in addition to the issue of recruitment of the male population for raising the labour corps. Punitive action by the British succeeded in producing a sense of devaluation among the native cultures. This was manifest in undermining the spirit of native resistance by the British. The 'rationale' by the British for penalising the Kukis was not the said Rebellion but the raids that they conducted on the Nagas. The British intention was to stop such raids by punitive measures, which would ultimately subject them to surrender before the rule (Mackenzie 1999: 80–81). Such apparently justified pleas made by the British served their ulterior purpose of colonisation, but they knew very well how to disguise the actual purpose behind the veil of such justifications given to repressive measures. The ulterior purpose of colonisation became evident when the British displaced the same Kukis to various places as a front against other tribes.

The Kuki Rebellion was a testimonial account of resistance from the hills of Manipur against the colonial rule and its policy of expediency. The resistance was against domination and exploitation of the coloniser, an event of anti-colonial movement, which was truly a manifestation of the perspective of the colonised. Some native scholars in their different accounts remarked that the Rebellion was not only a valiant assertion by the Kukis for their rights but also an act of avenging the Khongjom War of 1891 on behalf of all the Manipuris (Kipgen 2005). It also sowed the seeds of future resistance movements, which were led by Haipou Jadonang, Gaidinliu and Hijam Irabot, and the second *Nupi Lan* (Parratt 2005: 27). But most importantly, the Rebellion sowed the seeds for perfection in guerrilla and jungle warfare and stands as an edifice of honour for one's way of life as is currently witnessed on the soil of Manipur. Today, the cry for justice against forced labour, as one witnesses during many of the military 'operations' to flush out 'insurgents', is evocative of the Kuki resistance against British colonialism.

Nupi Lan, 1939

Assertion of Manipuri women in the economic sphere in particular, and the public domain in general, was accompanied and entrenched by its constant encounter and resistance to colonial impositions. In 1904, thousands of women demonstrated in Imphal to protest and disobey the order of the British Superintendent who decreed that the general public must supply bamboo, cane and so on, free of cost. The *Nupi Lan* of 1939 – popularly known as the Women's War – is another illustration when women revolted against the king and British authority to stop the export of rice from Manipur. The spirit and legacy of the two struggles can be interpreted as follows: 'where there is oppression, there is resistance'.

The *Nupi Lan* of 1939, fought under the leadership of Manipuri women against British colonial policy, culminated in the struggle for the establishment of self-rule. The legacy has generated an unwinding path of resistance against all forces of oppression. What was taken as a war cry against colonial atrocity has in the course of the struggle duly become an epitome of the relentless struggle against all forms of repressive agents.

> It was a milestone; a battle where each wound inflicted by colonial oppression echoes the cry of the undying will; each step a milestone of resistance in the sojourn of all forms of atrocities so

forth; each cry beckons the never-ending harrowing memories of these voices that shall find the spirit whenever the undaunted will embark upon all stark forms of oppression.

(Hidam and Meetei 2008: 1)

Colonial free trade policy produced famines of 1920 – that sparked off the Bazaar Boycott – and of 1939. An important factor that aroused feelings of disgust among the Manipuris against the Marwari merchants was their utter disregard for people's suffering at the altar of profit. Although Marwaris were allowed to export rice from Manipur subject to the condition that they should stop rice export when the price of rice rose up to Rs 3 per maund, most of the Marwari merchants, without considering the needs of the public, had always tried to avoid the restriction under cover of the Red Pass. Red Pass was a special permit issued to certain Marwaris to export rice for the Government purpose even during the time of prohibition (Singh 2000: 112).

Consequently, there was widespread starvation all around while the unceasing free trade policy further aggravated the food scarcity to such an extent that people had to feed on stems and roots. On 12 December 1939, Manipuri women started fighting the colonial apparatus to bring an end to the colonial exploitation and artificial scarcity of rice by stopping rice export from Manipur. In the words of Salam Tomba Singh, 'We begged for rice and in return received bayonet wounds and wounds from the gun-butts. For one handful of rice we paid two handfuls of blood' (quoted in Hidam and Meetei 2008: 1). Consequent to the War, E. F. Lydall remarked, 'The Women's War caused a breakdown of the administration, manifested mainly by the inadequacy, both in numbers and efficiency of the State Police' (quoted in Singh 2000: 57).

The general parlance of *Nupi Lan* heralded the unshakeable ground whereof all continuing processes of struggle till date has found the will to fight against all unjustifiable wounds and atrocities or forms of institutionalised atrocities. Nevertheless, although the struggle for emancipation from all oppression has seen ups and downs, the overall approach of struggle never took a backseat. This is rather an obvious fact since Manipur was annexed to the Indian Union in 1949. From that moment onwards, Manipur has been a witness to repressive policies of the Indian State. Since 1958, the continuing force of resistance against the Armed Forces (Special Powers) Act, 1958 (AFSPA) has taken undue grievances in many forms of glorious sacrifices, mortifications and abnegations. The 26 years of resistance that the Manipuri women instantiated in the form of the *Meira Paibi* movement has today become a proven capacity to challenge the oppressive measures of the Indian State. The trepidation that stirred one of the greatest awestruck sight, and has found its place in the pages of the history of resistance against state terrorism, is the nude protest at Kangla on 15 July 2004. The nude protest represents the bulwark of resistance against the savagery of the AFSPA. In this relentless struggle, it would not be overrated to highlight the long struggle of Irom Chanu Sharmila. It is not a struggle of one woman; it is a voice of that human will; a voice of the wounded that has been leashed incessantly; the fate of justice that has been sealed prolonged to the people of Manipur. The *Nupi Lan* finds its torchbearer in the struggle of Irom Chanu Sharmila who has been on fast since November 2000 demanding the complete repeal of AFSPA. The legacy of *Nupi Lan* has today been epitomised in the undying struggle of Sharmila and *Meira Paibis* (Women Torchbearers).

Conclusion

History is made to exist in the public consciousness by producing the accounts of the past in such a way that characterises omission and inclusion of events and figures as unpopular and popular. What has to be accounted and narrated of the past, and commanded as a history, has been one of the foremost tasks of the historian. This task of talking about the past, especially of the colonial past, should be linked to understanding the operation of domination and oppression in the present for as long as practices of exploitation and domination exist, the necessity to intervene in these practices will remain an agenda of any form of historical writing. It would definitely amount to an erroneous belief if we declare that decolonisation in the world has been completed, negating the existence of various insurrection, which is predominant across the globe. With massive underdevelopment and economic backwardness persisting in the postcolonial 'ex-colonies', the relationship between the erstwhile colonial structures/Western power and the ex-colonies becomes a focal point of critical debates on the 'pastness' of colonialism. The more recent global triumph of capitalist states and other forces produces new forms of imperial agents and forms of domination. It is also true that with the establishment of a monolithic and hegemonic global economy controlled by the West and shared by its comprador allies, erstwhile colonies – or what is known as the Third World States – have been in deepening crisis. The problem that is enduring with most of the ex-colonies is that they have inherited the colonial structures of rule and domination and hence, forms of resistance to these new forms of colonial agents bring out the need to understand these structures in the less visible parts of the world.

References

Amin, Samir. 2005. Empire and Multitude, *Monthly Review*, Vol. 57, Issue 06, November.

Carey, Bertram S. and H. N. Tuck. 1896 (Reprinted 1983). *The Chin Hills: A History of the People, Our Dealings with Them, Their Customs and Manners, and a Gazetteer of Their Country.* New Delhi: Cultural Publishing House.

Chatterjee, Partha. 'Towards a Postcolonial Modernity: Interview with Partha Chatterjee', http://www.asiasource.org/news/specialreports/chatterjeeprint.html.

Cohn, Bernard S. 2002. *Colonialism and Its Form of Knowledge: The British in India.* New Delhi: Oxford University Press.

Dena, Lal (ed.). 1991. *History of Modern Manipur: 1826–1949.* New Delhi: Orbit Publisher.

Griffiths, Martin and Terry O'Callaghan. 2002. *International Relations: The Key Concepts.* London: Routledge.

Haokip, P. S. 1998. *Zale'n-gam: The Kuki Nation.* Kuki National Organisation. Imphal

Hidam, Praem and M. Bobby Meetei. 2008. '*Nupi Lan*: Continuing the Struggle', *MSAD Newsletter*, 1(5): 1–8.

Kamei, Gangumei. 2004. *A History of the Zeliangrong Nagas.* Guwahati: Spectrum Publications.

Kipgen, Donn Morgan. 2005. 'The Great Kuki Rebellion of 1917–19: Its Real Significances', *The Sangai Express*, December 21.

Lenin, V. I. 1917. *Imperialism: The Highest Stage of Capitalism.* Petrograd: Znaniye Publishers.

Mackenzie, Alexander. 1999. *The North-East Frontier of India.* New Delhi: Mittal Publications.

Paokai, Sithou Mangjel. 1995. 'The Kukis', in Naorem Sanajaoba (ed.), *Manipur, Past and Present: The Ordeals and Heritage of a Civilization (Nagas & Kuki-Chins), Volume III*, pp. 232–45. New Delhi: Mittal Publications.

Parratt, John. 2005. *Wounded Land.* New Delhi: Mittal Publications.

Reid, Sir Robert. 1942 *History of the Frontier Areas Bordering on Assam from 1883–1941.* Shillong.

Said, Edward W. 1994. 'Introduction', *Culture and Imperialism.* New York: Vintage Books.

———. 1995. *Orientalism: Western Conceptions of the Orient.* London: Penguin.

Shakespeare, L. W. 1980. *History of the Assam Rifles.* Gauhati: Spectrum Publications.

Singh, Karam Manimohan. 2000. *Nupi Lan.* Imphal: K. Premlata Devi.

Singh, N. Lokendra. 1998. *The Unquiet Valley: Society, Economy and Politics of Manipur (1891–1950).* New Delhi: Mittal Publications.

Singh, R. K. Jhalajit. 1965. *A Short History of Manipur.* Imphal: O.K. Store.

Singh, Thingnam Kishan. 2006. *Rethinking Colonialism.* Delhi: Worldview Publications.

Tarapot, Phanjoubam. 2005. *Bleeding Manipur.* New Delhi: Har-Anand Publications.

Vaiphei, Prim S. 1995. 'The Kukis', in Naorem Sanajaoba (ed.), *Manipur, Past and Present: The Ordeals and Heritage of a Civilization (Nagas & Kuki-Chins), Volume III*, 126–33. New Delhi: Mittal Publications.

4

COLONIALISM AND MOVEMENT FOR DEMOCRACY IN MANIPUR

Konthoujam Indrakumar

It is commonplace to receive the post-renaissance period as a history of hegemony and its counterfoils. This 'commonplace' became 'highly sweeping' as hardly any part of the world's territory was left unoccupied. Occupation became a dominant ideology to be realised for there was a Eurocentric notion of a universally superior, represented by the West, and a universally lacking, represented by the non-West. Such ideology was meant to rationalise the colonial conquest of other peoples and cultures across Asia, Africa and Latin American continents besides incorporation of peripheral areas of the globe into world economic networks centred on the more industrially advanced countries (Skocpol 1999: 20). This chapter is not intended to delve into a detailed account of the economic and political historiography of European colonialism as it aims at a focused understanding of how democratic ideas began to make its mark and consequent movements were shaped against the backdrop of colonial exploits and already existing undemocratic political authorities and socio-economic norms. The present chapter is an attempt to locate the democratic movement in Manipur within the broader socio-economic background from the late 19th century to the late 1940s.

To put into perspective, the chapter touches upon two important phases of the colonial and resistance history of Manipur. One aspect is to discuss events in Manipur up to 1930 with an introduction to how colonialism was played out, and the other is to examine the developments from 1930 to 1948 as there was a strong tendency to consolidate the democratic questions in terms of a movement.

Political conditions of Manipur

The advancement of colonialism in Manipur was heightened in the wake of frequent animosity and fratricidal killings among the royal blood for the throne. Manipur's geopolitical position played a pivotal role for outside intervention. In addition, the Burmese devastation, which came to be known as *Chahi Taret Khuntakpa* (the Seven Years' Devastation) (1819–25) in its history, was the result of an alliance formation in pursuit of the throne. The British account of Manipur and later accounts by Manipuri historians cite innumerable instances of such fratricidal feuds and killings among the princes of Manipur. The ensuing fragmented polity and lack of unity among the princes led to interference from external powers, especially British and Burmese, into the sovereignty of Manipur. However, it is not to be assumed that external interventions were the outcome of internal fragile politics only, but it was also a result of the overall imperial expansion all over the world. An overview of Anglo-Manipuri relations from 1762 to 1891 throws significant light on strategic concerns of the Manipur State and the British Empire. Manipur needed friendly diplomatic relations with the British to protect its sovereignty against Burmese invasion and to keep itself in good terms with the British. On the other side, British alliance with Manipur was essential to advance and protect her imperial interests, both political and commercial, in her colonies in Burma and Assam. Rajas of Manipur used to supply men and food to the British. The British and Manipuri soldiers even took joint expeditions such as the Burmese expedition in 1825, Naga Hills expedition of 1879 and the third Anglo-Burmese War of 1885–86. Thus, Manipur was frequently used as a partner to fulfil British imperialist interests. By 1835, a new beginning in the Anglo-Manipuri relation was affected by appointing a political agent 'to act as a medium of communication between Manipur and the British Government' (Allen et al. 2005: 615). It can be said that the appointment of a political agent marked the beginning of direct British control over Manipur. Gradually, the political agent acted more like a 'de facto administrator of the state' (Joykumar Singh 1991: 31).

The British policy towards Manipur was essentially to transform it into a buffer state between the British Indian and Burmese Empires in order to enhance the interests of the British Indian Empire (Dena 1991: 9). The Palace rebellion of 1891, and subsequent outbreak of the Anglo-Manipur war the same year, can be located within the above-mentioned framework. On the economic aspect, the Empire was prepared to exploit the economic possibilities in Manipur. For example, an agreement on silk trade was signed between Messrs A. Wright & Company, Calcutta and the Maharaja on 29 November 1906, for a term of 30 years. According to the terms of the agreement, Raja Churachand Singh of Manipur agreed to grant necessary land for the successful operation of the factory free of land revenue. The Raja also agreed that the state would not levy any tax or duty on cocoons, silk or silk waste exported by the firm (ibid.: 86). Besides, British rule had created a non-local trading class in Manipur that seriously affected the economy of Manipur. Under the British rule, Marwari traders were granted monopoly right to conduct trade on rice that seriously undermined the agrarian economy of the state.

Native settings, alien rule and manipulations

After the defeat of Manipur in the Anglo-Manipuri War of 1891, the British kept the state under its suzerainty without directly annexing it. The British instead appointed a minor called Churachand as the Raja of Manipur to suit their imperial interests on 15 May 1907. Although legally the rein of administration and power of the state belonged to the Raja, the British through their political agent were the *de facto* sovereign. Administrative arrangements initiated under British colonial rule were more akin to having two sovereigns with respective spheres of influence. A perceptive reading testifies to a manifest British policy of making Manipur a vassal state of the Empire. Suffice it to say that there was a combination of feudal and colonial rule over the people where exploitation was extraordinarily heightened. The burden of this combined oppression fell on the shoulders of poor subjects, including peasants and small traders, who were later to become the springboard for anti-colonial, anti-feudal and pro-democratic reform movements.

In other words, the abolition of the previously existing exploitative system such as *lallup*[1] was replaced by a sophisticated tax system that levied an annual house tax of Rs 2 per homestead in the valley and Rs 3 per household in the hills. The land revenue was also assessed at a uniform rate of Rs 5 per *Pari*[2] and the decennial *patta* system introduced during the period of Maxwell's political agency; most of the oppressive system of taxation remained intact and was sometimes reinforced vigorously.

On the administrative aspect, the British rule also brought the hills and valley of Manipur under a separate administration. Significant modifications were made in the administrative set-up of the state after the installation of Churachand as the Raja of Manipur. On the whole, the

administration was not transparent and pro-people, and was now conducted by

> His Highness the Maharaja and the political agent through a
> Darbar, which consisted of an Indian Civil Service (ICS) Euro-
> pean officer, formerly deputed by the local government of
> Assam. All the six Darbar members (3 ordinary, 3 additional)
> were nominated by the King and most of them had "near rela-
> tion" with His Highness
>
> (Manimohan Singh 2006: 170)

Manipur society then was a stratified one with British colonial agents,
the Raja, members of the Manipur State Durbar, other high rankings state
officials and monopolist Marwari traders occupying the higher echelon
in the socio-political and economic hierarchy. In sum, they combined to
form an exploitative governing class. The poor state subjects who formed
the bulk of the population were subjected to various forms of taxes,
whereas the ruling class was exempted.

Under the native rule, taxes were collected in kind and the main sources
of revenue were taxes on land, houses, fisheries, elephants, forest produce,
imports and exports, oilseed, silk, cotton, sale of offices, tea seeds, rubber,
ivory, and bee wax. In addition to paying taxes, people were also subjected
to the *lallup* system. The poor and downtrodden were the greatest sufferers
under this scheme. Under the combined rule of colonial power and native
king, the public had to bear the burden of many taxes such as land revenue, road, fisheries, forest toll station, water, cycle, vehicles (lorry), *wakhei
sel* (settlement fee), *Mangba–Sengba*,[3] *pandit loishang* (board of pandits, for
marriage purposes), *chandan senkhai* (tax for wearing the *tilak* on forhead),
kunja sen (attire taxation) and tax for singers. All the taxes were not added
to the revenue of the state – some were meant for the private expenses
of the Raja of Manipur and other state offices (Manimohan Singh 2006:
170). Although *lallup* was abolished, *pothang*[4] continued in the State. This
was prevalent in Manipur long before the installation of Churachand
as the Raja of Manipur, but the system was found to be executed in the
severest manner during his reign. The villagers strongly protested against
the system of *pothang* carriage, *amin-chakthak*[5] and attendance by the villagers at night to guard the collected revenue (*yairek sentry*), etc. Besides,
there was the system of *mangba–sengba*. The system of *mangba–sengba* had
given extra power to the *Brahma Sabha* and its head – Raja Churachand
Singh – and additional burden to the poor subjects of the State, especially people who had adopted Vaishnavism as their creed. The system

was frequently used against the persons who defied the authority of the *Brahma Sabha* and it had transformed into an instrument of exploitation directed against the poor and downtrodden state subjects. However, an outcast or excommunicated (*mangba*) person could become pure or can be purified (*sengba*) by paying a certain amount of money. The amount to be paid, however, also varied depending on the authority who declared the person an *amangba* (impure one). For instance, if a person was declared *mangba* by *Ratnas*,[6] he or she had to pay rupees 50; if the *Brahma Sabha* declared a person *mangba*, the payment was rupees 85 and 23 paise and if the order for *mangba* was issued by the Raja, then the person had to pay rupees 500 in order to revoke the order (Bir 1990: 4).

Growth of political consciousness

Before the dawn of the 20th century, there were no organisations of political character to initiate a sustained resistance movement against the then-existing combined oppression of feudal – colonial authority. However, there were sporadic cases of opposition to the British policy and feudal oppression as evident in 1904, Thoubal villagers' refusal to perform *pothang* services in 1909, the 1913 protest against the oppressive system of taxation, and the Kuki Rebellion of 1917 against the forced labour. The Kuki Rebellion (1917–19) against the British, though short-lived, undoubtedly represents a great episode in the history of Manipur. It exposed the limitation of British rule over the hill territory of Manipur. Although the rebellion was suppressed with the military might of the British, it helped in spreading anti-British feelings among the Kukis of Manipur. Dena (1991) ascribed the wrong administrative approach as the long-standing cause of the rebellion. As a result of the rebellion, a major administrative reorganisation was effected in Manipur. A new scheme for the administration of the hill area was floated in 1919. But these movements lacked political organisation having mass base to leadership and ideology for a sustained movement to overthrow the oppressive regime. The Zeliangrong Movement was initially based on the socio-religious agenda of cleansing the traditional Kabui religion from evil elements. The movement took an anti-Christianity stand. To quote Gangmumei Kabui:

> Christianity had come to the hill and started challenging the traditional religion, its old values and ideals of Zeliangrong people. Being religious minded he (Jadonang) wanted to eliminate the evils that had crept in his own religion as practiced by the

common people. By 1929, Jadonang movement had gained momentum and took a semi-military, semi-religious and political character.

(Kabui 1991: 135–37)

Subsequently, the movement was suppressed with the execution of Jadonang in 1931 and arrest of Gaidinliu in 1934. However, these movements had left a significant impact on the history of Manipur. The anti-British and anti-feudal sentiment inherent in the movement led to wider consciousness about the various forms of exploitation prevailing during the period and it also led to formation of many political organisations along the length and breadth of Manipur at a later stage. The ground for the growth of a middle class was laid down during the British colonial rule and it became more pronounced and vocal during 1920–40, a period that was characterised by growing economic and socio-cultural problems (N. Lokendra Singh 1998: 113). The growth of a politically conscious middle class produced a collective movement against the injustices of an alien colonial rule and excesses of feudal rule in Manipur. It was during this period that pioneering magazines like *Meetei Chanu* founded by Irabot in 1922, followed by prominent newspapers like *Yakairol*, edited by Ningthoujam Leiren in 1930 began to appear; three years later another magazine *Lalit Manjuri Patrika* came out. The increasing journalistic activity began to introduce political as well as cultural issues to the wider public. In the ensuing decade, the first two daily newspapers *Deinik Patrika* and *Manipur Matam* appeared (Parratt 2005: 28).

The increasing publications and journalistic activities show the emergence of a politically conscious educated middle class. Such awakening led to the formation of various politico-economic organisations that subsequently initiated socio-cultural reformation movements and the movement for democracy in Manipur. The culmination of cultural awakening and political consciousness among the literate section of Manipuri society, particularly amongst the Meitei/Meetei, found expression in the formation of the *Nikhil Hindu Manipuri Mahasabha* (henceforth, NHMM) in 1934. At its early stage, NHMM activity was focused on socio-cultural and economic upliftment of Manipuris. However, such activities laid the foundation for more intense political agitations at a later stage. Soayam Chhatradhari Singh opines that the Mahasabha is the first political organisation or party in Manipur. The main objectives of the NHMM's activities were to bring unity among the Manipuri (Meitei) diaspora settled in different parts of the world in order to make a strong and independent nation (1996: 38).

To reflect briefly on the NHMM, its first session was officially opened on Friday, 30 May 1934, in the Ras Mandal (dancing hall) of the Palace with Maharaja Churachand as its president. The session took 22 resolutions concerning mainly socio-cultural and economic aspects of Manipuri (Soaym Chhatradhari Singh 1996: 38). Over 300 delegates from the Meetei/Meitei diaspora of Cachar (Assam), Tripura, Dacca and Burma participated in the session. The main concerns of the first session were cultural and educational. The session asked for the adoption of Manipuri as the language of education for Manipuris both within and outside the state, and for the teaching of Meetei *Mayek* (script). The state was also requested to establish more high schools (Parratt 2005: 30). The second session of the NHMM was held at Silchar (1936) and the third at Mandalay, Burma on 2–3 March (1937) with Irabot Singh as chairman. Mostly, the Manipuris in Burma and a few other delegates from Assam and Manipur attended the session. The delegates seriously deliberated on various socio-economic and religio-cultural problems faced by the Manipuris in Burma and passed 15 resolutions.

Meanwhile, despite consistent effort of the Mahasabha to eradicate socio-religious problems, *mangba* and *sengba* scandals had swept over the state. In 1938, several individuals were excommunicated or outcasted by the Brahma Sabha. The NHMM became a radical and politicised organisation in 1938 by omitting the word 'Hindu' in order to make it an all-Manipur organisation. The turning point came in the fourth session of NHMM at Chinga Hill, Imphal, on 29–30 December 1938. This session radically changed the content of Manipur politics. As Karam Manimohan Singh perceptively wrote: '[T]his session brought into Manipur the first consciousness of a political party as well as the meaning of democracy and social justice to the public' (1989: 70). The Chinga session, which took place amid the increasing *mangba–sengba* scandal, decided to omit the word 'Hindu' from the NHMM and the Mahasabha was rechristened Nikhil Manipuri Mahasabha (NMM). By this time, the Raja had distanced himself from the NHMM and Irabot had been appointed as its president.

It was the realisation of various socio-political issues developed within and outside Manipur and the coming of the organisation under the influence of radical leaders – particularly, Hijam Irabot – that led to the transformation of the Mahasabha into a radical socio-political movement opposing feudal rule, religious oppression and colonial injustices. The fourth session of the Mahasabha passed some politically significant resolutions which to a great extent paved the way for a popular movement for a responsible government in Manipur, representing both the hills and valley

COLONIALISM AND MOVEMENT FOR DEMOCRACY

of Manipur. The Chinga session manifested the understanding of political development in various parts of British India and princely states. It was evident from the fact that the session expressed its sympathy for those who had suffered in the agitation for the 'struggle for freedom' in some of the native states. The session, among other things, urged the Government on the release of Kabui prophetess Gaidinlui; abolition of *Yairek Sentry, Pothang*, etc.; establishment of a panchayat in every village; restoration of self-rule in Manipur; a unified system of administration for the hills and valley, etc. (Soaym Chhatradhari Singh 1996: 47). Even though the resolutions on the whole remained fairly deferential to the Maharaja himself, the NMM did condemn the petty humiliations, which it perceived many of his subjects suffered, such as having to remove shoes and kneel in court, and it attacked the compulsory payments to court officials. There were particularly two resolutions in the Chinga Session that struck at the heart of the feudal and colonial governing of Manipur. Resolution 10 of the session addressed the issue of separation of the hills from the valley under the British administration. The NMM argued that the Meeteis and the Hill people had always been one. 'The hill men and we, the Meeteis, have never been separated and cannot be separated in language, in culture and commerce' (Manimohan Singh 1989: 76). The session resolved that the 'Government of India should be approached to return the hills to the state administration. This was a direct challenge to the British power and expressed the desire of the people that full sovereignty be restored to Manipur and the hills reintegrated with the valley.

Another significant resolution that struck at the very foundation of the feudal system of government by the Maharaja and his Durbar was 'resolution number 11' demanding the setting up of an elected legislature: 'The NMM also demands the fulfilment of the claim of the Manipur state subjects for the establishment of a Legislative Council for the attainment of the representative form of government for which they have already submitted an application' (Manimohan Singh 1989; Lokendra Singh 1998; Parratt 2005). This resolution was reflected in Irabot's outspoken presidential address. In his address to the gathering, he had pointed out that the Manipur State Durbar (MSD) members (with the exception of the president, who was a colonial officer) were all personal appointees of the Raja and had no public mandate. He argued that only elected members would satisfy the wishes of the people in general (Parratt 2005: 35–36). Thus, the Chinga session of NMM (1938) had brought several changes in the political perception and worldview of the Manipuri middle class by expressing desire for a responsible elected legislature and visualising a united Manipur in administration, which was segregated by the British under their divide and rule policy. By any account, the leaders of NMM had taken up radical steps towards gradual abolition of a combined feudal – colonial rule in Manipur. They had laid the foundation for various socio-political movements, which were to be launched in Manipur by radicalising and politicising the people.

As a follow-up action, the new Secretary of the NMM, Chingakham Pisak, forwarded an English version of the resolutions to the PMSD (President of the Manipur State Durbar) MacDonald in February 1939 with request for action. In the same month, about 350 leading Manipuris petitioned the Maharaja to set up an elected Legislative Council. Since the resolutions were a direct challenge to British colonial power and feudal monarchy, the main demands of the NMM were rejected by the Durbar. The Durbar, however, was prepared to concede that some of the members of the MSD could be appointed through elections. The proposal, however, did not materialise. As the colonial system of administration or any oppressive rule entails the suppression of radical political formation, the Durbar took action against the NMM on 15 February 1939 and branded it a political organisation. The government banned all meetings and processions within the British Reserve. Against this heightened political consciousness about the injustices and exploitative rule of feudalism and colonialism, women's participation grew and gave tough challenges to the British Empire.

The Women's War, or *Nupi Lan*, of 1939, where thousands of women spontaneously raised their voice against the export of rice from Manipur by Marwari traders, which had caused an artificial scarcity of food grains, manifested the growing political conscience. The *Nupi Lan*, which began on 12 December 1939, was the result of accumulated grievances against the exploitation of rice economy by Marwari monopolists and the long-standing suffering of the common mass under the combined feudal and colonial rule. It is worth mentioning that the Marwari merchants, Mangal Chand Megharaj and Co. of Imphal and Mangal Chand Kisturchand of Imphal held the contract of the Cart-tax Monopoly. The total quantity of rice exported from the Manipur state from 1 June to 30 July 1939 by Mangal Chand Kisturchand, the Cart-tax Monopolists, was: rice – 371,174 mounds and Chira – 198,558 mounds (Manimohan Singh 2006: 165). As early as in the second decade of the 20th century, people began to demand the halting of rice exports from the state. Slogans like 'Price of rice has gone high because the Marwari merchants and the shopkeepers purchase it in great quantity';'Turn out the Marwari merchants and shopkeeper from villages of Manipur: they (Marwaris) take money from the illiterate state subjects by force' were already heard by the Manipuris in

COLONIALISM AND MOVEMENT FOR DEMOCRACY

the late 1920s (Manimohan Singh 2006: 163). Another causal factor was the establishment of electric run mills by the Marwaris and some natives for husking rice that seriously undermined the income of the women folk. The movement was strengthened and turned into a political agitation under the leadership of Irabot and his colleagues.

In tune with the British colonial theses of 'civilising mission' the 'natives' who were yet to be fully appropriated by the 'colonial modernity' as backward were certified to be incapable of ruling themselves. The then British officers in Manipur argued that the time was not ripe for wider political participation. In a letter to Raja Churachand in July 1939, the then political agent of Manipur, Grimson pointed out that Manipur had no tradition of democracy and that he did not believe that there were enough politically aware Manipuris to make it work. British officials were contemptuous of the ability of the Manipuris and Grimson is on record saying that he did not believe any Manipuri of the time would have been appointable even as an assistant commissioner (Manimohan Singh 1989: 96). However, by the following year, Maharaja Churachand himself was putting forward a plan of his own for a Legislative Assembly, with an appointed Prime Minister and 27 members, 16 of whom would be elected, the rest appointed by him. But by that time, the state was being disrupted by the 'Second Women's War', and soon after became the eastern front in the Second World War (Parratt 2005: 37). The growth of political consciousness and awakening can be seen in the hills area of Manipur also. The growth of organisations such as the Tangkhul Long (Tangkhul Assembly) in 1919, Kabui Samiti of Ruongmei in 1934 (later renamed Kabui Naga Association in 1946), Vaipei National Organisation in 1944, Hmar Association in 1945, Zeliangrong Council in 1947, Manipur Zeliangrong Union in 1947, and the Kuki National Assembly (KNA) in 1947 left a significant imprint in the history of Manipur.

Growth of political parties and movement for responsible government

The post-Second World War period marked the growth of various political parties in Manipur and more intense agitation for self-rule through elected representative government. The political movement in the post-war period was mainly focused on the issue of responsible government elected through universal adult franchise. The period experienced the growth of political parties such as the Manipur Krishak Sabha (MKS), a rural-based party, the Manipur Praja Sangha (MPS) – the party is popularly perceived as the urban counterpart of the MKS – and the Manipur

State Congress (MSC), which was mainly constituted by the urban elites. Manipur politics during this period was polarised on the two strands of ideology visualised by the MKS and the MPS on the one hand, and the Manipur State Congress Party (MSC) on the other hand. The political turmoil in the state was reflective of political changes taking place across the British Indian Empire in the face of eminent British departure from the subcontinent. The years from 1945 to 1949 can be regarded as the most critical, challenging and active period in the 20th-century politics of Manipur whose legacy found resurrection time and again in the politics of Manipur today.

It is, therefore, pertinent to analyse the political developments and challenges during this period and the response of the politically conscious class to the challenges in order to locate the various movements of contemporary Manipur in their proper historical perspective. The enormous changes brought by the Second World War necessitated a radical socio-political program in Manipur. By the end of the war, it was evident that British departure from the subcontinent was eminent. Hence, the Indian National Congress (INC) began to take keen interest on the political activities in the princely states. The immediate attention of politicised elites in Manipur was focused on the demand for installation of a responsible government through adult franchise. The democratisation of polity was the central focus of the movement for every political group in the state. The momentum of political activities in the state increased when Irabot was allowed to return to Manipur in the early part of 1945 on the grounds of his mother-in-law's illness. In Manipur, Irabot tried to galvanise the masses by reorganising the mass fronts such as Mahila Sanmelani, Praja Sanmelani, Praja Mandal, Krishi Sanmelani, and Chhatra (Student) Federation. As such, strong voices were raised against the idea of forming Crown Colony, comprising the hills of North East India and Burma proposed by Andrew Clow, the then governor of Assam and Sir Reginald Coupland, a British constitutional expert. Any attempt to include Manipur into alternative political arrangement or formation was met with stiff resistance. For instance a joint meeting of the Nikhil Manipuri Mahasabha and the Praja Mandal held at Wangkhei on 5 April 1946 opposed the inclusion of Manipur into the proposed formation of the North-Eastern Frontier Province. It was argued that the proposal was an act of continuation of imperialism and pledged to make 'Manipur a free nation within a free India' (Irabot Celebration Committee 2000: 40). However, the idea of making Manipur a free nation within free India and the nature of its relation with India calls for detailed study.

COLONIALISM AND MOVEMENT FOR DEMOCRACY

In the meantime, the Krishi Sanmelani, which later on became the Krishak Sabha, began to play a crucial role in the history of Manipur people's struggle for socio-economic and constitutional changes between 1946 and 1952 (N. Lokendra Singh 1998: 193). In the second conference of the Krishi Sanmelani, which was held at Nambol in May 1946, Irabot Singh was elected as its president, while O. Ibomcha continued to serve as secretary. The conference demanded the installation of a fully responsible government in Manipur, setting up of Panchayats in the villages, etc. (Manimohan Singh 1985: 179). Again, in a working committee meeting of the Mahasabha held in August, a resolution was passed demanding an immediate declaration for the early establishment of responsible government in Manipur and to take steps for setting up of a constitution-making machinery with public leaders (Resolution of the Working Committee Meeting of NMM, 2 August 1946). In a significant development, the leaders of both the Praja Mandal and the Praja Sanmelani held a joint meeting on 21 August 1946 and floated the Praja Sangha by merging the two organisations. R. K. Bhubansana and Irabot Singh were made president and general secretary, respectively.

The first general body meeting of the Praja Sangha held on 1 September 1946 resolved to support the popular demands of the various organisations for a quick installation of responsible form of government in Manipur. The meeting also decided to urge for the formation of a committee representing different organisations in the state for ascertaining the views of the people on the nature and type of the 'Legislative Assembly' that they wanted for Manipur (Naorem 1998: 195). The growing strength of the Praja Sangha and the Krishak Sabha alarmed some of the elitist leaders of the Mahasabha who were determined to outwit the two organisations in the struggle for power. There was systematic planning for isolating Irabot from the political landscape of Manipur. The fateful moment came on 4 October 1946, when a joint meeting of all the organisations in the state was called by some pro-Mahasabha students to discuss the feasibility of forming a united party. The conference was held at the Aryan Theatre with R. K. Bhubansana of the Praja Sangha presiding.

The conference decided to form a single party by merging all the organisations and it was also agreed that three representatives each from the Mahasabha and the Praja Sangha, two from the Krishak Sabha, two from the organisers of the conference, and five from the general public would be appointed as members in the working committee of the new organisation. Not surprisingly, when the Praja Sangha and the Krishak Sabha selected Irabot as one of their representatives, a section of delegates of the conference arbitrarily rejected him on the grounds of his membership to the Communist Party of India. Sensing the undemocratic nature and duplicity of the conference, the representatives of the two organisations, except for R. K. Bhubansana of the Praja Sangha, walked out. The remaining members, including Bhubansana, formed the Manipur State Congress with Bhubansana and Khoimacha appointed as president and secretary respectively. The stage was thus set for an intense struggle towards capturing political power in Manipur.

The process of formation of the MSC through political machination 'set in train a culture of grasping for power and personal aggrandisement, through cynical and undemocratic manipulation, which has bedevilled Manipuri politics ever since' (Parratt 2005: 96). Meanwhile, Maharaja Bodhchandra on 12 December 1946 issued an order for setting up of a Constitution Making Committee (CMC) along with its composition. The composition of the Committee was meticulously arranged to reflect the interests of the hills and valley as well as the Palace. The PMSD was to be chairman of the proposed Constitution Making Committee. Election was held through an indirect method and two voters from each of the five-valley tehsils elected their representatives. As was expected, the Congress Party candidates were elected in the valley area. As for the Hills, the PMSD nominated five members, viz., (*i*) A. Daiho *ii*) R. Suisa, (*iii*) Teba Kilong, (*iv*) T.C. Tiankham and (*v*) Thangopao Kipgen, as members of the Committee. Finally the 16-member committee, including five nominated from the Durbar and one nominee of the King, was formally inaugurated on 3 March 1947.

However, the Praja Sangha and the Krishak Sabha did not take part in the election in protest against the undemocratic nature of the formation of the CMC. Spelling out the reasons for their protest, Irabot Singh exposed the undemocratic method of forming the Committee in his presidential address to the Third Annual Conference of the Praja Sangha held at Khurai from 16 to 17 March 1947. The task of the CMC was completed in July 1947, two months before the scheduled date of submission. The recommendation of the Committee visualised elections with full adult franchise to a Legislative Assembly, with no required qualification for voting either in terms of land ownership or education. The Manipur State Constitution Act (MCA), 1947, in the words of Parratt, 'was a remarkably enlightened and liberal piece of legislation. It provided, for the first time on the Indian sub-continent, for a legislature to be elected by full adult franchise under a constitutional monarchy' (2005: 100). The Constitution (1947) visualised an elected Legislative Assembly having a term of three years. The composition of the Assembly was proportionally divided to accommodate the plural character of Manipur. Under it,

30 seats were allotted as general seats (valley), 18 seats were meant for the Hills and 3 seats for the Muslim communities. Besides, there was provision for two seats representing education and commerce, respectively, to be elected by a limited franchise (The MCA 1947).

The later part of 1947 witnessed certain political problems in Manipur that affected the autonomous existence of Manipur as a distinct territorial and political entity. At this time, the Mao Naga Party, under the leadership of Daiho, came under the influence of the Naga National Council under President A. Z. Phizo, and the party advocated the consolidation of Nagas under one administration, even though its support base was limited. Meanwhile, the Mizo Union, in the southern part of Manipur, initiated sporadic agitations for the union of Kuki areas with the Lushai Hills. At this critical historical juncture, Irabot along with M. K. Shimray of Tangkhul Long, Lunneh of Kuki National Assembly, Kakhangai of Kabui Association, and some organisations from the valley of Manipur tried to form a united front to fight the election. However, the plan did not materialise. In the meantime, another political party, the Praja Shanti, emerged in the political spectrum of Manipur immediately before the Assembly elections. It was widely believed that Maharaja Bodhchandra floated the Praja Shanti Party (PSP). Not surprisingly, the party was pro-royalist and fiercely anti-Congress and anti- merger (N. Lokendra Singh 1998; Mayengbam Anandamohon Singh 2004; Parratt 2005).

As envisaged in the Manipur Constitution Act of 1947, the election to the Manipur (State) Assembly started from 11 June to 27 July 1948. The election produced a hung Assembly as no single party could get absolute or simple majority. In the election, the Krishak Sabha won 6 seats, the Manipur State Congress won 14 seats, the Praja Shanti Party won 12 seats and 18 seats were won by representatives of the Hill areas of Manipur. The election outcome was a shattering blow to the state Congress' grand design of wresting power in collaboration with the Indian National Congress. A coalition government led by the Praja Shanti Party, which was supported by the Krishak Sabha and the Hill representatives, came into existence. The first ever democratically elected 'Assembly' was formally inaugurated on 18 October 1948 by Maharaja Bodhchandra with M. K. Priyobarta Singh as the Chief Minister.

Conclusion

During the first half of the 20th century, Manipur witnessed a plethora of political alterations, new social formations and several democratic questions. Colonialism, combined with oppressive systems of the native Kingdom, had started to face several challenges. These challenges resulted in a mass movement, irrespective of gender, community, etc. The trajectory of the movement can be cited as anti-feudal, anti-colonial and democratic. Within these trajectories, the people's resistance against oppressive tax systems, *Nupi Lan*, Kuki resistance, Zeliangrong movement and movement for democracy that continued throughout the first 50 years of the 20th century can be mentioned. While revisiting these trajectories of resistances, there is a significant dent towards a united fight against colonialism and other forms of oppressive regimes, for oppression became extremely generalised. In the 1940s, Manipur also witnessed the movement to save itself from attempt to dislocate her historical existence as distinct cultural and territorial entity. It was evident from the fact that there was fierce resistance to the Coupland Plan of 'Crown Colony' and the Indian National Congress' plan of forming 'Poorvanchal Pradesh' combining 'Cachar, Manipur and Tripura'. Most of the political parties and organisations rejected the proposal as it would undermine the distinct cultural and historical identity of Manipur. The given period also witnessed political machinations to weed out progressive elements from Manipur politics. A significant feature of the political movement in Manipur is that it was informed by the ideology of Marxism, liberalism and the idea of nationhood.

Notes

1 *Lallup* was a system of forced labour prevalent in Manipur until it was abolished by Major Maxwell, the then British political agent in Manipur, on 29th April 1892. Under this system every male between ages 17 and 60 was required to place his services at the disposal of the State without remuneration for a certain number of days in each year. The number of days thus placed nominally at the disposal of the State was 10 days in every 40.

2 A *Pari* is a land area of nearly 2½ acres, and was roughly 120 yards by 100 yards. A *Pari* of land, on an average, produced from 40 to 80 pots of *dhan*. A *Pari* of land is equivalent to 7 *bighas*, 2 *kattas* and 10 *leshas* (about two and half acres). Two *sangbais* made one *Pot*. One *Pot* = 50 seers.

3 It was a practice widely prevalent in Manipur during the reign of Raja Churachand. It refers to the practice of declaring people of villages as *Mangba* (outcast or excommunicated) by well-to-do Brahmins of the *Brahma Sabha* (Council of Brahmins) and again offering for a consideration to have them declared *Sengba* (or purified) under certain fee whether of cash or kind.

4 It was a practice of carrying belongings of Manipuri officials free of cost by the villagers when the officials took tour from village to village.

5 Under this system villagers provide free food and lodging to *amins* and peons.

6 One of the leading members of the Brahma Sabha.

References

Allen, B.C., E. A. Gait, H. F. Howard, and C. G. H. Allen. 2005. *Gazetteer of Bengal and North-East India.* New Delhi: Mittal Publications.

Bir, Thockchom. 1990. *Comrade Irabotki Maramda Kharadang (Some Words on Comrade Irabot).* Imphal: Progressive Literature House.

Dena, Lal (ed.). 1991. *History of Modern Manipur, 1826–1949.* New Delhi: Orbit Publishers.

Irabot Celebration Committee. 2000. 'Communistsingna Manipur Kankhiba Numit' (in Manipuri), in Thangjam Babu (ed.), *Milleniumsida Jananeta Irabot.* Imphal: Khaollao Publication Sub-Committee.

Kabui, Gangmumei. 1991. Zeliangrong Movement under Jadonang and Rani Gaidinliu, 1930–49', in Lal Dena (ed.), *History of Modern Manipur, 1826–1949.* New Delhi: Orbit Publishers.

Parratt, John. 2005. *Wounded Land: Politics and Identity in Modern Manipur.* New Delhi: Mittal Publications.

Singh, Karam Manimohan. 1989. *Hijam Irabot Singh and Political Movements in Manipur.* Delhi: B.R. Publishing.

———. 2006. *Nupi Lan (Women's War of Manipur).* Imphal: K. Premlata Devi.

Singh, Mayengbam Anandamohon. 2004. *Shillong 1949.* Imphal: Mayengbam Akshey kumar Singh.

Singh, N. Joykumar. 1991. 'Political Agency, 1885–1890', in Lal Dena (ed.), *History of Modern Manipur, 1826–1949.* New Delhi: Orbit Publishers.

Singh, N. Lokendra. 1998. *The Unquiet Valley: Society, Economy, and Politics of Manipur (1891–1950).* New Delhi: Mittal Publications.

Singh, Soayam Chhatradhari. 1996. *Manipurgee Itihasta Irabot (Irabot in the History of Manipur).* Imphal: Soayam Publication.

Skocpol, Theda. 1999. *States and Social Revolutions: A Comparative Analysis of France, Russia, and China.* Cambridge: Cambridge University Press.

Part II

LITERATURE, POPULAR CULTURE, AND RELIGION

5

RELIGIOUS REVIVALISM AND COLONIAL RULE

Origin of the Sanamahi Movement

Khuraijam Bijoykumar Singh

The evolution of Meitei religious life has a long history of conflict and confrontation between the two religious systems of the ancient Meitei faith and Hinduism. Successive kings, in order to exercise control, attempted to draw legitimacy from religion (associated institutional structures), thus resulting in the legitimisation of two systems of religious authorities such as the maiba and maibi (priest and priestess) and the Brahmin, each representing different sources of legitimacy, respectively. The most important characteristic of the Meitei society has been its adjustment to every force of change and the retention of traditional values in every sphere of society till today. Hinduism was enforced as the state religion in 1714 CE by King Garibaniwaz (also named Pamheiba, 1709–48). From this period, Manipur had closer contact and relationship with the Ahom kingdom of Assam and other neighbouring kingdoms of Tripura, Cooch Bihar, Sylhet etc. Matrimonial and military alliances were major forms of relationship between the Meitei king and these Hindu states (Brara 1998: 4). Though the Meiteis formally adopted Hinduism, they simultaneously retained their traditional religion as the core of their faith.

The king, in the traditional state, was recognised as the ultimate authority in the spheres of politics, society, economy, culture as well as religion. Governance or control of the subjects, in addition to police, military and civil administration, included cultural projects wherein religious functionaries such as the *maiba – maibi* and the Brahmins were used by successive kings. Cultural forms and patterns in society were reconstructed and transformed through various means in the way Edward Said terms as a 'method of controlling people' (1995: 59). State control over the subjects was so strong that cultural identity or collective consciousness was shaped by the categories provided by the state. For example, the formation of the Meitei state under the Mangangcha *salai* (clan) in Manipur was not merely through the political supremacy that was established over the remaining *salais*. It was made successful and then strengthened by cultural politics of the Mangang rulers. Therefore, state is not merely a form of political control over the people but also becomes a form of cultural project to control its people. However, with the defeat of Manipur in the Anglo-Manipuri War of 1891, colonial regimentation introduced newer forms of control and administration.

An interesting loophole in the existing scholarship on the Sanamahi Movement comes out glaringly as it fails to connect the politics of revivalism and the realities of colonised political economy in Manipur. Gangmumei Kabui predominantly refers to Hinduism as the only factor that brought about an identity crisis among the Meiteis of Manipur and was the root cause of the Sanamahi Movement (Kabui 1991: 101–02). At the same time, he calls the process as 'Sanskritization' (Kabui 1991: 90) instead of Hinduisation, which I feel is more appropriate, as the Meiteis were never part of the Hindu worldview before the beginning of the 18th century. Such an overarching underpinning of a singular force excludes other factors – for instance, the frequent invasions made by the Burmese in Manipur and their occupation of Manipur from 1819 to 1826, known as the *Chahi Taret Khuntakpa* (Seven Years' Devastation) that have had an impact not only on the political and economic life but also on the identity of the people. The occupation resulted in the development of communalism between the Hindu and the Muslim. Moreover, the British occupation of Manipur from 1891 to 1947 also provided an equal degree of impact on the identity of Manipur and helped in the consolidation of Hinduism. Thus, while looking at the problems and issues of identity formation and the Sanamahi Movement, it is pertinent to look at other political forces that helped change the identity and culture of the people.

Behind this background, the chapter seeks to analyse the emergence of the Sanamahi Movement as a result of dual administration (hitherto unknown) under the British and the native ruler. More specifically, an attempt is made to investigate why 'revivalism' emerged as a cultural and religious reaction against the king and the *Bramasabha*, a Hindu religious body, and not against British colonialism. Three key focus areas are identified for the purpose of the chapter: (*a*) socio-political context in which the native ruler struggled to sustain power through the manipulation of socio-religious institutions; (*b*) the context in which 'nativism' in the form

RELIGIOUS REVIVALISM AND COLONIAL RULE

of Sanamahi Movement started and (*c*) the forms of resistance made by the rulers as well as the people against British colonialism.

Burmese occupation and the socio-religious life

The history of Manipur is a revealing tale of the people's love for independence. Their skills and martial ability helped them safeguard their freedom against repeated incursions from neighbouring countries. Till the reign of King Garibaniwaz, who engaged in the highest number of wars (up to 64) with the Burmese, Manipur could protect her independence and sovereignty. After the death of Garibaniwaz, the Burmese conquered the throne. As a result, Manipur came under Burmese suzerainty for seven years from 1819 to 1826. Before this period, there were no clear evidences of impact of the Burmese invasions on the socio-religious life of the Meiteis. British ethnographer T. C. Hodson writes, 'The Shans under Samlongpha who invaded Manipur in the beginning of the fifteenth century seem to have left no trace of their occupation of the State upon religious belief of the people' (1984: 97).

However, the Seven Years' Devastation or the occupation uprooted the socio-religious and political life of the people, as noted by Gang-mumei Kabui: 'Repeated Burmese invasions had uprooted the social and economic life of people. . . . Thousands of people fled to Cachar (in Assam) for refuge; and many more (were) taken as prisoners and deported to Ava (in Burma)' (1974: 54). Sir James Johnstone also remarks of this event: 'Manipur at this time contained 2,000 inhabitants, the miserable remnants of a thriving population of at least 4,00,000 or probably 6,00,000 that existed before the Burmese invasions' (1971: 86).[1] Regarding the immediate change on the part of people's socio-political and religious life on account of the Burmese invasion, M. Gojendra Singh observes:

> The Burmese king sent a large force under General Mahaban-dula in 1819 and Marjit Singh (the then king of Manipur) fled to Cachar. He took a large number of his people to Cachar. He was received warmly by his brothers Chourajit and Gambhir (who were already there in Cachar leaving the country due to Bur-mese aggression started since 1755). Marjit took the royal deities *Gobindaji* and *Brindabanchandra* with him. The three Manipuri princes Chourajit, Marjit and Gambhir divided the whole of

southern Cachar among themselves and large numbers of Manipuri followers were given settlement there.

(1989: 41–42)

Flow of human traffic outside Manipur subsequently had an impact upon the life of Manipuris, especially on the socio-cultural aspect of the people. People of Manipur interacted with the people in Cachar, Tripura and West Bengal. While staying with Bengali Hindus in Cachar, they learned many new cultures from them, which were introduced to their people on their return to Manipur. For example, King Bhagyachandra (1759–98) introduced *Ras Lila* and many other Hindu festivals after he returned from Assam. Similarly, new festivals were also introduced after Meiteis returned from Cachar. It is also said that King Gambhir Singh (1825–34) introduced rituals like the *Ratha Jatra* (chariot pulling ritual), etc.

The reconsolidation of Hinduism under Chandrakirti Singh (1850–86), which had lost much of its hold on the people during the said period of the Burmese occupation (Hodson 1984: 95), brought many new values of orthodoxy from outside Manipur where there had been a long history of Hindu and Muslim conflict.

The coming of (new) Brahmins, especially after the Burmese occupation, was also the main reason for the increasing religious orthodoxy and hostility among the Meiteis and other communities. While staying outside Manipur, Meiteis adopted many new cultural and religious values from the places they took refuge in. The Meiteis who adopted few basic beliefs and practices of vegetarianism, purity and pollution by virtue of a few Brahmin representatives in the country then became 'better Hindus' with a greater degree of orthodoxy.

The new religious orthodoxy, which developed after the event of the Seven Years' Devastation, was prevalent not only among the Meitei Hindus but also among the *Pangals* who were also exposed to the outside Muslim world. The Manipuri *Pangals*, after they came back from Cachar, revived and consolidated their Islamic faith by establishing various mosques in Manipur. They also brought many changes not only in the religion but also in the cultural sphere. Orthodoxy was manifested in the form of Islamic revivalism, which is under way till today among the Manipuri *Pangals*. They constructed the first mosque in 1873, which was the foundation of Islamic culture in Manipur. Then, the first trained Manipuri *Maulavi* returned to Manipur in 1910 and started a strict adherence to Islam (Kabui 1991: 100). Before that, there was no sign of Islam in Manipur. R. Brown wrote in 1869, 'They were ignorant of their

Islamic religion. Their womenfolk did not have *purdah* system' (Brown 2001: 90).

On account of the Burmese occupation, visible transformations occurred in religious practices and identity, mainly on account of people's interaction with outsiders in other parts of India. Orthodoxy among the communities was the notable one. However, evidences of Burmese rulers solidifying the orthodoxies or communalism are not found.

British colonialism in Manipur

The frequent invasion of Manipur by the Burmese in the late 18th century and early 19th century forced the rulers of Manipur to seek the help of the British, who themselves were looking for a partner to counter the Burmese. Later, Maharaja Gambhir Singh became a party to the First Anglo-Burmese War resulting in the Treaty of Yandaboo (1826) and liberating Manipur from the Burmese force. Following the Treaty, the office of the British Political Agent was established in Manipur in 1835. This marked the beginning of the involvement of Manipur in the field of conflict between the European colonial forces and those in South Asia and South East Asia. As a result, the British increasingly started interfering in the kingdom's internal affair, which created a tussle between the Maharaja and the British, which finally led to the Anglo-Manipuri War in 1891. In this war, Manipur was defeated by the British force and thus ended the friendly relationship between two sovereigns, resulting in the British occupation of the native state of Manipur till 1947. The British occupation of Manipur for more than 55 years had a profound impact on the political and economic life of the people. However, it also helped in the consolidation of the socio-religious institutions of the people.

Crafts of the colonial rule

Institutions such as the church, schools and hospitals played a predominant role in the development and strengthening of the colonial powers. Thus, the colonial government as elsewhere had two crafts: military and religious (Dirks 2003: 9). The spread of Christianity and the establishment of modern formal schools and hospitals helped to consolidate the British administration in the native state of Manipur in two ways. First, with the help of these institutions, a new 'socio-cultural industry' was set up to produce a new category of elites who would support the colonisers and challenge the traditional authority. Second, the colonisers, in order to get full control and command over the resources, needed to displace the native people from their own culture and belief; native culture and belief had its own principle of ownership towards their environment and resources. For example, the native people's belief in forest grove and totemism is a particular system, which not only satisfies but also regulates and limits the needs and demands on the one hand and supplies and sustains on the other (Richards 1932; Malinowski 1978).

The beliefs associated with the native people had a strong resistance toward the access of resources by the colonisers. An incident during the colonial period illustrates this point. A British engineer is reported to have taken a number of Gurkha jawans (soldiers) belonging to the Assam Rifles to cut down pine trees from the compound reserved for lord Wangbren (in Meitei belief, a deity or guardian of the south; and one among eight guardian deities of the eight directions). The local people warned the officer not to cut down the trees without first offering due homage to the deity and also without taking permission from the same. The said engineer disregarded the warning and started felling the trees. Mysteriously, that very night many of the jawans died. Coincidence or not, it is reported that the said incident did occur and the engineer had to reconsider his step. Thereafter, before giving further orders to cut down the trees in the compound, he stood in front of the deity with folded hands and prayed:

> Lord Wangbren, I know the jungle and all the trees are your property, but I need them for the welfare of the state and your people. Allow me to cut them down. Stop punishing my men and I promise you that for every tree cut down, I will plant two saplings so that you will get back your family of trees in due course of time.
>
> (Singh 1972: 35)

After this prayer, the jungle was cleared without further mishap befalling the jawans. In fulfilment of his promise, the state engineer planted two saplings in place of each tree felled.

The story reveals that religious and cultural beliefs acted as powerful sites of resistance to colonialism. Cultural beliefs allowed the people to contest the violation being done to their territories and resources. Therefore, in order to get full command over the access of resources, the colonisers had to eliminate native culture and belief, which denied the coloniser access to these resources. This view is different from Edward Said's definition of 'conversion', which he regards as a process of displacing the native people from their own culture and belief (1995: 68). The effort of the colonisers to eliminate native culture included a process of creating a new and alternative system of belief through which they could gain access to the resources freely.

Socio-cultural changes in Manipur

During the colonial period, two processes of change are observed in the arena of culture and tradition in Manipur. Each of these processes had their own origins and was affected by different forces having their own process of change. In the first place, there was a trend of modernisation in various socio-cultural spheres. The force working in this process was the British colonisers. Second, there was the rise of orthodoxy among the native people to resist the increasing power of the colonisers. The force working in this arena was the institution of Brahmasabha, patronised by the king. The above mentioned processes of change are clubbed together as an exogenous model of social dynamics. However, the increasing trend of modernisation did not retard the process of Hinduisation; instead, both interplayed simultaneously and, to some extent, the increase in the modernisation accelerated the process of Hinduisation (Singh 2002: 9). For instance, the process of modernisation and development of roads and other infrastructure enabled people to interact with the rest of the Hindu world frequently through pilgrimages to Vrindaban, a Hindu religious site in Agra, Uttar Pradesh, and other holy places.

Responding to the new religious and cultural invasion, there started a process of Sanamahi 'revivalism' of the pre-Hindu identity, which I term as Sanamahism, a belief system that resembles ancestral worshiping. The force working behind this endogenous process of social change was the Meitei Marup association, which was started as a counterforce to the rising power of Brahmins especially in the socio-religious arena. There was an increasing tendency among the new elites and some socio-religious groups, who were mainly deprived by the new system, to emphasise their own in-group identity through isolationism and nativism. They were not merely the outcome of the cultural differences but emerged from the latent structural tensions in the social system produced by a sudden rise in Brahminical domination after the consolidation of *Brahmasabha* and the emergence of modern elites and their effort to dominate each other. The emergence of the Meitei Marup organisation is the manifestation of an age-old conflict between the two socio-religious values of Hinduism and Meiteism. The reason for the strengthening of *Brahmasabha* during the colonial period was an expression of challenge primarily against the socio-political deprivation of native people by the British colonisers. At the same time, colonisers also offered another means to some sections of people to break the monopoly of the king and Brahmins by reducing their political and economic significance in the new system. Therefore, the native people's resistance to colonialism was manifested as anti-Hindu, too.

Thus, the study of the nature and dimension of socio-cultural changes during the colonial period found a complex phenomenon where the three forces of modernism, Hinduism and nativism interplayed together to bring a new order in the area of religion, polity and economy. However, orthodoxy among the traditional authorities was a by-product of modernisation, which again produced another counterforce of nativism. It is, however, pertinent to mention that while modernising tendencies influenced all the socio-cultural and political spheres, which had undoubtedly changed many aspects of the traditional Manipuri society and culture, they had not destroyed the basic structure and pattern of traditional society. Instead, they gave the Meiteis a new alternative and some new choices for their future politics.

Dual government and politics of the *Mangba–Sengba*

The direct result of British colonialism in Manipur was the emergence of a dual government run by the British and the Maharaja in the political and socio-cultural arena, respectively. Each of the systems had their own interest and area of operation. The British, in order to reduce the Maharaja's political power, undertook various measures. First, *lallup*, which was the only political and military institution of the Maharaja, was abolished in 1892. Moreover, a new system of land holding was introduced in the state. The peasant who enjoyed fertile lands after the payment of tax in kind was given *patta* for rightful ownership of the land. Thus, this particular policy ended the economic power of the Maharaja and, thus, changed the whole economic relationship between the Maharaja and his subjects. It reduced the Maharaja's power not only in the economic sphere but also in the political sphere.

However, the Maharaja was given the power in the socio-religious sphere, which was subsequently used to consolidate his power. The Maharaja started strengthening his power through the consolidation of traditional socio-religious institutions (especially the Hindu institutions, such as *Brahmasabha, Panji Loishang, Jagoi Loishang*, etc.) and as a cultural project to retain his power. He also established a Hindu institution, the Nikhil Hindu Manipuri Mahasabha. Through this institution,

RELIGIOUS REVIVALISM AND COLONIAL RULE

the Maharaja could control the educated Hindu Meiteis. In the name of religion, the Maharaja with the aid of Brahmins collected various strange taxes. Thus, the colonial government produced a dual government, which brought two parallel forms of exploitation – one in the area of politics and another in religion.

In the political sphere, there was particularly a new system of oppressive measures, which created a feeling of bondage among the people of Manipur. The British, after the introduction of the *patta* system in land ownership, started imposing various other taxes like land revenue, house tax, and other odd taxes such as dog tax, cycle tax, conscription known as *pothang senkhai*, and forced labour system known as *pothang*, all of which had a serious negative impact on the traditional village economy of Manipur. These obligations were made compulsory for every household even when they were not in a position to pay. The common peoples suffered from the two obligations which were the direct substitution of *lallup*. Whenever an officer toured, the nearby villagers were forced to carry the luggage of the officers. And when an officer visited a village, the villagers were obliged to contribute food and other requirements of the officer. To avoid these two obligations, many villagers shifted their village to places that were not close to the roads. This is still evident today in the village settlement patterns in the valley.

In the religious sphere, the Maharaja and his council of Brahmins started imposing various odd taxes in the name of religion, such as the *chandan senkhai* (tax for wearing a *tilak*), *napet senkhai* (tax for cutting hair), *lugul senkhai* (tax for wearing sacred thread), etc. Above all, the Brahmins also exercised various powers in the area of religion and culture. The most painful oppressive system in the religious sphere was the practice of *mangba* and *sengba* (or *amangba* and *asengba*) (impurity and purity), according to which the Maharaja and Brahmins could declare any person as *amangba* (polluted). For *sengtokpa* (a purification rite), the Brahmin demanded money from the person; otherwise the subject is not to be allowed to participate in any social gathering.

Dual politics of mangba–sengba: *resistance of a different kind and production of religious subjects*

The atrocious practice involved in the systems of *mangba* and *sengba* became quite widespread especially during the Maharaja Churachand Singh's reign (1891–1941) in connivance with the *Brahmasabha*. The establishment and consolidation of the *Brahmasabha* could be observed in two ways. First, it provided the native ruler with an alternative method of controlling and exercising his supremacy over the politically and militarily superior British colonisers. In the absence of political power, the *Brahmasabha* was the only institution for the Maharaja to remain in power. It is said that during their long stay in Manipur, the British officers were not allowed to enter the temple of the Hindus. Whenever they interfered with the religious space, a new site was created – the Hindu Meiteis considered the British as polluted. In this regard, B.C. Allen remarks, 'The profane foot of Europeans must not enter even the compound of a Brahmin, and if . . . steps on the verandah of an ordinary villagers, the house will be instantly abandoned and another erected in its place' (1905: 61). Thus, a form of protest and non-co-operation was initiated in the cultural domain.

Second, failing all other political means to exercise his power over the people, the king then used socio-religious means to produce a new category of subjects, especially 'religious subjects'. These factors led to the emergence of an exploitative system of *mangba* and *sengba* politics, which consequently paved the ground for the emergence of a counterforce of social movements under Irabot and revivalist movement under Naoriya Phullo during the colonial period. Thus, the politics of *mangba* and *sengba* became one of the most important factors for the widespread dissatisfaction and dissent especially among the Meiteis. Thus, religion during the colonial period was a method of controlling the masses as well as a means for resistance to secular power of British colonisers by the native rulers.

The second category of politics is closely associated with an alternative source of income for the king, after he lost control over taxation in economic affairs. Taxation on socio-religious grounds was the only option open to him to meet the royal expenditure and, thus, extorted money from his subjects (Saha 1974: 100). By directly or indirectly supporting the Brahmins, he secured a major share of the money collected through the *Brahmasabha* of which he was the president. The king established many socio-religious institutions to generate new taxes to pay for the maintenance of his offices.

By the 1920s, in order to increase the number of socio-religious taxpayers, and on the *Brahmasabha's* advice, the king passed a policy to increase followers of Hinduism by absorbing the hill tribals into the Hindu fold. Therefore, a society known as the Gour Dharma Pracharini Sabha was established at Imphal in 1924 by the late Lalita Madhab Sharma and Banka Behari Sharma to spread Hinduism especially in the hill areas of Manipur (Kabui 1991: 100). They tried to establish Hindu religious schools and encouraged the learning of Sanskrit among the hill tribes. However, the said project was unsuccessful.

RELIGIOUS REVIVALISM AND COLONIAL RULE

Similar method of establishing more religious centres especially in the rural areas was started along with a wider distribution of Brahmin settlements in every possible area. The new process of increasing Brahmin settlement was to mainly enable the state to collect religious taxes.

An official report of 1939–40 recorded, '[W]ell to do Brahmins had gone round the village informing people that the Brahma Sabha had declared them "Mangba" or outcast and (they) offered for a consideration to have them declared "Sengba" or purified' (N. L. Singh 1998: 116). Another British political agent, MacDonald, in the beginning of 1940 also observed:

> The plague of black mail recently again swept over Manipur. Gangs of bullies have been quartering the country demanding money from the public and threatening those who refused to pay with religious excommunication. Many thousands of rupees had been squeezed by these scoundrels from the poorest and the most helpless of the population.
>
> (Singh 1998: 131)

On account of these impositions, people gradually became hostile towards the Maharaja and Brahmins. Persons who resisted mostly belonged to the educated section of society. The educated class discarded the Brahminical coercions. The educated class composed hymns in the Meitei language.

The Brahmins of the *Brahmasabha* strongly reacted to this new response from the few Meiteis. In 1934–35, the *Brahmasabha* issued a resolution against those persons who performed their rites and rituals without Brahmins. Accordingly, many Hindu Meiteis were declared as *amangba* and forbidden to cremate the dead body of their relatives and compelled to bury them. No *Sradha* ceremony for the dead according to the Hindu custom could be performed. But those ostracised persons or locality could be readmitted to Hindu society after payment of Rs 80 and 4 annas. If the order of the ostracism was passed by the Maharaja himself, then the person or locality had to pay Rs 500, if it was by the elder brother of the Maharaja then it was Rs 200 and if the order was passed by 'Ratan', the highest-placed official in the *Brahmasabha*, then it was Rs 50. The money, which was collected by the Brahmins, went directly into the private pocket of the members of the *Brahmasabha*. Thus, the people of Manipur in those days felt that they were culturally, religiously as well as politically colonised by the Brahmins. Such socio-religious atrocities were also stronger in the rural areas. On account of such inhuman practices of

85

the Hindu religious institution in Manipur, many Meiteis attempted to return to their pre-Hindu religious belief and practices in order to escape from the Brahminical influences.

Revivalist resistance to religious hegemony

One of the biggest challenges to Brahminical coercions came in the form of Sanamahi Movement that had its origin outside the present Manipur as Manipuris were historically spread all over South and East Asia. The cause of the movement in Cachar was primarily due to the humiliating experience of Meiteis in the Bengali-dominated Cachar district of Assam. The acculturation pressure due to interaction with a culturally more dominant Bengali community produced a state of resentment and confusion, which led the Meiteis to resist or reject the former. The main objective of the movement was to revive and adopt the Meitei culture, tradition, belief and script.

But the origin of this movement among the Meiteis in Manipur was attached to the feeling of safeguarding their distinct culture and belief that have been constantly threatened by various factors of Hinduisation, colonisation and, finally, modernisation as discussed earlier. This tendency among the Manipuris is highlighted in a play, *Pebet*, directed by Heisnam Kanhailal, a prominent theatre personality. The play depicts a popular Manipuri folktale in which a mother *pebet* (small mythological bird) guards her nestlings by circumventing the predatory attention of the cat by flattery until her nestlings are able to fly and protect themselves. Once they could fly, the mother *pebet* plans *to* defy the cat. However, in their attempt to flee from the captivity of the cat, the youngest among the siblings fails to escape. Rustom Bharucha interprets the play as portraying Hindu indoctrination of the Meiteis by the immigrant Brahmins in the 18th century and says, 'The real fear of the mother *Pebet* is not that her nestlings will be killed and eaten by the cat but rather they will be absorbed into "cat's culture"' (1991: 749).

In the initial stage, the Sanamahi Movement appeared to be a purely socio-religious movement. But today it has assumed other political goals of the Meiteis and stands symbolic of the forced merger of Manipur with India and provides sustenance to the movement against the merger. It is, therefore, a claim for a political space defined by a particular identity and history, which is also free from the influence of outsiders. Or, in other words, it stands for an imagined political space defined by a particular history, culture and identity. Moreover, the Sanamahi Movement is a search for a socio-political space, which can safeguard the Meiteis'

RELIGIOUS REVIVALISM AND COLONIAL RULE

distinct identity and also ensure equality to all the ethnic communities of the region. Thus, the main cause of the Sanamahi Movement among the Meiteis in Manipur is of their historical experiences of the past that threatens the uniqueness of culture, polity, territory and ethnic harmony among various groups. The Meiteis felt that the socio-political status that they had enjoyed in the past was deprived at different stages of history by the Burmese occupation (1819–26), the British colonialism (1891–1947), and the Indian Union (1949 onwards). It is more clearly proved that when an independent kingdom, having its own existence from 33 CE, ended with British colonialism in 1891 and integration of independent Manipur (1947–49) again in 1949 to the Indian Union. Manipur's integration with India reduced Manipur's political status further to a Part C State until the statehood was conferred in 1972. All these political upheavals and developments in the history of Manipur stirred many youths to establish a political space defined by their historical and cultural identity.

Conclusion

The origin of the Sanamahi Movement among the Meiteis in Manipur needs to be located within two frames of understanding, which nevertheless are interconnected. The first relates to the inspiration to safeguard their identity – culture as well as belief – which has been constantly threatened by a wave of exogenous factors. An overall analysis of Manipuri society shows that basic structural and functional transformation had taken place in different historical periods. It is also observed that in all the stages of these transformations, major changes occurred in the areas of culture and identity. Therefore, it is commonly felt that culture, tradition, religion, polity, and territory has been constantly threatened by various exogenous factors like Hinduism, the Burmese invasion and British colonialism. These experiences inspired the Manipuris to safeguard their identity from such powerful forces. Thus, the Sanamahi Movement in the initial stage appeared to be a socio-religious movement, which attempted to remove the Brahminical domination in the socio-religious spheres. Later on, it assumed political dimensions such as a claim for political space defined by identity and history – a space also free from the influences of the outsiders.

The second understanding related to the origin of the Sanamahi Movement was the issue of resistance in the form of native revivalism. Here, the term of reference is how the king used religion as a tool for control or rather as a source of legitimacy of power. The motive behind the strengthening of the Hindu values through the institution of the

87

Brahmasabha during the colonial period was the use of socio-religious means by the native ruler to retain his power. This trend produced a third force, seen in the form of the native revivalist movement of Sanamahi religion, which has continued to sustain till today. Thus, the rise of the Sanamahi Movement during the colonial period, and more strongly at present, is also the result of the rise of the Brahminical power during the colonial period. These new trends indicate that there are aspects of Meiteisation, which do not conform to the process of Hinduisation and modernisation of Meitei society and culture. The increasing tendency among the new generation, especially among some socio-religious groups of Sanamahi Meiteis, to emphasis their own in-group identity through 'isolation' and 'nativism' reveals the rejection of the new socio-political process of dominant India. Contemporary forces working in this movement, like the Meitei Marup, Lainingthou Sanamahi Thougal Kanglup, Meitei National Front, or Sajal, are not merely cultural bodies; they really emerged from latent structural tensions in the socio-political system ingrained in the in-group conflict and rivalry for power and domination in the history of Manipur. The Sanamahi Movement, therefore, is the manifestation of an old conflict between the two socio-cultural values – Hinduism and Sanamahism. However, at present it is reshaped by the prevailing socio-political system. It is the product of interaction between the native people and mainland India in the new socio-political system of post-independent India.

Regarding the functional role of the Sanamahi Movement in contemporary times, my conclusion is that it has come out to restore a moral force that has been neglected by the modern 'secular' state. In the traditional society, both the State and religion co-existed and performed two different functions. The State, with the help of its military, defended the territory and sovereignty of the country from any possible external threat. And religion provided a moral binding force of the people, thus reducing any possible threats to the territorial integrity and sovereignty by its own people. They also legitimised the status quo of the monarch not only as the legitimate ruler of all the peoples, but also as the protector of the people. The coronation ceremony of a king, which was supported by religious authority, bestowed legitimacy to the king as a divine incarnation of Lord Pakhangba. Besides, other annual rituals like *Kwaktanba*, *Mera Hou Chongba*, *Cheiraoba*, and *Lai Haraoba*, with functionaries from diverse ethnic groups, also provided the basis of legitimacy of the monarchy. All these elements established power and institution of the kingship. Finally, the position of the king is equated with the position of God or as a person nearest to God. This position provided the cultural and ideological context in which men and resources could be controlled. Thus, religion functioned as an instrument of legitimising structure of authority and power in ancient and medieval Manipur. Therefore, any nation, in order to minimise possible threats to its sovereignty and territory from within, requires the co-existence of the State and religion. The absence of one increases the chance of threatening its boundary and sovereignty either by outside forces (in the case of a weak defence) or by its own people (in the absence of religion).

However, the problem of the co-existence of religion and State is that the State, by its nature, is very dynamic as its function is to respond to the external forces, and religion by nature is very rigid as it is the body of belief. That is why the State adopted different religions in different historical periods of time in Manipur. But the so-called modern 'secular State' has left religion in the companion of another entity called the Constitution. However, it is questionable whether the given Constitution can perform the same function that was performed by religion. The same problem is also being faced by the Indian State today. Thus, the Sanamahi Movement has come out to restore this moral force that was neglected by the modern secular State.

Note

1 The author is aware of the 'problematics' inherent in colonial texts. Citations referred here do not necessarily mean uncritical acceptance of the views expressed in colonial texts. On account of limitation of space, investigation to see how terms, data, ideas, categories, etc., appear in the texts is excluded.

References

Allen, B.C. 1905. *Naga Hills and Manipur, Assam District Gazetteers*, Vol. 9. Calcutta: Baptist Mission Press.

Bharucha, Rustom. 1991. 'Politics of Indigenous Theatre: Kanhailal in Manipur', *Economic and Political Weekly*, 26(11–12): 747–54.

Brara, Vijaylakshmi. 1998. *Politics, Society and Cosmology in India's North-East*. Oxford: Oxford University Press.

Brown, R. 2001 *[Reprint of 1874]. Statistical Account of the Native State of Manipur and the Hills Territory under Its Rule*. New Delhi: Mittal Publications.

Dirks, Nicholas B. 2003. *Castes of Mind: Colonialism and the Making of Modern India*. Delhi: Permanent Black.

Hodson, T. C. 1984. *The Meitheis*. Delhi: Low Price Publications.

Johnstone, James, Sir. 1971. *My Experiences in Manipur and the Naga Hills*. Delhi: Vivek Publishing House.

Kabui, Gangmumei. 1974. 'Social and Religious Reform Movement in Manipur in 19th and 20th Century Manipur', *Bulletin of the Division of History*. Imphal: Centre of Post-Graduate Studies, JNU.

————. 1991. 'Socio-religious Reform Movement', in Lal Dena (ed.), *History of Modern Manipur, 1826–1949*. Delhi: Orbit Publishers.

Malinowski, Bronislaw. 1978. *Magic, Science and Religion and Other Essays*. London: Souvenir Press.

Richards, Audrey I. 1932. *Hunger and Work in a Savage Tribe*. London: Greenwood Press.

Saha, R. K. 1974. 'An Ethnic Movement in Manipur Valley', in K. S. Singh (ed.), *Tribal Movements in India, Vol. I*. New Delhi: Manohar Publishers.

Said, Edward W. 1995. *Orientalism: Western Conceptions of the Orient*. London: Penguin.

Singh, M. Gojendra. 1989. 'Brief History of Manipur', in *Nehru and Manipur*. Imphal: State Level Committee.

Singh, N. Lokendra. 1998. *The Unquiet Valley*. New Delhi: Mittal Publications.

Singh, N. Tombi. 1972. *Manipur: A study*. Delhi: Rajesh Printing Press.

Singh, Yogendra. 2002. *Modernization of Indian Tradition*. New Delhi: Rawat Publications.

6

POLITICS, SOCIETY AND LITERATURE IN MODERN MANIPUR

Arambam Noni

The history of modern Manipur, like many other societies, is significant for it was marked by various developments including alteration and devaluation in political status and power re-configurations with the advent of British imperialism. Frequent internal animosity and treachery between blocks of native princes had provided easier conditions to the Empire's faster colonisation of Manipur. The British opted to be more strategic in colonising Manipur as the Empire kept the state (Manipur) under its suzerainty and did not opt for a complete annexation. It was due to this political approach that the British ruled over Manipur by appointing a minor, Churachand Singh, as the titular head (Raja) in 1907. Under such a strategic approach of effecting political hegemony, the brunt of the regime over the common masses had become harsh. In other words, the spheres of influence exercised by the Empire, feudal lord and monarchy had resulted in the colossal hegemony, exploitation and restrictions over the people and society.

Keeping such a social and political milieu at the backdrop, the chapter revisits the modern literary history of Manipur[1] particularly focusing on the period of British colonialism. Among the important questions that the work poses with regard to the said period are the way forces of colonialism, feudalism and monarchy were unleashed and ordered, on the one hand, and the literary produces and their responses to wholesome socio-political and economic environment on the other. The chapter discusses the nature of literary – mainly poetry and novel – trends with a perspective to study the overall themes, issues of relevance with the time, criticality, and originality as reflected in the literary works. Nevertheless, this work is not an exhaustive study on all kinds of modern literary texts.

ARAMBAM NONI

Colonialism, responses and literature

With the introduction of Western education and subsequent emergence of a literate class,[2] there began a new phase of Manipuri literature in terms of poetry, songs, prose, novels, epics, etc. By the second decade of the 20th century, Manipuri literary genres began to extensively refer to the literary works of other societies, especially Bengali and English. Once colonialism became an inescapable reality, the material objectives, values and arrangements on which the Empire stood began to produce immense exploitation of the populace. The coming of the British witnessed several changes in administration and economic policies. Mention can be made of the abolition of *lallup*, which was only to be replaced by more rigorous taxation systems such as house tax, both in the hills and the valley, and further ethnicisation of the hills and valley of Manipur due to the separate administrative arrangements.

Under the dual authority of the British and titular king, the public had to shoulder various atrocious taxation systems such as road, forest and water tax, and even taxation on ritual practices and entertainment. In addition, there was extensive exploitation and coercive use of labour. The *pothang* (compulsory unpaid carriage service to the State) system and *yairek sentri* (guarding of official revenue) can also be mentioned. Reminiscent of the imperial strategic neutrality elsewhere, in Manipur the Empire did not intervene in the social and religious exploitation that continued to be the stamp of monarchy. Continuation of the *mangba–sengba* (impurity – purity) and *chandan senkhai* (religious tax for wearing the *tilak*) testifies the non-intervened areas of the Empire.

The emerging middle class, with their newly acquired sensibilities through modern education, had shown their discomfort towards the continuing religious burden and increasing exploitation by the imperial administration. On the other hand, a direct confrontation of the burden and exploitation was also to come from the suffering common masses. It was not long after the British Empire was consolidated that the first *Nupi Lan* (Women's War) of 1904, Thoubal Resistance of 1909 against oppressive labour systems, Kuki Rebellion of 1917, and various other resistances occurred one after the other. In addition, Western values, particularly colonial education, rendered through colonialism began to immensely influence the beliefs, values and knowledge systems of the then Manipuri society. The condition of instantaneous exposure to colonial knowledge and 'autonomy' of resistance seem to enormously influence the sensibilities of the literary pioneers in terms of their reference, usage of metaphor, vocabulary, symbol (religious, cultural and ethnic), objectivity and critical reflexive positions.

POLITICS, SOCIETY AND LITERATURE IN MODERN MANIPUR

By the turn of the early 20th century, most of the prominent (Meetei) literary pioneers had obtained English and Bengali education (and Sanskrit to an extent), in addition to religious and cultural acquaintances with Hinduism. The literary history of the first quarter of the 20th century was largely set against the backdrop of sensibilities acquired from Bengali literary trends and Western education. With the introduction of the Empire's education system, waves of liberal sensibility began to gain ground in Manipuri society and literary products. During this period, a significant number of youths educated outside Manipur had returned home with their newfound educational degrees and acquired sensibilities. Consequently, they began to write poetry, songs, novels, epics, interpretation and translation of religious texts etc.

Literary conceptions:
Genre and subject matter

The first quarter of 20th-century Manipur is significant mainly for the evident shifts and changes that came into existence in the society. British colonialism brought in a new set of political arrangements, exposure of resources to the world market, changes in values and belief systems, etc. In the hill areas of Manipur, the change in literary sensibilities was a result of spreading evangelism and colonial education. It is recorded that on 10 February 1897, the first elementary school was established at Ukhrul by William Pettigrew, an English missionary. Pettigrew, by 1912, had managed to educate and convert several Tangkhul youths and Thadou Kuki youths (Dena 1991: 115). The first literary offshoot was seen in the form of translated works as the missionaries translated the Gospel of St John into native language(s) and dialects of Manipur. The early phase also witnessed several international Christian missionary organisations sponsoring religious literary works. The publication of the Tangkhul New Testament in 1926 and Thadou Kuki translation of the same in 1928 were significant literary manifestations of the Christians in Manipur. The early literary settings of the hill communities in Manipur were largely on Christian religious texts, such as preaching, theological reading, translation, etc. Thus, throughout the first half of the 20th century, Christian literary works in Manipur remained largely confined to the consolidation of religious writings and translations. The Tangkhuls, Kabuis and Thadous are considered to be among the hill communities who played significant roles in the early literary movements of Manipur.

Consequently, there was a simultaneous growing acquaintance with the modern social and political values, on the one hand, and denouncement

93

of feudal social structures and oppressive apparatuses, on the other, among the newly emerging Christian literate class. This class was to become a political force more evidently towards the 1940s when several crucial political conjectures were unfolding along with the looming departure of the Empire.

Another important trajectory of early modern Manipuri literature is found in the *Pangal* (Manipuri Muslim) literary history. Towards the last quarter of the 19th century, the *Pangals* began to travel outside Manipur for Islamic education. Religiosity remained a predominant undercurrent of Muslim literature in Manipur as far as the first half of the modern century is concerned. It is considered that the first trained Manipuri *maulvis* returned to Manipur in 1910 and started Islamic revivalism in Manipur (Kabui 1991: 100). The *maulvis* were the pioneers of Muslim literary history. They were more into the appropriation and reproduction of Islamic knowledge. The history of the early *Pangal* literary journey was exclusive such as that of the early literary trend of the hill communities as it was largely focused on religious verses, Islamic etiquette and learning of languages such as Urdu, Arabic and Persian.

Regarding formal modern education, by the early 20th century, around 15 primary schools were established, and during 1913–14, a middle school was upgraded to high school in the valley area of Manipur. During this period, Bengali instructors, clerks and officers from other parts of British India were brought into Manipur to assist in the Empire's administration and education. As colonialism and increasing influence of the (British) missionaries went hand in hand, several schools were established in the hills and valley. There was also a growing number of learners who could afford, and opted, to study outside the State.

The dawn of a state press towards the close of 1920 and pioneering writings for school textbooks were some of the important developments that helped in the speedy emergence of Manipuri modern literature. The early literary works were not products of higher learning and research as education was a costly affair. In addition, there was non-availability of higher institutions for learning in Manipur. The initial days were also marked by unavailability of the required native instructors and literary materials in the indigenous language.

There was a great dependency on foreign scholarship, teachers, reading materials and translators. For instance, Makar Singh's *Manipuri Primer* and Munal Singh's *Second Primer* in Bengali script were published in Cachar. These two works became leading literary references

POLITICS, SOCIETY AND LITERATURE IN MODERN MANIPUR

for the Manipuri literary pioneers during 1910s. It is believed that through these works produced by the outsiders, the first generation of Manipuri literature became familiar with Bankim Chandra Chattopadhyay, Sarat Chandra Chattopadhyay, Kali Prasanna Ghosh, Rabindranath Tagore, etc., in Bengali, and William Shakespeare, Sir Walter Scott, Lord Alfred Tennyson, Thomas Babington Macaulay, etc., in English (Manihar 1996: 218). Introduction of such a wide range of literary figures and their works left an impact on the nature of literary genre, styles, themes and literary sensibilities, which were to emerge in the years to follow in Manipur. Poetry, novels and other forms of literary genres were largely the replication of such sensibilities. For example, poems were devotional in character and vocabularies remained highly influenced by Sanskrit and Bengali, while presentation of novels and themes of the epics was predominantly derived from renowned Bengali works.

Khwairakpam Chaoba and Hijam Irabot are some of the prominent pioneers whose works were officially recognised. The main feature of the writings that came up during this period deals with ethics, morality, values and recovery of 'Mother Manipur'. Chaoba's *Chhatra Macha* (Student) (1924), *Seidam Seireng* (Introductory Poetry) (1924) by Hijam Irabot and *Basanta Seireng* (Spring Poetry) (1931) by A. Minaketan Singh can be mentioned in this regard. In terms of scope and methodology, these writings remained indirect in picking up the immediate political and economic concerns of the then Manipuri society. The extensive abstraction of poems and the plot of historical novels hint at such tendencies. For example, Chaoba was one of the first literary figures to be recognised officially. His *Chhatra Macha* was an authorised text for school level reading. Chaoba, in his *Chhatra Macha* and *Thainagi Leirang* (Flower of Olden Days) (1933), expresses his concern and love for 'Mother Manipur'. His writings mainly eulogise the richness of *Meeteilon* (Manipuri language). In the words of Chaoba:

> *Lairabi ironni*
> *Khangdabana haibani*
> *Meitei kavi lakhini*
> > (*Thainagi Leirang*, 1932)

> (Loose translation)
> A poor language, they call it
> Ignorant are those who demean it
> The Meitei poet(s) is coming for sure

Chaoba's vocal eulogisation of the Manipuri language was expressive of his concern over the excessive intrusion of and dependence on 'foreign' languages, particularly Bengali and Sanskrit. To Chaoba, indigenous language was rich enough to explicate all kinds of literary urges, complexes and ideas, and compete with other advanced languages of the world. Such a focused commitment of Chaoba was distinctive for his rootedness in comparison with other contemporary literary personalities for his pioneering perspectives on linguistic nationalism.

Lamabam Kamal , a doctor by profession, can be regarded as another pioneering literary exponent whose writings set a new trend. Kamal's *Madhavi* (1930) is considered to be the first novel written in the contemporary theme and style. Being educated outside the state, Kamal had a wider exposure to several shades of literary works, mainly Bengali and English. *Madhavi* is a romantic novel with contemporary sensibilities particularly on society and the plight of women. The problems created by the then-existing social hierarchy finds a running theme in *Madhavi*. The novel unfolds the social disequilibrium and its influences even on interpersonal affairs, including men and women. Through *Madhavi* Kamal denounces social stratification and draws a picture of the sufferings and worries that dominates our world particularly pointing out to the socially enforced helplessness of women as aptly enacted through his lead female characters such as Urirei and Madhavi. Another significant social trajectory that Kamal successfully brings out in the novel can be seen in the lead character Madhavi, a young woman who is depicted as the protagonist denouncing exploitation and confinement of women in most aspects of life. The flip side of *Madhavi* is about untold sufferings meted out on the people at the margins of society. The resistance that come from Urirei's father and her friend Madhavi exemplifies the undercurrents of social resistance in Manipuri society (Kamal 1999: 199). At the ideological plank, sensibilities in *Madhavi* remain largely original as Kamal expresses his discomfort when true love and sacrifices made by Urirei were not acknowledged by the 'English educated Biren' (ibid.: 122). Kamal's writing evokes extensive interest among readers and researchers till date.

However, one can critique that Kamal somewhere oversees the political questions of the then Manipur, perhaps for the reason that he was a doctor by training. Another obvious trajectory for this 'miss out' was the strong strictures that a writer like Kamal came across. It is also a matter of concern that despite Kamal's ability to critique social orthodoxy and the plight of ordinary Manipuri women, *Madhavi* fails to come out of the status quo of the then-existing social framework which constructs women

POLITICS, SOCIETY AND LITERATURE IN MODERN MANIPUR

as comparatively weak, true, honest, pure, etc. Perhaps, it would not be wrong to say that even the name Urirei symbolically implies dependence, such as a vine or creeper.

The coinciding literary developments with *Madhavi* were the emergence of (monthly) literary journals such as *Yakairol* (1930), *Lalit Manjuri Patrika* (1933) and *Meitei Chanu* (1922). The periodicals provided a significant platform to the budding literary practitioners. In this regard, mention can be made of the first two daily newspapers in Manipur; *Deinik Manipur Patrika* and *Manipur Matam* (Parratt 2005: 28). For the Manipuri Muslims, *Message of Islam, Creed of Islam, Traditions of the Prophet*, and *Day of Judgment* were some of the important religious texts that were (re)produced during this period, (noted by Sayed Ahmad in the *Poknapham* daily on 16 October 2006, Imphal), *Musalman-i-Manipuri* (1934–36) in Urdu by Maulana Rahimuddin Ahmad, and *Pulsiratki Pambei* (1938) by Amanullah in Manipuri are considered to be pioneering literary works of *Pangals* in Manipur (Rahman 2003). Till around the 1940s, consolidation of *ulemas* and institutionalisation of madrasas remained an important aspect of Muslim literary manifestations. The coming up of the *Madrasa Alia* at Lilong in 1944 and the *Jamiat-ul-Ulema-e-Hind* in the 1960s can be cited.

In the following years, new literary genres were attempted, which came in the form of epics such as Arambam Dorendrajit's *Kansha Vadh* (1945), Chaoba's *Tonu Laijing Lembi* and Hijam Anganghal's *Khamba Thoibi*. Dorendrajit, Chaoba and Anganghal are well known for their literary contributions in this regard. *Kansha Vadh* is considered to be the first epic written in *Meeteilon*. Dorendrajit's work is interested in drawing out a replication of the great epic *Mahabharata* while exposing the constant conflict between the good and evil in which the good overcomes the evil. The same period also witnessed significant political developments in Manipur and the world. For instance, there was a growing movement for responsible government, *Nupi Lan* (1939), and the beginning of the Second World War. This was also the period when Hijam Irabot (1896–1951) was emerging as a social reformer and, ultimately, a revolutionary political leader. The literary works which came out during this period had begun to shun social hierarchies and growing materialistic values in human relationships. One understandable condition which enforced such limited horizon of Manipuri literary setting was due to the highly restrained socio-political environment created by the British colonialism and native monarchy. Similarly, the parameter of colonial education was limited for there was an apprehension of a newly emerging critical class who were suspected of potentially subverting the colonial interest.

If Chaoba, Kamal, Anganghal, Dorendrajit etc., represented a new literary trend, Irabot represents a unique aspect of modern Manipuri literature. The initial works of Irabot were not distinctively political, possibly because he was a member of the then State *Durbar*. Irabot is credited for introducing the first Manipuri literary journal, *Meitei Chanu*. His collection of poems *Seidam Seireng* was prescribed as a school textbook. *Seidam Seireng* is expressive of the mundane aspects of human society. The first poem, *Ayuk Anganba* (Dawn), describes the beauty of nature and the hope with which it comes to humanity every morning. The poem is also a wake-up call for the peasantry to work hard and carry on with their daily activities. Irabot's growing clarity on social concerns can be seen in the following passage of a poem called *Lairaba* (Poverty):

> *Mayai karingei senna*
> *Matam amada,*
> *Lairaba anangbabu*
> *Tukkatchakhi eina*
> > *(Seidam Seireng 1986: 5)*

(Loose translation):
While intoxicated with material comforts
In the times gone by,
The poor, destitute, helpless
I dealt (them) with abhorrence.

In *Seidam Seireng*, Irabot deals with the issues of poverty and deprived conditions of his time. These questions were to gradually constitute his political articulation and consistent fight against oppression of all kinds. *Imagi Puja* (Worship of Mother) is considered to be one of his important works. This work is devotional in nature with undercurrents of patriotism. Like many of his contemporaries, patriotism was more expressive in the form of recovery of the past glory of Manipur. Irabot's critical writings, mainly in terms of social reform and political rights, began to show more clarity once he denounced the official position and properties accorded to him. Since then, he began to fill up the gap left by many of the literary pioneers of modern Manipur. In the latter half of the 1930s, Irabot denounced official status and privileges accorded to him by the state. For example, it was in the *Ching-nga* Declaration of 1938 that the word *Hindu* was omitted from the Nikhil Hindu Manipuri Mahasabha (NHMM) in order to make it an organisation for people from all social backgrounds in Manipur. Irabot's full-fledged activism banking on communist ideologies gave his literary writings a new trajectory and shift from what was hitherto dominant. Irabot's writings question the feudal social structures, imperial economic exploitation and monarchy at later stages.

Reclaiming of the 'glory and the richness' that we encounter in the literary works of the early 20th century is indicative of the desire to recover the historicity of Manipuri civilisation, cultures, languages and historical legends, etc. Such a style of recovering the past continues to find favour from the contemporary nationalists' discourses in Manipur. A strong imprint of this literary aspect is found in the Manipuri historical novels. *Nar Singh* (1941) is one example. Lairenmayum Ibungohal Singh's *Nar Singh* is a historical novel about a warrior who drove away the Burmese from Manipur in the 19th century. Nationalist recovery has shown strong currents to appropriate the legendary historical figures. Similar recovery and tribute are given to those who fought in the 1891 Anglo-Manipuri War. Though defeated in the war, the sacrifices and valour with which the then kingdom fought continue to evoke legacies of patriotism and nationalist articulation in contemporary times. It can be said that the contemporary Manipuri nationalists' discourses generally usurp the 1891 War as a heroic incident of anti-colonial resistance, love for independence and sovereignty.

Post–World War II times and literature

Towards the second half of the 20th century, there were significant developments in international politics and methodology. The first quarter of the 20th century witnessed intense debates on approaches to economics, social reality and politics, which were reasoned against the growing complications in international economics and politics. The outbreak of the First World War and the Great Depression of 1929 led to the questioning of the strength of positivism. Positivism was criticised for having failed to pre-empt the First World War of 1914 and predict the Great Depression of 1929, which demanded alternative methods of studying society, politics and economics. Such trends were a challenge to the continental philosophical tradition mainly from American scholarship. Unlike the methodological trends in European social sciences, there were no serious empirical methods followed in the literary works in Manipur, especially the writings on society and politics. In the West, the literary concern of the 20th century was more of a new age of experimentation. The early literary works in Manipur were not sufficiently reflective of such tendencies. The early modern Manipur that one often talks about, by European standards was in many ways trailing by several decades.

Like many other societies, World War II is considered to have given a hitch to the literary developments in Manipur. However, there were important conceptions of newer literary thinking and production, especially in short stories and novels. Mention can be made of Hijam Guno's *Laman* (Obligation) (1958) and Hijam Anganghal's *Jahera*. The time of publication of these novels happened after the time frame that the chapter refers to. Guno and Anganghal are acknowledged to have conceived the ideas of the novels during the 1940s. *Jahera* and *Laman* are distinctively bold, particularly in terms of theme and appropriateness. Comparatively, *Jahera* is thematically complex for it is a bold discussion on contemporary society. Anganghal, born in 1892, did not have the opportunity to go for formal education and higher learning due to his humble social background. He is considered to be comparatively rooted in the native language, culture and social settings. *Jahera* is thematically sensitive as it is based on a love relationship between a young Manipuri Muslim girl, Jahera, and Kunjabihari, a Meetei Hindu. *Jahera* is a bold literary venture because when he was writing, Manipuri society was struggling to come out of the enormous religious orthodoxy and closed inter-community relations. Anganghal deserves to be credited for his ability to speak about the religiously bound social relations, particularly between communities. With true love for each other, the plot of the novel enables Jahera, a Muslim, and Kunjabihari, a (Meetei) Hindu, not to succumb to the sectarian strictures embedded in the society.

In *Jahera*, Anganghal resists sectarian predilections that loomed large in Manipuri society as Jahera and Kunjabihari are adamant to uphold their love for each other and even face social ostracisation from their respective communities. Ultimately, the tragic death of Kunjabihari and Jahera adds to the melodramatic impact, which the author uses as an occasion to warn the society to come out of their sectarian social conceptions. To many, *Jahera*, in other words, continues to represent the liberal literary concerns of 20th-century writing in Manipur. The author indirectly recognises the plurality of Manipuri society and boldly questions religious orthodoxy and sectarian attitudes. The tragic end in the novel cautions the trailing fabric of Manipuri social consciousness. The unexpressed empathy and support shown by Jahera's mother Tombi Miya, Amir, Gopal, and Ibemcha to the entire complexities involved in the Jahera–Kunjabihari relationship confirms the growing acceptance of different cultural values and belief systems.

POLITICS, SOCIETY AND LITERATURE IN MODERN MANIPUR

The limitation in *Jahera* is that Anganghal fails to completely shed the usage of dominant symbols and typology of plot setting in his storytelling. In addition to the then-existing closed social order, Jahera and her mother, Tombi, face the maximum brunt of their community's pressure as the author mainly imposes the burden of imbibing dominant cultural practices, such as planting *tulsi* (holy basil) in her courtyard, and applying *chandan* (sandalwood) and *sindur* (vermillion) on Jahera. In addition to these burdens, there is a poor taste of projecting community values, stereotyping of characters and sexuality. Despite Anganghal's ability to wobble up the sectarianism and social orthodoxy of his times, he proves to be insensitive to the several aspects of social hierarchisation and the orthodoxy inherent in most traditions and belief systems. Anganghal appears to have succumbed to the baggage of the dominant psyche that he was informed by. Quite similar to the concerns shown by Anganghal, Shitaljit's novel *Thadokpa* (Sacrifice) is also a sensitive work dealing with social division and economic disparity of his times, and challenges the then growing notion of status, class distinctions and artefacts of modern prosperity.

Laman (1958) can be considered as a distinct literary contribution. The novel rigorously brings out the political landscape of Manipur touching upon the hill and valley relationship, devastation caused during the Burmese aggressions, monarchical exploits and the distrust that grew along with the political instability that was experienced in different phases of history (Guno 2006: 24). In terms of ideational concerns, socio–political relevance and originality in articulation, Guno is effective in questioning the monarchy and feudalism in the then Manipur. The novel beautifully portrays the displacement and hardship faced by a woman, Tamubi, and her infant son, Pari. Another crucial dimension of *Laman* is that it denounces slavery as an inhuman system (ibid.: 30). Locating the theme of the novel in the 19th-century political landscape of Manipur, the author successfully brings out the undercurrents of patriotism and appeals for an organic relationship between the hills and valley (ibid.: 120). The originality that we find in Guno's articulation is reflective of his own political experiences of the 1930s and 1940s, such as the second *Nupi Lan* of 1939 and democratic movements.

Like *Laman,* Guno in *Eikhoigi Tada* (My Brother) (1966) impressively reflects on the social order of 1930s Manipur. Guno aptly summarises the idea of the novel in the following words:

> The plight of the peasants and toil of the toilers who reeled under the heavy weight of scheming land-holders, money-lenders and

the kind of justice meted out to them by the so called guardians of justice and the underhand dealing which form part of the fabric which dispenses justice and last of all, the social taboo, are some of the salient features woven together to make up this story.

(Guno 2009)

Eikhoigi Tada is a fitting critique to social stratification and plight generally meted out to people from a poor social background.

Conclusion

The early literary trends in Manipur can be said to have not been sufficiently bold or direct in anchoring the then-existing social and political questions, such as the seeding legacy of women's movement, democracy, feudalism, and colonialism. In the case of *Meitei Pangals* and Christians, literary works were predominantly religious. As a result, there was no substantial engagement with the social, economic and political realities of the period. Given the colonial and monarchical impediments, the early literary seeding was not highly experimental in their explorations unlike the trend that was seen during this period in European literature. The pioneering literary generation of the 20th century was more or less to work within a limited norm stipulated by the Empire and monarchy, which can be called as the 'official opening' of literary thinking. Corroborating the official stipulation, the initial writings, including poems and essays, were largely for school-level reading, mainly as textbooks. The critics, therefore, would always struggle to find immediate (political) corresponding relevance between literary works and the particular material time. The limitations we find in the early literary works were perhaps for the main reason that the rendering of theme and style was largely derived from and influenced by literary genres that were not originally developed in Manipur, in addition to the discernible encumbrance that came from the monarchy and the Empire. It is suggestive that the early literary figures had to immensely struggle for originality and ways to resist uncharacteristic authority. The wholesome impact was the restraining of creative thinking and clipped literary freedom while dealing with social reality, political hegemony and economic exploitation.

Due to the official strictures and surveillance on the lives of people in general, the literary environment and production were largely retrained.

The first quarter of the 20th-century literary practices was, therefore, limited to specific segment of writings mainly making it confined to

POLITICS, SOCIETY AND LITERATURE IN MODERN MANIPUR

devotional, religious, fictional, mythical, and descriptive writings that mainly lacked scope for critical engagement of the then social realities.

Towards the 1940s, literary urges, ideas and productions became more concerned and vocal towards social, economic and political issues. The first half of the 20th century is an eventful period for the people of Manipur and elsewhere for the important political questions that come up along with the anti-colonial struggles and subsequent decolonisation. The works of Irabot, Guno and Angranghal signify such literary currents.

Notes

1   Here, the term 'modern' is used only in the sense of general periodisation of history, say, the period of British colonialism. The term is not employed to implicate Manipuri literary genres *per se*.
2   I am using the term 'literate class' in the context of the early 20th-century Manipuri politics and society. The literate class, here, implies the section of people who were introduced to the colonial education system of British India. It also implies those who were educated, beneficiaries of colonial administrative support and officials of native origin.

References

Dena, Lal (ed.). 1991. *History of Modern Manipur, 1826–1949*. New Delhi: Orbit Publishers.
Dorendrajit, Arambam. 1945. *Kansha Vadh*. Imphal: P.S and Tamra Publications.
Ibungohal, Lairenmayum. 1941. *Nar Singh*. Imphal: Panthung.
Irabot, Hijam. 1996 [1924]. *Seidam Seireng* (Introductory Poetry).Imphal: Naharol Sahitya Premi Samiti.
Kabui, Gangumei. 1991. 'Socio-religious Movement and Christian Proselytism in Manipur', in Lal Dena (ed.), *History of Modern Manipur, 1826–1949*. New Delhi: Orbit.
Kamal, Lamabam. 1999 [1930]. *Madhavi*. Imphal: Manipur Sahitya Parishad.
Manihar, Ch. 1996. *A History of Manipuri Literature*. New Delhi: Sahitya Academi.
Parratt, John. 2005. *Wounded Land: Politics and Identity in Modern Manipur*. New Delhi: Mittal Publications.
Rahman, Mohammad Abdur. 2003. *Pangal Amasung Manipuri Sahitya* (Manipuri Muslim and Literature). *Pambei*, October. Imphal.
Singh, Hijam Angranghal. 2004. *Jahera*. Imphal: Sahitya Akademi
Singh, Hijam Guno. 2006 [1958]. *Laman* (Obligation). Imphal: Lamyanba.
———. 2009. *My Brother*. Imphal: Ningthou Printers.
Singh, Khwairakpam Chaoba. 1956 [1932]. *Thainagi Leirang* (Flower of the Olden Days). Imphal: The Government Press.
Singh, Nilakanta E. 1993. *Fragments of Manipuri Culture*. New Delhi: Omsons.

7

DESIRE, DISGRACE AND COLONIALISM

A reading of *Bor Saheb Ongbi Sanatombi*

Rajkumari Smejita

Theoretical and political shifts involved in the strategies of theorising colonialism have recently focused on the issue of sexuality, desire and intimacy under colonialism (McClintock 1995; Stoler 1995; Young 1995; Dollimore 1997; Looby 1997). By locating the chapter within the same theoretical perspective, I am intending to examine how the notions of desire and disgrace circulate in M. K. Binodini's (hereafter, MK) careful delineation of the story of a native princess, Sanatombi, who falls in love with a white man during a period when British colonisation takes a sharper shape and position in Manipur following the Anglo-Manipuri War of 1891. The novel portrays a fictional reconstruction of a love affair that leads into a final culmination with formal conjugality.

The chapter seeks to offer an interpretation of how the protagonist's relationship with the political agent can be discerned within an ambivalent relation of attraction and repulsion of the colonised 'other'. Thus, an attempt is made is to locate the love affair within the colonial fantasies, which is imbued with a desire for the 'native' and 'exotic' beauties. The chapter explores the constitution of the body and territory under the conditions of colonial rule as the site and object of colonial desire. Another focus of the chapter is to see how an inquiry into the intimacy with the 'colonial desire' offers a possibility to recover instances of disgrace and shame as subversion, which only end up in serving the colonial libidinal economy of desire (possession as well as exploitation of the possessed; explained in subsequent sections). In this case, an exploration of how the stigma of becoming a 'fallen woman' that Sanatombi

DESIRE, DISGRACE AND COLONIALISM

bears to witness till her death can be 'questionable' if her disgrace is to be interpreted only in the context of the moral vicissitudes of that time. The chapter suggests that the question of disgrace and shame under the condition of colonial rule should rather be studied by taking into account how these categories were socially organised within the notion of the colonised otherness and colonial racialisation, as the novel shows, though implicitly.

The novel delineates the story of a princess, Sanatombi, who is married to a colonial ruler, the then political agent, Colonel Maxwell. The story weaves around the gradual development of the protagonist, Sanatombi, from her early childhood days until she becomes a contested figure on account of her relationship with the white man. Sanatombi is the eldest daughter of Maharaja Surchandra and Rani Jashumati. Before she meets Maxwell, she is in the throes of a failed marriage with Manikchan, a petty trader. She is the one who maintains close ties with all the kin in the royal clan, to mention a few, her uncle Koireng (Tikendrajit, and Ningthempishak (Churchand, her 'brother' from a different genealogy of the royal clan). Her quintessential love for her father, the fallen state of the kingdom and her being lonely in the deepest recesses of her mind give a dimension of a complex character throughout the story.

The author engages in building up the protagonist amidst the stringent decorum and rivalry of a royal family and the turbulent phase of Manipur's political scenario, which more or less informed the protagonist to evolve a personality of her own. Sanatombi is a woman who suffers the most sordid form of loneliness which gradually dissipates her following the encounter with the colonial agent, and at the end she succumbs to this melancholia. In a short span of her lifetime, Sanatombi is remembered for her daring spirit, strong-headedness and the infamous act of elopement with Maxwell, the *Bor Saheb* (white groom).

MK meticulously portrays the events that bring Maxwell closer to the life of the protagonist. And in the penultimate of the novel the author says:

Aduga Maxwell gee maramda eina hangkhiba chaoraba wahang gee paokhumdi ei phangle. Ei mabu chingnadre.

(Binodini 1976: 254)

(Loose translation):
I have got the answer to the big question that I have asked about Maxwell. I am not doubtful about him anymore.

105

The answer for her is:

Maxwelna Sanatombibu nungsi, Meiteisingbu nungsi.

(ibid.)

(Loose translation):
Maxwell loves Sanatombi and Manipur equally.

It shows the significance of the author's enterprise to reconstruct the coloniser from a different perspective, which is central to the novel's narrativisation. Sanatombi and Maxwell are two lonely figures wrapped up in a time that is not destined for them, a place where they cannot call their own, a bond that fails to gain recognition, an emotion that is eroded before it springs. MK, in naming the title of the novel as *Bor Saheb Ongbi Sanatombi*, has rightfully placed Sanatombi as the betrothed to the *Bor Saheb* and, therefore, suggesting the rich interplay of desire and disgrace from the very beginning.

Intimating colonial desire

Recent scholarship in the field of post-colonial theory has revealed the extent to which colonialist notions of essential racial difference were organised through the complex relationship between the desire of the coloniser of being (sexually, culturally) intimate with the colonised and the construction of the intimacy as inferior attraction that leads to its being finally abandoned (Young 1995). Such relation exposes the racialised, gendered and sexualised dimensions of colonialism. The sensibilities to this dynamics under the condition of colonial rule have been well articulated in postcolonial theorising of colonial knowledge and power. This body of knowledge has enabled us to see the role played by desire and sexuality in the constitution of the colonised as inferior and gendered (feminised) subjects.

In the following sections of the chapter, an attempt is made to explore a possibility to revisit the issues involved in the portrayal of desire, intimacy and disgrace under colonial rule and, thereby, suggest ways to interpret the very inscriptions of power in the ways it figures in narrating them in fictional mode, as MK does in reconstructing Sanatombi in the novel. The novel sensitises in bringing up a woman protagonist who represents the object of colonial desire. She depicts the intrusion of this desire and its reception in Manipur in the end of the 19th century and the initial period of the 20th century. What is noteworthy about the novel is that it

DESIRE, DISGRACE AND COLONIALISM

shows certain representations of colonial desire both in terms of how it intrudes and how it is received in an exotic site(s) (bodies, sexuality, place, the 'palace', etc.). Such depiction throws light on the way the protagonist's body becomes both a symbolic and discursive site of colonial desire.

By transforming the native's relationship with the colonial agents as that of an object of desire and the spectator who finally consumes the object, the world of the native under colonialism thus represents a particular manner in which desire is invoked, used and put into service for the colonial male interests.

Colonialism, understood as the very process of inscribing this 'desiring machine', when applied to MK's novel, makes visible the extent to which the body of Sanatombi as well as the colonised territory are inscribed as sites of colonial fantasies and erotic desire for the exotic other. The palace, the land, scenic beauties of nature, and the body of the protagonist altogether represent as the totality of the site of this desiring machine.

The author renders Sanatombi as one such figure who remains mysteriously present in the history of the royal family of Manipur. In her attempt to render Sanatombi as a charismatic enigma in her stature, the author carefully tries to restore the protagonist both in the historical and fictional dimensions. As a historical person, Sanatombi belongs to that particular era of turmoil and devastation under colonial rule. She has experienced both the pangs of being a part of the thwarted privileged class, the 'unheroic' defiance of the norms of the moral fabric of that time with her intimacy with a colonial agent, a white man.

On the other hand, as a fictional figure, Sanatombi appears in the larger canopy of a woman who lives an unlikely rugged life behind the seams and frills of a colonial enterprise and a much fantasised and suspicious public gleam. MK consciously employs particular sources as tools to reconstruct Sanatombi in a fictional mode. By employing these tools, she goes deeper in understanding the psyche of Sanatombi – her most enlivened moments of life, her agonising experience in one of the most turbulent phases of Manipur. Through Sanatombi the author gives a picture of the power of the royal family as well as the colonial establishment in the most undiluted, unflavoured and intimate manner.

Then, coming to Sanatombi's gradual evolution of becoming intimate with Maxwell, the novel reveals an undeniable force of necessity that is demanded by the situation. Along with the situations, the protagonist's strain of fulfilment in conquering intimacy that is endeared to her and the vengeance that she wants to take for the irretrievable loss of her loved ones begin to fuse into union . Within the sphere of the desiring machine, she thrives both within and without the colonial grid, continually slipping in the fissures of her divided 'selves', divulging a 'condition' that obliterates the fixity of her existence. It profoundly impacts her up to the last moment. She cannot deny her inexorable presence as the 'racialised' other; yet, the impossibility to completely diffuse and emerge from the tension of becoming both an autonomous desiring subject and, most particularly, the object of colonial desire. As delineated in many situations in the novel, she also figures in the clash between the western modernity (that she had encountered) and the indigenous culture. What is glaringly accountable is the way she becomes the site of this encounter whereby the colonial master enforces his accumulated knowledge of hygiene, medicine and disease, which contrasted with the ethos of the colonised. For example, Maxwell urges Sanatombi to boil water to protect against typhus. He also teaches her the advantages of moving to more hygienic habits, such as the use of a smoking pipe and change in her dietary habits. Sanatombi willingly overrides all cultural taboos and begins to adhere to the newly acquired habits of living. The coalescence reflects how the colonised other is made to affirm and mimic new territories of values, knowledge, practices, and identity that were for the natives in the colony considered as taboo, impractical, 'unknown' and obnoxious. Indeed, the protagonist's parodic performance of the role of a wife of the colonial agent and her reassertion of the identity of the colonised other invoking the lost position of the royal clan reveal the tension of this mimicry in holding the two divided selves within herself.

However, MK does not fully recover the fluidity and slippages of Maxwell, which she does appertaining to her narrative strategy and shows a conscious effort in doing so in the novel. The author gradually recounts the different aspects of the protagonist. However, in delineating Maxwell, the matter lacks magnitude and certain fissures arise reflecting the laxity of such a projection. It cannot be denied that the resources are limited but more arresting are the various conjectures of the author that captivate the colonial master in a limited frame of characterisation and largely amplifying the emotional state of this persona. Through this weakness or rather, in a way, the productive strength of her technique in recounting the white man, the author evokes the subtlety of Maxwell as the reformed colonial agent, an ordinary man who can make mistakes and liable to be punished and devoid of his stature – sentimental, deep thinking, benevolent ruler and an emancipator. One such instance is the long retribution he pays after clearing Sanatombi's doubt:

> *Ashonba piklaba Manipur nakhoigee naphamda chaokhatlaba kallaba ekhoi lankhre.*
>
> (Binodini 1976: 157)

DESIRE, DISGRACE AND COLONIALISM

(Loose translation):
[. . .] we the mighty, the civilised have wronged to the weak and
small Manipur . . .

However, the question of colonial desire is involved at this stage to the
extent of being hybridised and transmuted in such a scale that Maxwell
becomes a disgrace to his own political stature, the moral baggage of the
Victorian metropole and the larger cultural image of the British Empire
in general. His actions begin to be questioned by his fellow colonisers and
he risks his own reputation. When Maxwell is ready to perform all the
customary practices required for a man to marry a woman, other British
officers find his action 'ridiculous' (Binodini 1976: 195).

Such questioning is grounded in a long tradition of organising the
system of Western knowledge and power in relation to the non-West categories, especially the East or the Orient, as understood by Edward Said in
Orientalism. While the notion of the Orient, according to Said, does not
correspond to what the Orient is, the construction, however, provides a
framework of rendering the Orient intelligible to Western consciousness.
The discursive construction of the Orient within the Western consciousness as a place of 'inordinate sensuality and sexual pleasures' reveals how
erotic desire in the colonies are organised through the racial epistemol-
ogy of the 'Oriental' knowledge produced about the Orient (Said 1978).
What appears is that Maxwell's desire for the princess is not innocent
of power and the historical context of colonialism and its conditions of
rule, and is, therefore, imbued with the operations of colonial knowledge
and power. In other words, the colonial desire cannot escape entirely its
rootedness in the racial structure of the relation between the coloniser and
the colonised.

While drawing the other side, Maxwell is the *Bor Saheb* for the masses.
He is the ruler and the master who 'loves' Sanatombi, which causes disgrace to her following her elopement to his place in a spring of delusional
madness. He is the one, as some locals believe, who by using black art
induces Sanatombi to a madness of desire for him. However, Maxwell is
never a disgraceful figure to the author and his desire gets due weightage
and implication in its pretext. The projection of a colonial agent's desire
is undermined and is subdued in tone due to the narrative implication of
the author, or rather it is diluted under the wrap of a heightened romantic
theme and by recreating a characterisation of the protagonist as a willing
subject of desire. The narrative gives way to merely creating a love interest
out of the colonial master and highlighting the character of a subtle son-
in-law of the royal clan. Maxwell only simmers in the text to bring out

the situations and character in Sanatombi's life. Much of his accounts are delimiting, which fail to show the colours of his character, the uncourtly act towards Sanatombi, the final voyeurism and the infamous elopement, the curtailment of Sanatombi from serious political issues, the final departure to never return etc.

Barring the plight of how a dethroned king's daughter is treated and disregarding the reprimand of customary rules and authority, Maxwell encroaches where the mark of disgrace is unprecedented; the mark of disgrace, which the protagonist carries to her grave. He displays his desire with no panache of shame or glory. His desire over the colony is emphatic in the way he expresses his feeling to even have a place of his own and this idea is explicated in the way he unfolds the path of acquiring his object of desire. He seems to exhibit an exultation of heightened emotions about the land: eulogising the place; empathising with the plight of the people; bearing to be guilt conscious of the flaws of the Raj and making a final overture of his senses and desires upon Sanatombi. His love for 'this painfully beautiful country' explicates his entrapment into the interplay of both attachment and detachment of the colonised and 'exotic' territory, and the very object of his desire. And he thinks 'there is no way out' in his letter to his metropole home (Binodini 1976: 190).

It is at this juncture that the author implicitly tries to acknowledge the coloniser's desire for his lover that would have arguably resulted in the repudiation of his identity as a racially and sexually pure white man and in his self-constitution as a hybrid subject – the white man's racist disavowal of his desire and reassertion of his 'white' identity. His attachment to 'whiteness' and the object of his desire, the princess, highlight the oscillation between identification with and attraction to the colonised other and repulsion of this other as well. Such a messing up of the dichotomised boundaries between his white colonial self and the colonised other and the anxiety provoked by this messiness is implicitly shown in Maxwell's silent agony. The conjectures of MK do not fully attempt to capture her fictionalised presentation of the white coloniser's inner world in order to understand the racial identifications, which, in the words of Diana Fuss, are always 'caught in a system of cultural relays that make assumptions of racial identity both necessary and impossible' (Fuss 1994: 38).

The question of disgrace

Pre-colonial Manipur experienced the hegemonic and hedonistic fiesta of the powerful kings of numerous lineages. The royal family is shown as a replica of purity, refined and the image of decorum for all. Royal women bet their luck in bearing a son as it will bring them honour, title

DESIRE, DISGRACE AND COLONIALISM

and priority and a steady rise before the public. Gaiety and fun are curtailed before specific person and place, and has to be carried out only after authority permits. Mannerisms are strictly to be observed especially by the womenfolk; they have their own separate space and cannot enter a man's domain without permission. However, Sanatombi experiences an altogether different ambience; at an early age she reconciles herself to being the subordinate sex, which she more or less defies. She abhors the stringent rules for women inside the palace and grows up guarding her much hard-earned love of a few people. She is also a witness to the emotional vacuum and continuous kinships rivalry for the crown. To a free-spirited person like Sanatombi, it is like living in a cage; she commits several misdemeanours though when she fights this subjugation.

As the princess of the last ruling king, Sanatombi witnesses the luxury of her childhood and youth along with the shaping of her understanding of being a woman within the limited scope of freedom inside the four walls. She grows up rebellious and strong-headed, but as one who speaks her mind. These attributes go a long way in shaping her personality. MK delineates the tryst of this unforgettable character from her early childhood to bring out the real essence of Sanatombi's character – her values, spirit, rebelliousness, and daring – which shape her personality as she grows up. Sanatombi is shown in all her vagaries as a mixture of fiery spirit and someone endowed with the capability of appropriating the condition she is confounded with.

Sanatombi's first marriage is loveless; and it was an arranged marriage. But this never serves as an alibi for her second marriage, which becomes an event that marks crucial changes in her life: a symbol of disgrace and ostracisation. Her intimate 'desire' for the colonial master is a fallible act, unsuitable for a woman of her standing. It is a desire that is socially unacceptable and interpreted in an overtone of sexual implicitness, a failed marriage and morally mortifying act committed by a royal lady. She is condemned and her social ostracisation is carried out from the utmost close royal clan to the scale of public disgrace. She remains an outcast among the royal circuit and she accepts this with much humility. It was as her mother said, 'A public scandal on the one hand and the question of disgrace on the other' (loosely translated). In Manipuri the text runs as '*Amaromda leibak wathok, amaromda jattaba*' (Binodini 1976: 195).

Norms of society define the coterie of royal women besides being a symbol of worth simulating for the public. The private life of Sanatombi becomes malignant if seen with the moral standards of the royal family. She cannot be free despite being a princess or living with the then

RAJKUMARI SMEJITA

authority by her side; she cannot escape the determining norms of society. The hue and cry against her is that she marries a detested culture and defiles the royal blood. However, her act can be understood in a more symbolic plane as subversive.

It is questionable whether Sanatombi is a fallen woman because of the disgrace she brings upon herself and to the ethos of the royal clan by marrying a white man. I suggest that Sanatombi's disgrace lies in her mimicry of subversion. She cannot fully recover her past stature and can never completely reconcile her newly acquired condition of being the hybridised 'other' living at the threshold of those boundaries, one that is wiped out forever and the other that was never written in her fate. Her desire for the white man shows an insidious de-identification with her being a married woman in a patriarchal society.

Sanatombi's subversive mimicry of the role of the wife of a white man ends up reinforcing conventional power relations between Western colonial desire and Oriental 'woman' rather than challenging them. This is quite vivid in one incident that evokes Sanatombi's realization of both her strangeness and her proximity to her husband. During a dance party in one of their outings, she experiences the anxiety of being alienated and the feeling of anonymity and this strange feeling makes her recognise the very condition of her existence. She cannot truly become a part of the culture she adopts nor can she let go of her powerful feeling for the man she loves. At the party at a tea estate in Shillong, 'Maxwell wore a smile and Sanatombi found herself too small' (Binodini 1976: 224). She merely let her feeling dissolve and accepts her 'otherness' and Maxwell's pacification of the incident only shows that she is now distant from the things that she cares the most.

She is unable to transcend the positions of being the princess who is married to a commoner and of being the 'racialised' wife of a white man. The fluctuating positions that she is never able to reconcile are trapped in an ambivalent structure of colonial libidinal attraction to and repulsion of the other. This trapping must be understood as central to the dynamic of the coloniser – colonised relation that is manifest in a more symbolic realm of colonised femininity and sexuality. By performing the role of autonomous female subject and subverting the conventional female identity strictly encoded in the mores of being a daughter of the former king of Manipur, the protagonist makes the white man the object of her desire. In so doing, she forces herself to mime the image of a desiring female subject, an image that challenges the role of women as weak, submissive and subordinate within the confines of the palatial strictures and larger social standards of moral constriction. Forcing her to mime which is detestable

DESIRE, DISGRACE AND COLONIALISM

is her subversion and at the same time, subjugating her assertive identity to the colonial power is her disgrace. Sanatombi's self-constitution as the desiring female subject is dependent on her appropriation of the racialised image implicated in her being the wife of colonial officer. Thus, her attempt to distance herself from a traditional society through her deviant endearment for the white man conjures up the colonial power relations from which she is never able to escape. Her relationship to the white man as recounted in the novel, however, is made to work in the service of colonialism.

Conclusion

M. K. Binodini states in her 'Foreword' to *Bor Saheb Ongbi Sanatombi* that her colossus is not a historical or biographical account of Sanatombi, the eldest daughter of Maharaja Surchandra. Rather, it should be read as a work of fiction. The work is shown as a fictional representation of the events narrated through Sanatombi's life. She, however, uses both oral and written accounts including conversation, letters, photographs, and memories inherited through official and unofficial sources. An interesting aspect of this novel is that the novel seeks to recreate the real life of an actual historical person who lived in a period that is not of so distant past.

In other words, the authorial sieving of the events and persons becomes possible through her encounter with the images, memories, conversations, written accounts, and sentiments accumulated when she intended to gather these sources. It is how they represent the reconstruction of the event and the characters. These seemingly innocent sources, however, are not so when they are made to tell and retell the stories of the past. This is significant, though the chapter does not focus on it, in the way telling and retelling of such stories speak of how colonialism is registered, memorised and received.

The point is to see how in the novel intimacy, repulsion and subversion are retained and refreshed. As we find in the character of Sanatombi, we may ask more questions on how we imagine our own contemporary plight of repression, dehumanisation and shame. I suggest that Sanatombi being dejected, abandoned and disgraced, and condemned even after her death, can be seen in two ways. One is to consider disgrace itself as a mode of resistance to the structures of colonial intimacy and desire. By considering Sanatombi as a fallen woman it is through this dishonour that colonialism is resisted. This can be retrieved from various sources that MK used when she wrote the novel. The other point is that disgrace is subversion. What I am trying to put forth is that the protagonist's

113

conjugal relation with the officer makes her a seemingly rebellious agent of subversion, rather than being a mere object of colonial desire. It is the reconstruction of her female subject as a desiring subject that somehow subverts the colonial ambivalence of 'desire', as well as the traditional moral conditioning in a monarchic society. About the novel itself, we may add another feature of imagining colonialism as we seen in the novel. MK's effort to clear some of her own personal doubts about Sanatombi being drawn as condemned princess may be seen also as recounting modernity through which to receive, rethink and reproach colonialism and its outcome. Desire is itself a subversive form, and this could be both disgrace and resistance.

References

Binodini, Maharaj Kumari. 1976. *Bor Saheb Ongbi Sanatombi*. Imphal: Published by the author.

Dollimore, Jonathan. 1997. 'Desire and Difference: Homosexuality, Race, Masculinity', in Harry Stecopoulos and Michael Uebel (eds), *Race and the Subject of Masculinities*. Durham: Duke University Press.

Fuss, Diana. 1994. 'Interior Colonies: Frantz Fanon and the Politics of Identification', *Diacritics*, 24(2/3): 20–44.

Looby, Christopher. 1997. 'As Thoroughly Black as the Most Faithful Philanthropist Could Desire: Erotics of Race in Higginson's "Army Life in a Black Regiment"', in Harry Stecopoulos and Michael Uebel (eds), *Race and the Subject of Masculinities*. Durham: Duke University Press.

McClintock, Anne. 1995. *Imperial Leather: Race, Gender and Sexuality in the Colonial Contest*. New York and London: Routledge.

Stoler, Anne L. 1995. *Race and the Education of Desire*. Durham: Duke University Press.

Young, Robert. 1995. *Colonial Desire: Hybridity in Theory, Culture and Race*. London: Routledge.

8

JESTERS OF POPULAR GENRES AS AGENTS OF RESISTANCE THROUGH REFLEXIVITY

Ksh. Imokanta Singh

Cultural performances are exposed to the process of both conscious and unconscious forces of temporal exigencies, brought through the dynamism of both endogenous and exogenous cultural traits. This means there is the vulnerability of cultural performances being immersed into the cultural, religious, political and economic terrains of the society which they are a part of. However, this does not discount their propensity to rise above/ against these terrains; to fix them in the synchronic time frame; to take them to the world of mythology and history and also to the yet unseen future with their own prognosis. Then cultural performances cannot be labelled just as a product devoid of values, because 'taste is a deeply ideological category' (Storey 2001: 5) for both the giver and the taker. Raymond Williams (1965) is of the view that the changes and conflicts of a whole way of life are deeply implicated in its systems of learning and communication, with the result that cultural history is far from being a mere province of idle aesthetic interest. Cultural production involves a tacit understanding, between the producer and the consumer, of a shared meaning. If there is an endeavour, through this, to possess a certain cultural, political and religious element within the societal location, then this very process may be a pointer to the dispossession or to 'othering' of the elements, which are perceived as detriment to the well-being of that certain community or the cultural producers. Pierre Bourdieu sees the cultural production and consumption as 'predisposed, consciously and deliberately or not, to fulfil a social function of legitimating social differences' (quoted in Storey 2001: 5).

In this backdrop, this chapter will try to discern the various courses the performing art forms, in general, took during colonialism in Manipur. Specifically, this venture will try to study the attempt to resist and actual resistance by jesters of the popular theatre form, which is known today as *Shumang Lila*,[1] against the overindulgence of power controlled by the twin forces of colonialism and feudalism. These popular genres served as a mouth to voice the dissension of the powerless majority against the powerful minority. Such expression of resistance, both passive and active, was comparatively more open in popular genres than in proscenium theatre, which might be categorised as 'elite theatre' because the latter was more meticulously screened and participated by the ruling minority. So, the popular genres were cloistered to the peripheries in the power structures. These performers might be seen as poor cousins of the artistes in 'elite theatre'. However, this periphery was utilised as a vantage point to strike at the powers that be at the centre, through their various tools of satire and parody.

The jesters of the popular genres performed with an ardent sense of agency laced with a responsibility to speak for the powerless majority. They did not act just as a mirror which only reflected how the society and polity behaved. So, popular genres as cultural performances reflexed upon 'the mundane, everyday socio-cultural processes, domestic, economic, political, legal and the like' (Turner 1986: 21–24). For Victor Turner, this relationship (between mundane processes and cultural performances) is not unidirectional and positive – in the sense that the performative genre merely 'reflects' or 'expresses' the social system or the cultural configuration, or at any rate their key relationships – but that it is reciprocal and reflexive – in the sense that the performance is often a critique, direct or veiled, of the social life it grows out of, an evaluation (with lively possibilities of rejection) of the way society handles history. He also asserts that performative reflexivity, too, is not mere *reflex*, a quick, automatic or habitual response to some stimulus. It is highly contrived, artificial of culture not nature, a deliberate and voluntary work of art (Turner 1986: 21–24). This is why these jesters relied on what may be called *reflexive politics*, to question, critique and finally resist the unwarranted moves from the side of both the societal and political systems.

Colonial intervention

Study of colonial Manipur needs to also take into account the monarchical power structure as the two systems had mixed equations, sometimes converging and sometimes diverging. Manipur is clearly the last eastern post which fell into the hands of the British Empire in the subcontinent. It remained as a sovereign kingdom and a trusted ally of the British even when her surrounding territories including Burma were already a part of

British India. The sovereignty of this kingdom finally came to an end in 1891 when the British defeated Manipur after a fiercely fought battle.

Manipur then 'became a tributary State and had now to pay an annual tribute of Rs 50,000 to the British Government' (R.K.J. Singh 1992: 307). The British chose Churachand Singh, a minor boy of six years, as Raja of Manipur. He was a symbolic king, as the administration was completely manned by the British. So, the British kept Manipur under their 'direct rule' from 'September 13, 1891 to May 15, 1907', a period known in history as 'Manipur under British Management' (K.M. Singh 1989: 5). Subsequently, the British started gaining control over the elites as they were the ones who could rise against them. As a part of their tactics, the Raja was sent to Mayo College, Ajmer, in 1895 (till 1901) where he was given a modern (British) education and the English way of life so that he could be physically and ideologically sculpted in the English mould. This era was the beginning of the 'profanation' of the concept of the 'divine kingship' starting from the 'Divine' King Pakhangba. Here, it is noteworthy to suggest that Manipur presents a case in hand when it comes to the marriage of history and mythology in its attempt to establish the linear diachronic connection of events and epochs, which make its synchronic world credible.

Churachand Singh was again handed over the charge of administration on 15 May 1907 (K.M. Singh 1989: 5–8). The Manipur State Durbar was formed on the same day, with the Raja appointed as President, W.A. Cosgrave as Vice President and three others as Ordinary Members. . This body was entrusted to run the administration of the state. Though the king was the head, the major power was reserved for the British officer holding the post of vice president. There are so many angles from which this era can be seen but what is of interest here is the cultural side, which, in a way, was enmeshed with political and economic undertones. By now, the outside cultural elements started influencing the Manipur elites directly through the Bengalis who came with the British as clerks and administrative and judiciary officials. Early 20th century was also the time when a native educated middle class emerged in Manipur. The new class was accommodated to the state services so that they also were ideologically merged to the ruling class.

The new middle class tried to carve out its own niche as different from the majority class of peasants and common people. Such an endeavour gradually helped this class create the so-called elite culture in Manipur. The modern literate culture imported from Bengal, where it was originally imitated from the British, became a marker for its class difference. The same class became the one defining cultural and societal values, including patriarchy. This way the British in convergence with the Bengalis were, considerably, able to control the political and cultural discourses of the elite and the middle class so that these values might be diffused to the rest of the population.

As the Raja was also politically and economically sidelined, he had to find a way of hegemony in the cultural and religious fields. There were impositions of taxes and services on common Meiteis (Manipuris) – the hill people were fortunately not part of this ordeal – who were kept aloof from the king and his nobles by the British. The taxes were partly to meet the amount of tribute to be paid to the British annually and partly to consolidate his authoritarian legitimacy in the minds of the people, which seemed to have waned, vis-à-vis the British power. These taxes included *chandan senkhai* (tax on using *chandan*, the sacred mud used to apply the Vaisnavite religious marks on the forehead and other body parts) which reasserted the practice of *mangba–sengba* (pollution-purity); *Kangthouri* (a subscription of half an *anna* per house collected from all the common Meiteis instead of collecting *kangthouri*, the rope to pull the *rath* (chariot) during the *kangchingba* (*rathjatra*) ceremony); *Chabok Wangol* (collection of one paise per house of all the common Meiteis on the eve of the birth of the king's child) etc. (K. M. Singh 1989: 30–31). Above these, there were free services offered to the king and his officials by the common Meiteis. They included *yairek sentry* (duty by the villagers to guard the tax money collected by state officials from the villagers); peon and *amin chakthak* (free feeding of visiting state officials by the villagers); *dolaireng* (carrying of government peons on the *dolai* (palanquin) by the villagers during rainy season) etc. Though these practices consolidated the monarchical assertion, they, however, built a passive dissension among the masses, which further distanced them from the ruling class.

After strong movements against both the colonial and the feudal powers by various groups and political parties, King Bodhchandra Singh, the son of Churachand Singh, conceded to form a responsible democratic government. In March 1947, the Constitution Drafting Committee was formed with members from both the hills and the valley. On 15 August 1947, Manipur became independent. On 26 August 1947, the Manipur Constituent Assembly adopted the Manipur constitution, which introduced a democratic set-up with a constitutional monarchy in Manipur. Elections based on the universal adult franchise were held in 1948. Thus, under the universal adult franchise, the people of Manipur enjoyed the fruits of democracy, the first of its kind in the entire Indian subcontinent. However, this euphoria ended when the Indian government and the king signed the controversial 'Manipur Merger Agreement' on 21

September 1949. As a result, the Assembly was dissolved on 15 October 1949 from which date the Agreement came into force. The kingdom was then reduced to a mere 'Part C State' within India, administered by a chief commissioner appointed by the President of India.

Manipuri performative genres

There is no bone of contention in Manipur's luminous place in the firmament of cultural performance traditions. There is a convergence between what we generally call religious/ritualistic and non-religious forms. This categorisation takes into account the texts and contexts of performance; the audience structure and behaviour etc. This is not to deny the fact that, especially in most of the traditional societies, the cultural is entwined with the religious. Keeping this in mind, Manipuri performing art forms can be loosely grouped into 'religious' and 'non-religious'. The religious genres are mostly constituted by dance dramas. The ritual festival called *Lai Haraoba*[2] is replete with intricate representations of mythological events and the nuances of practicality of the community life, predominantly through various forms of dances called *jagoi* performed by the *maibi*s[3] (priestesses). Apart from this, there are other Vaisnavite genres like the *Rasa Lila*s,[4] *Gouralila* (drama enacting the childhood of Gouranga Chatanya Mahaprabhu, mainly by children), *Sanjenba* (an episode from Krishna's childhood when he reveals his true self and played mischief with the *gopi*s while grazing cows in the Vrindavan), *Udukhol* (an episode from Krishna's childhood) etc. In the non-religious category, Manipur has *Phampak* or Stage *Lila* (proscenium theatre) and Shumang Lila (courtyard theatre) genres.

Stage Lila could be considered as 'elite theatre', and genres, which came within the present-day Shumang Lila, as 'popular'.[5] The latter predated the former in their historical emergence. Stage Lila is a colonial contribution to the theatre scenario of Manipur. Manipur was introduced to proscenium theatre by the Bengalis who in turn learned it from the British in the 19th century. The first proscenium play, *Pravas Milan* (A.S. Singh 1980: 31), was performed in 1902 in Bengali by Manipuri artistes. Since the very beginning, the plays were performed and organised by some amateurs from the new middle class, but the viewership was open to all. On the other hand, the indigenous popular forms like *Phagee Lila* (comic play)[6], which could be incorporated within present-day Shumang Lila, were prospering too. Understandably, the tradition of jesters, who were an indispensable part of the Phagee Lila, was absent in Shumang Lila. Nevertheless, there were no deliberate attempts to liquidate the popular forms from the side of the middle class, unlike in Bengal of the 19th century. In case of Bengal, where there was a rapid rise of Bhadralok culture,

> from the mid 19th Century, educated Bengali males attempted to rouse public opinion through articles in newspapers, meetings in city halls, and often through books, against these popular forms [*like Jatra*] and against their performers. By the beginning of the present century [*20th century*] they had succeeded, to a large extent, in driving them away from the precincts of "respectable" urban society.
>
> (Sangari and Vaid 2006: 148; italics mine)

In case of Manipur, there was an acceptance of popular forms, by the middle class, as a parallel form of theatre.

This period of the first half of the 20th century was also a period when *sanskritization* of the literary and spoken language, especially among the new middle class, started. The more Sanskrit or Bangla words a sentence had, the more the writer or the speaker was considered to be 'cultured' and educated. For instance, in the sentence *Kulachandrana nataktugi nayikagi abhinay toukhi* (Kulachandra took on the role of the actress in the play), the important words like *natak*, *nayika* and *abhinay* are all Sanskrit words (A. S. Singh 1980: 35). This trend was starkly witnessed in proscenium theatre and also in the religious performing art forms like *sankirtan* singing.[7] In Manipur, initially, all the plays of Stage Lila were performed in Bengali. The extreme example of cultural hegemony was witnessed when there was an ideological campaign against using Manipuri language in Stage Lila and other Vaisnavite religious performances including sankirtan singing, which relegated the language into a status of being impure. This was a clear sign of how the cultural discourses were controlled by the hegemons from both within and without Manipur. The cultural hegemony was so deep that a new style of dialogue delivery was institutionalised in Stage Lila, which later percolated to the popular forms. Manipuri dialogues of the plays were made to be delivered in accents imitating the way the Bengali directors spoke Manipuri.

Most of the plays of this era were historical and mythological in theme. The king was already deeply involved in this new cultural import from the very beginning. He, at the same time, began to feel a little apprehensive of the direction Stage Lila was headed when all the plays were in Bengali with very few local elements. So, he became reflexive and realised what Stage Lila was doing to the language and culture of Manipur. Subsequently, there was a subtle counter-hegemonic attempt against Bengali

JESTERS OF POPULAR GENRES AS AGENTS OF RESISTANCE

cultural hegemony. He personally advised artistes to come out with a true
Manipuri play – in terms of language, text, context, acting style, dialogue
delivery style, costumes, props etc. So, the first true Manipuri play, in
all aspects, was a historical play 'Nara Singh' (A.S. Singh 1980: 41–42),
performed in 1925, based on the life of a king of the same name. This
play was important in as much as it traced the history of an independent
Manipur when Nara Singh was the king. Again, it carried a patriotic
theme, which also aroused political consciousness during that colonial
era. So, the play had such patriotic songs as, *Meitei leibak ibema, nungshibi
ima Manipur, khudang pifam teiduna hikna hikna kapliba* ('motherland of the
Meiteis, Manipur, my love, crying incessantly for having been subjugated')
(A.S. Singh 1980: 42). It is evident from the line that it does not have
even a single Sanskrit, Bengali or Hindi word unlike most of the plays of
this era.

Stage Lila being a cultural space controlled by the middle class, the
British considered it as a potential site for critical political engagements.
This was evident when censorship was provoked when a play became too
political. As a result, every play had to obtain *parvana* (permission) from
the king who was monitored by his colonial masters. That was why 'the
play "Tikendrajit" based on the 1891 events was performed only in 1950'
(gathered from Lokendra Arambam in a personal interaction). The fear of
the authority of this middle class turning against it was proven true when
Irabot, an active member of theatrical movement in Manipur, later turned
against the combined force of the British and the feudal structure.[89]

Jester and grotesque realism

The popular theatre genre called Shumang Lila of today has its roots in the
jester traditions which were known by different names during the 19th
and the beginning of the 20th century. The significance of this genre is its
dependence on the verbal and semiotic representations of the characters
and the narrative, with no, or minimal, help from props. There is also
profuse employment of improvisation depending on the context and
audience response, which sometimes may seem to fragment the integrity
of the narrative, but the craftsmanship of the performers often comes in
to weave the narrative suitably.

The era of jesters in popular forms started before the advent of colonialism in Manipur. However, its contemporary existence with colonialism and the still-thriving feudalism gave further impetus to enrich
this art form, since the two formidable powers gave an ample amount
of situations which it could address and critique through parody. It

KSH. IMOKANTA SINGH

was, and still is, a site of resistance, contestations, protests, and critiquing of the internal societal imbalances and irregularities, and hegemony of both the internal and external forces. All this was communicated through its seemingly insignificant puns and gestural expressions. Its importance was felt mainly in its involvement in the 'reflexive' politics through its conscious participation in the process of self-analysis and self-assertion in the cultural and religious fields vis-à-vis a hegemonic force that was projected as the 'other'. In this project, there was also a deliberate employment of agency to subvert the 'other' and to eulogise the 'indigenousness'.

The tradition of jesters is also regarded as a culmination of both Sanskritic and native clowning elements. The native elements were quite abundant in the *Tangkhul-Nurabi Loutaba*[10] repertoire of Kanglei Lai Haraoba and the social institution of *phunganai* (domestic slavery). The latter

> was a mild form of slave-labour in which the slave was owned by the nobles to do odd jobs, to run errands, to accompany their masters in community dining and social gatherings . . . But they were also exposed to the behaviour and manners of the court elite.
>
> (Lokendra Arambam 1990: 127)

They were also known as *achanba* (court favourite) and performed skits for the royal members and nobles, sometimes imitating the latter's various behaviours. They, by the middle of the 19th century, emerged as court jesters. The Sanskritic elements were the adaptation of the *Vidushaka* character, such as Balabasu who accompanied Narada in *Gosth Lila*.[11]

The reign of Maharaja Chandrakirti (1850–86) is considered to be the era when this genre of theatre adopted a relatively systematised structure. The king's court had court jesters who were masters of *chin kangjei* (verbal repartee). It is said that the court jesters Abujamaba Saiton and Kharibam Laishuba, one day, enacted a skit that made fun of one Thokchao, a court favourite, who had amusingly large heels (Arambam 1990: 130–31). The two enacted a scene of stumbling upon footprints of an elephant. When they followed the trail, it turned out to be not the footprints of an elephant but those of Thokchao. Very pleased with the extempore performance, the king ordered them to give public performances during the Durga Puja festival. This marked the emergence of the genre from the private space of the king's court to the public sphere (of Durga Puja).

122

JESTERS OF POPULAR GENRES AS AGENTS OF RESISTANCE

Such performances even included caricatures of the king and nobles. Nevertheless, the performances of these jesters were so conjuring that the king pardoned such minor misadventures and even enjoyed them. In this manner, Phagee Lila, which was the forerunner of present-day Shumang Lila, was born in the court of Maharaja Chandrakirti. This was a period when there was no strict categorisation of theatrical performances into 'elite' and 'popular'. The acceptance of this genre by the palace exemplifies the point in hand. But it became 'popular' at a later stage with the introduction of Stage Lila, which represented the 'elite' culture.

Phagee Lila's popularity across the classes of Manipur can be documented from the words of Ethel St. Clair Grimwood, the wife of Frank St. Clair Grimwood, the political agent (1888–91) (L. I. Singh 1987: 225). She writes narrating an event of gymkhana:

> To wind up there was a play; the Maharajah had three jesters, exactly like the old English fashion of having court-jesters to amuse royalty. The Manipuri specimens were very funny indeed. Their heads were shaved like the back of a poodle, with little tufts of hair left here and there; and their faces were painted with streaks of different-coloured paints, and their eyebrows whitened. They wore very few clothes, but what they had were striped red and green and a variety of shades. . . . [T]he play was beginning to be *rowdy and the dialogue vulgar.*
>
> (Grimwood 1975: 126–28; italics mine)

Since the occasion was a public event, a large number of common spectators, along with the royal members, were also present. It is also evident, from her statement, how she and other British spectators felt about the 'rowdy and vulgar' contents of the play. It clearly highlights the baggage of categorisation of these local cultural forms as 'inferior' and theirs as 'superior'.

As Phagee Lila had already been exposed to the public space, it then broadened its reach by performing on *shumang*s (courtyards). This did not mean that it was completely shut out from the royal court. Phagee Lila then started representing the lived world of the people who were in the periphery, both in terms of physical and power structure. Through its folk humour it scaled and then inverted the strict hierarchical social structure practised by the people and patronised by the king. Such conscious effort was also directed towards the British. This sowed the seed of resistance through performances which directly impacted upon the conscious public.

It was a moment for the people in general and the artistes in particular to look at themselves in a different relationship between the subject and the object. Here, the subject itself becomes object. This can be related to Victor Turner's idea of 'public liminality' and 'subjunctivity'. Many propositions are subjunctive and liminal

> in the sense that they are suspensions of daily reality, occupying privileged spaces where people are allowed to think about how they think, about the terms in which they conduct their thinking, or to feel about how they feel in daily life. Here the rules are themselves the referent of the knowing; the knowledge propositions themselves are the object of knowledge.
>
> (Turner 1984: 20–22)

In this 'reflexivity' during the 'liminality', i.e. during performance, there is identity of subject and object. In the Phagee Lila tradition, the performer (subject) himself also became the object of reference. Such engagement was also carried forward by other comic performative forms of this era. Apart from looking at themselves, these genres were also trying to look at others so as to make a critical analysis of the individuals and the system, reflex upon them and resist them if they and their actions were in contradiction to the interest of the majority. One example was that of *Chengba Phagee* (Chengba's comic play). Like many court jesters, Chengba, the leader of the troupe, also caricatured the royal family from time to time. It is said that one day when the Maharaja Churachand (1891–1941), his elder brother Sanakhwa Ahal (Dumbra Singh) and some of his family members and nobles were seated in a room, he took permission to perform some skits to entertain the gathering (narrated by Ningombam Angouton in a personal interaction). With the consent of Sanakhwa Ahal, an obese man, Chengba, emerged from behind, where the group of royals were seated, with a bulging stomach stuffed with clothes underneath his shirt. When asked where he was heading for by one of his co-performers, he replied with screwed face as if smitten with pain, '*Sanakhwa ahaldu angang unagadoure, aduna manakta chatlibani*' (Sanakhwa Ahal is giving birth to a child, so I am going to enquire about it). Such an unexpected gesture shocked and also amused everybody in the gathering. Sanakhwa Ahal also was taken aback but remained silent as he had already given his consent. So such was the carnivalesque milieu created by those jesters.

Popular comic plays in their various forms scaled their height during the first half of the 20th century. In the midst of this,, when the British colonial power made its presence felt in the social, political and economic

JESTERS OF POPULAR GENRES AS AGENTS OF RESISTANCE

spheres, a new form of protest play came up. It began to be known as *Kabul Lila* (Kabul play), which was predominated by dances caricaturing the behaviour and body language of the Pathans who came as part of the British army from the side of Burma. It began as satire of the misrule of the British and the petty-minded Kabuli traders. The verbal text was deliberately made nonsensical to mock the foreigners. It had a mixture of English, Bengali, Hindi, Manipuri, Burmese, and even Brajabuli, all put together in one sentence. It was a sounding attempt to deconstruct and resist the power structure through linguistic tools of art, when open expression of dissent against the powers that be was not expected in real public spaces like marketplaces. The play made fun of the British, making them tonsured, which is a way of punishing or insulting a culprit in Manipuri society (Samarendra n.d.). A Kabul Lila performance began with the blowing of a bugle. But due to the religious ethnocentrism of the people, patronised further by the king who regarded Vaishnavism as the superior religion to Christianity or Islam, Manipuris refrained from using any newly imported foreign musical instrument. So the bugle was made out of straws and the military tune was created using words in such a way that any listener would suspect them for meaningful ones. The words went like this:

> *Nambol kaibol kaibunai; Jhang Jhang petret petret pinao nao;*
> *Jhang jhang napui jhang; Guruna naptong guruna naptong;*
> *Phongai phongai, phongai phongai.*

(A. S. Singh 1980: 24)

In close line with the Kabul Lila was another politically loaded performance under the name of *Phadibi Lila* (play of tattered rags) during 1907–08 (Samarendra n.d.). Its specialty was wearing of the tattered *potloi* (female costume worn in Rasa Lila, and also by the bride during the marriage ceremony), *pheijom* (dhoti), *phanek* (sarong-like wraparound) etc., which symbolised the wretched condition of the people under foreign rule. The target was the British and their Bengali employees and merchants. The play was styled in dance and songs, mainly *Khubak Eshei* (a form of community singing with clapping of palms to give *tala*, which means rhythm) and *mal* (acrobatics). The dialogues were in Manipuri and had such lines as:

> *Bom kaappa, bomjao kappa*
> *Waskat litpa koijomba*
> *Mora phamba ningshumba*

(Loose translation):
One who fires bombs
Bearded men in waistcoat
Men with flat buttocks, who always sit on *mora* (a type of stool).

These lines are a clear indication of the pompous lifestyle of the people who were associated with the colonial power. They signify an attempt to counter and resist the hegemony of the cultural and political forces from above and outside.

Between the two world wars (1920s–1940s), there were also performances of some serious plays with different characters, and not jesters only. However, these plays had humorous interludes. For instance, in the play 'Sabitri Saitavan', there was one interlude called *Thengu Lila*. This became more popular than the play itself and thereafter the play started to be known as Thengu Lila. It used a *thengu* (a kind of wooden hammer) as a metaphoric tool to mesmerise a person so that he or she became the property of the user. In this skit, a village simpleton was pursued by a rich man with a thengu in his hand. The latter claimed that the former came out of his thengu and was his property. The villager was utterly out of his wits as to how a wooden hammer could be his mother. Resigning himself to his fate, the village simpleton imagined and said, 'How painful it might have been for the thengu to carry me inside it during the nine months' pregnancy!' He then thanked the rich man for his generosity in effecting his delivery from the thengu. Though it sounded superficial, the skit carried a deep structure of power and domination in the society when highly placed people in this structure were in liberty to exploit the powerless and uneducated for their personal ends.

One other popular genre of this era was the *Thok Lila* (con-trick play) (Arambam 1990: 136). It addressed the tribulations of the common people, mainly in the economic sphere. Initially, the troupe performed a satirical play on the 'water tax' levied on the people who used the Imphal River. It was a bold and open resistance against imperialistic designs and the exploitation of the already exploited masses. Learning about the content of the play, the king summoned Ibohal, the troupe leader, who was eventually incarcerated. Then he was made to perform in front of the king. Taking full advantage of this opportunity, he dressed himself up in a tattered *khudei* (a casual lower garment and a shorter version of the dhoti), an old and dirty *lukun* (sacred thread) and a dirty *urik* (a sacred necklace of *tulsi* beads), symbolising the sorry state of the people. He started his performance with his back to the king. Sucking in his stomach and feigning severe pain, he delivered his line, '*Papi machagi leinasida leiramdrabadiko*

(Had this cursed disease not been there in me!)'. This one-liner was sufficient to move the king personally as this clearly expressed the ordeal he was going through due to his suffering from piles. Then, Ibohal was given permission to perform whatever he wished. Such was the effect of a charismatic performer.

Thok Lila and many of the previously discussed genres came very close to the carnival laughter which Mikhail Bakhtin analyses as 'ambivalent: gay, triumphant, and at the same time mocking, deriding. It asserts and denies, it buries and revives' (Bakhtin 1968: 11–12). Apart from being pure satire, they parodied the obscurantist social norms apart from criticising the high-handedness of the authority. In this vein, 'he who is laughing also belongs' to the society (Bakhtin 1968: 11–12). So, there was a clear tendency not only to *laugh at others* but also *at oneself.*

As these genres continued to prosper, they, however, were made to face an identity crisis due to interventions from the middle class Manipuris. The etymology of the genres itself had to be redone. In the 1930s and 1940s, seeing *Jatra* of Bengal,12 they tried to equate the Manipuri theatre genres with Jatra, defiling the specific historicity and structure attached to these local genres. So, these Manipuri genres lost their names and got them replaced by Jatra, or the amusing term *Jatrawali* (those who play Jatra). Since then, the name Jatra became a generic term encompassing all those popular forms of theatre having the structure of the present-day Shumang Lila. Although they found an encompassing name in Jatra, they lost their individuality as the Phagee Lila, Kabul Lila, Thengu Lila, or the Thok Lila. Later, the reflexive politics spearheaded by local theatre persons found the name 'Jatra un-indigenous'. So, the Manipur State Kala Akademi, which was established in1972, formally intervened and replaced the name Jatra with Shumang Lila in 1973.

Conclusion

Theatre has always been a space for protest, resistance and contestation, a contestation within the text; between the text and the reality it represents; between the classes, ages, genders within its structure etc. More important is the propensity of theatre to strike and change both its system and structure with time so as to accommodate the changing trends of the wider society. In this sense, theatrical network works within the whole framework of cultural, ideological, ethical, and epistemological principles of the society of which it is a part. This dynamism itself is a reason for its growth and continuity. Theatre thrives as long as its communication with its audience is intact. Stage Lila and Shumang Lila tradition continued to tread

KSH. IMOKANTA SINGH

their own courses despite their varied relationship with the colonial and feudal powers, as both had their own spheres of influence within the system. This element of critiquing in its different forms makes theatre a vibrant cultural performance.

Notes

1 During this historical period, which this chapter delves into, this genre of theatre was not known as Shumang Lila, but by various names. This will become clearer as the chapter progresses. But to address the general issues and for convenience, the chapter will use the term Shumang Lila.

2 It is a festival of fertility, both societal and reproductive, in which the people of the *leikai* (locality) or *khul* (village) appease the deity and his consort for the same. It is also interpreted that the rejoicing by the devotees is a manifestation of the joy of the guardian deity for whom the Lai Haraoba is celebrated.

3 Maibis are the presiding priestesses in the Lai Haraoba festival. In this ritual festival, the role of the priests (*maibas*) is secondary to that of the priestesses. The term 'maibi' is also used for midwives.

4 Rasa Lila of Manipur is a form of dance drama started by King Bhagyachandra (1759–62 and 1763–98, two periods when the king ruled). It has different categories: *Basanta Rasa, Maha Rasa, Kunja Rasa,* and *Nitya Rasa.* The styles are taken from the Manipuri dance forms already present in Lai Haraoba ceremonies although the theme is Vaisnavite

5 'A discourse emerged in the late 1800s which distinguished elite or "highbrow" culture from the mass or "lowbrow" culture. Elite cultural objects and practices are those favored by the socially privileged and well-educated, who are believed to be uniquely capable of understanding and appreciating them. Lowbrow or popular culture is essentially everything that is not elite culture' (Harrington and Bielby 2001: 6–7).

6 This genre, which falls within the Shumang Lila genre of today, will be discussed in detail in the next section of the chapter.

7 Sankirtan singing is a form of community devotional singing and an invocation of the gods, performed in temples. It is a combination of dance choreography, songs and music. Traditionally, Rasa Lila is preceded by sankirtan singing. Also a part and parcel of marriage and death ceremonies, the stories of the eternal love between Radha and Krishna and the life history of Chaitanya Mahaprabhu are rendered through songs accompanied by *pung yeibas* (*mridanga* players).

8 Hijam Irabot was the Renaissance man – social reformer, poet, artiste, intellectual, sportsman, and revolutionary. During the pre-Independence era, he fought against the double forces of the feudal structure and the British imperialists mainly for the oppressed people. This invited dissent from both sides and he was sent to the Sylhet (now in Bangladesh) Jail (1942–43). He is now fittingly known as Jana Neta (leader of the people).

128

9 In this section I will be talking about 'popular' genres only. Wherever the category 'Stage Lila' comes in, I am talking about the 'elite' theatre of Manipur.

10 The Tangkhul-Nurabi Loutaba is performed on the night of the last day of Kanglei Haraoba, a form of Lai Haraoba. This is an enactment of the repartee between Tangkhul, the incarnation of lord Nongpok Ningthou, who dresses up in Tangkhul attire, and Nurabi, the incarnation of goddess Panthoibi, who dresses up as a Tangkhul lady, when they are out in the field for farming. This episode incorporates the philosophy of fertility in terms of reproduction. Again, it teaches the importance of work culture for a polity to sustain and progress. The whole episode is presented with a tinge of eroticism in dialogue and body movements.

11 Gosth Lila is 'a celebration of the tending of cows by the six-year-old Krishna, accompanied by his brother Balarama and their colleagues. Two demons – Dhenukasura and Bakasura – were killed in this chapter. The story was adapted from the tenth canto and the tenth chapter of the Srimad Bhagavad Gita (Arambam 1990: 127).

12 *Jatra* of Bengal is performed in a similar structure as that of the Shumang Lila, with the major use of songs, dance and poetry. 'They sang in temple courtyards, narrating the events of their patron god's life, and expressed their devotion with frenzied acting. . . . This singing with dramatic elements gradually came to be known as Jatra, which means "to go in a procession"' (Gargi 1996: 14).

References

Arambam, Lokendra. 1990. 'Tradition of the Clown in Manipur and Assam' in Birendranath Datta (ed.), *Traditional Performing Arts of North-East India*. Guwahati: Assam Academy for Cultural Relations.

Bakhtin, Mikhail. 1968. *Rabelais and His World*. Cambridge, MA: M.I.T. Press.

Gargi, Balwant. 1996. *Folk Theatre of India*. Washington: University of Washington Press.

Grimwood, Ethel St Clair. 1975. *My Three Years in Manipur*. Delhi: Vivek Publishing House.

Harrington, Lee and Denise D. Bielby (eds). 2001. *Popular Culture: Production and Consumption*. Massachusetts: Blackwell.

Samarendra, Arambam. Year unknown. '*Shumang lilagi hourakpham amasung makha tana chattharakpa mawong* (The origin of Shumang Lila and Its trend)', Seminar paper.

Sangari, Kumkum and Sudesh Vaid (eds). 2006. *Recasting Women: Essays in Colonial History*. New Delhi: Zubaan.

Singh, Ayekpam Shyamsunder. 1980. *Manipurgi Shumang Lila Amasung Theatre* (Manipuri Shumang Lila and Theatre). Imphal: Manipur Sahitya Parishad.

Singh, Karam Manimohan. 1989. *Hijam Irabot Singh and Political Movements in Manipur*. New Delhi: R.B. Publishing.

Singh, Lairenmayum Iboongohal. 1987. *Introduction to Manipur*. Imphal: S. Ibochaoba Singh.

Singh, R. K. Jhalajit. 1992. *A Short History of Manipur.* Imphal: Published by the author.

Storey, John. 2001. *Cultural Theory and Popular Culture: An Introduction.* Harlow: Pearson Education.

Turner, Victor. 1984. 'Liminality and the Performance Genres', in John J. MacAloon (ed.), *Rite, Drama, Festival, Spectacle: Rehearsals towards a Theory of Cultural Performance.* Philadelphia: Institute for the Study of Human Issues.

———. 1986. *The Anthropology of Performance.* New York: PAJ Publication.

Williams, Raymond. 1965. *The Long Revolution.* Harmondsworth, Middlesex: Penguin.

Part III

IMPERIAL STRATEGIES AND DISTINCT POLITICAL HISTORIES

9

SITUATING MANIPUR IN THE GEOPOLITICS OF IMPERIAL POWERS

Laishram Churchil

This chapter endeavours to explore the strategic importance of Manipur against the backdrop of colonisation of South and South East Asia by imperial powers. An account of Manipur's relation with the British and the Battle of Imphal, 1944, highlights Manipur's geo-strategic significance. Foregrounding the Battle of Imphal, the chapter interrogates the strategic importance of Manipur with regard to the geopolitics pursued by imperial powers such as Britain and Japan. This would help in comprehending the determining factors and impacts of the geo-strategic location of Manipur on its own history and destiny. No other factor has produced a more profound impact on the political history of Manipur than its geo-strategic location. Geographically, Manipur as well as North East India presented a buffer zone between the Indian subcontinent and South East Asia. Politically, the region acted as an interface among the imperial powers that were consolidating their domination on and across the interface. Though Manipur was never a geopolitical player by itself, it occupied a crucial site in the geopolitics of contending imperial powers. It was on account of its geo-strategic location that one of the bloodiest chapters in the history of World War II was fought in her territory. Britain's competition with France and the Netherlands, and later on with Japan, for the possession, consolidation and defence of their colonies in South East Asia had put Manipur in the centre stage of British and Japanese geopolitical thinkers particularly during the period of World War II.

Geopolitics through the ages

The term 'geopolitics' was coined in the last part of the 19th century by Swedish political scientist Rudolf Kjellén and is associated with the discipline of statecraft and realpolitik vis-à-vis the existing world order.

Therefore, it has its roots in the territorial states. To many classical geographers, geopolitics was an enigmatic, shadowy and contested discipline. There are many exponents of varied geopolitical theories and their interpretations are wide-ranging. But what is ubiquitous in most of the geopolitical theories is that the centre of a state is its military apparatus. The defining argument behind this thesis is that the behaviour of states (and, to a considerable extent, their structure as well) is determined from the outside, in state's act and reaction, in relation to the military capacities of those around them. The history of states is the growth, transformation and crisis of their military apparatus and of the organisational machinery constructed to support them. In all these processes, geopolitics plays a defining role. It defines the character and mode of interplay among different territorial (nation) states. The era of industrialisation and the onset of capitalist world economy gave a distinctive meaning to the term geopolitics.

Geopolitics as a discipline developed in Europe, which was coming to terms with both a new international order and disintegration of religion-based image of universal order dominant among its intellectuals and leaders. An insistence on taking charge of the world is a key feature of European modernity. Its realisation has changed significantly over time as the material context (dominant technologies) and mode of economic organisation affected scope of state organisation, thereby changing its capacity of violence (Agnew and Corbridge 1995). Geopolitics today is used freely to refer to international boundary disputes, structure of global finance, geographical pattern of election results, diplomatic rows etc. When we mention world politics, it must be noted that the term was invented in Europe only when it became possible to see the world as a whole and pursue goals in relation to the geographical scale. John Agnew remarks:

> [W]ays of thinking and acting geographically implicit in the sphere "world politics" had begun much earlier. However, when the intellectuals of statecraft of the European states (leaders, military strategists, political theorists) pursuing their interests had to consider their strategies in terms of global conditions revealed to them by the European encounter with the rest of the world.
>
> (quoted in Agnew and Corbridge 1995: 34)

Geopolitics: core of colonialism and imperialism

Geopolitics is an intricate blending of geography, the state and the military. The collection, collation and circulation of geographical knowledge in the form of maps, charts, surveys, and reports had much practical significance for the execution of state power (Bell et al. 1995). Randall Collins and David V. Waller traced back the modern story of geopolitics to the so-called military revolution that began around 1500 CE marked by the expansion of empires and multiplied expenses on armed forces. The result was that rulers started devising and executing policies and programmes for maximum revenue extraction. Then with the industrial revolution and expansion of maritime trade, the expansion of overseas empire began. Such policies of overseas imperial expansion was guided and sustained by geopolitics. Thus, geopolitics is at the core of imperialism, colonialism and, ultimately, wars between imperialist forces.

By the 19th century, a strong sense of nationalism was sweeping across Europe and politics was best thought of in terms of national states. The idea of distinctive national characters was, in fact, gaining ground. Soon there was fierce competition for economic and military dominance among European powers. This heralded a race for overseas expansion of empires. Between 1800 and 1914, major European powers, Russia and the United States of America (USA), went from controlling 35 per cent to 84 per cent of the earth's surface (Kennedy, quoted in Agnew and Corbridge 1995: 34). The process of imperialism or colonisation of Africa and Asia was a result of similar geopolitics pursued by the European powers, which was formulated in reaction to the real and imagined economic and political transformations of the late 19th century. Fearful that geographical size would determine national power, and aware that they would be unable to expand within Europe, the principal imperial powers embarked on a hectic scramble for imperial space from the 1880s onwards. Over 16 million square kilometres (20 per cent of the earth's surface) and 150 million people (10 per cent of the world population) were added to the European empires during the last 30 years of the 19th century. As Eric Hobsbawm puts it:

> Between 1880 and 1914 . . . most of the world outside Europe and the Americas was formally partitioned into territories under the formal rule or informal domination of one or other handful

of states: mainly Great Britain, France, Germany, Italy, the Netherlands, Belgium, the USA and Japan.

(Hobsbawm 2002: 57)

In the world of imperialism, geopolitics is the guiding principle of geo-strategy or military strategy. The pursuit of *Lebensraum* or expanded imperial space by nation-states has its manifest roots in geopolitics. Although all imperial states like Britain, France, Spain, Portugal, Russia, and the USA have their own set of geopolitics, the discipline earned its worst notoriety under Nazi Germany. The secretive *Institute fur Geopolitik* headed by Major General Dr Karl Haushofer was the principal architect of Nazi foreign policy. The institute had remarkable domination over Adolf Hitler. Haushofer and his geopolitical institute in Munich worked with its 1,000 scientists, technicians and spies. These men were almost unknown to the public even in the Reich. But their ideas, charts, maps, statistics of information, and plans dictated Hitler's moves from the very beginning (Sondern 1941: 45). The Nazi *geopolitik* was fairly successful in intellectual legitimisation of Nazism as well as marginalisation of all challenging voices of dissent against the Third Reich's hard-line militaristic state policy. Just as geopolitics was the driving force behind imperialism, colonialism and ultimately wars, it also sowed the seeds of a national liberation movement.

Geopolitics of colonial expansion was not based on immediate political or economic gain. It embraced a futuristic conceptualisation of state policies. Thus, the hectic colonial expansion by European powers in the 19th century was also an attempt to acquire comparative territorial advantage outside Europe with a view to sustain their states in the coming world order. The geopolitics of European powers did not end with the distribution of Asian, African and Latin American territories among themselves. It soon deflected on to Europe itself, leading to polarisation of powers within Europe. The evolving political development ultimately resulted in bipolar arrangements of power within Europe. The bipolar system was the direct reaction to Germany's economic and political expansion. German industrial productivity was second only to the USA on the eve of World War I. This newfound economic dominance was matched by a more aggressive imperial stance both within Europe, particularly towards the South, where Germany's ally, Austria–Hungary acted as a kind of 'Cat's Paw' for German territorial ambitions, and towards the East where expansion was sought at the expense of a sprawling but vulnerable Russian Empire. Anxious to contain Germany, the other European imperial powers – Britain, France, and Russia – suspended their traditional antagonisms and

SITUATING MANIPUR IN THE GEOPOLITICS

established an encircling alliance to counteract German expansion, an arrangement secured by the Franco-Russian treaty of 1894, the Anglo-French Entente Cordial of 1904 and the Anglo-Russian Accord of 1907. This was accompanied by an unprecedented arms race. The main European armies increased by an average of 73 per cent between 1880 and 1914 while warship tonnage grew by a factor of four, the latter primarily due to head-to-head Anglo-German contest for control of the seas (Herrmann 1996; Kennedy, quoted in Dodds and Atkinson 1988: 249–354; Massie 1991).

The changes in the global economic order, together with the fear of comparable political shifts, created the intellectual environment in which the new science of geopolitics gained unprecedented relevance in statecraft, more pronouncedly in foreign policies. In brief, geopolitics is roughly defined as the applied study of relationship of geographical space to politics. It deals with the reciprocal courses and impacts of spatial patterns, features and structures, political ideas and institutions and their interactions. In the early 20th century, geopolitics was a form of power and knowledge or statecraft directly concerned with promoting state expansion and securing empires. The project of geopolitics received widespread state patronage in the early 19th century, underscoring the belief that the changes taking place in the global economic and political system were seismically important.

The shift from an older industrial capitalism based on steam, coal and iron to a newer version based on gas, oil and electricity seemed to change the ground rules on which the world economy functioned. By the turn of the 20th century, the USA had supplanted Britain as the global economic and military hegemony, and on the eve of World War I, American factories were producing one-third of the world's industrial goods, a dominance Britain had claimed a mere forty years earlier. These changes seemed to foreshadow comparable transformations in the global political order. The fact that the USA was a continental-scale land power, with unprecedented rail and road connections linking major cities on both the Atlantic and the Pacific coasts, pointed towards a new relationship between space and state politics that was entirely at variance with the traditional European world order. This older system involved relatively small European states with distant, often chaotically scattered empires, 'spatch-cocked' together by the fragile sinews of maritime trade (Dodds and Atkinson 2000: 28).

Of the varied politics pursued by different nations, the geopolitics of Britain, Germany and Japan evinced keen academic and political interest because of their confrontationist style and content as well as the

137

catastrophic consequences and relevance to the region. As the geopolitics of each nation was manifested in the foreign policies, sometimes subtly, and at times quite obviously, there was virtually no discrete or exclusive geopolitical tradition. The history of inter-war geopolitics in Europe, for instance, was characterised by a series of intellectual exchanges and debates between geopoliticians in Germany, France, Italy, Spain and Scandinavia. Qualification for an imperial power depends on its ability to impose dominant representations and practices, its coercive power, the ability to force others to accept what it represents and propounds, as well as the capacity to write the political-economic agenda of inter-state relations with which others must conform. This was witnessed across Asia and Africa, which the European powers tried to justify with the ideological propagation of white men's burden of civilizing mission.

Manipur and British imperial interest

Manipur had always occupied a strategic position right from the days of the British imperial expansion into the region because of its location and its status of a regional power. The geopolitics of imperial powers, coupled with its strategic location, played a pivotal role in shaping the history of Manipur. After the Battle of Plassey in 1757, the British East India Company (hereafter, the Company) annexed the Chittagong Hill Tract in 1760 from the Nawab of Bengal. In subsequent developments, the Company acquired the *dewani* (authority to collect revenue) of Bengal in 1765 and gradually its power reached the borders of Sikkim, Bhutan, Cooch Behar, Assam and Arrakan, besides the Garo and Khasi Hills (Chaube 1999: 3). Since 1760, there was ceaseless expansion of the Company's power and influence over the well-functioning kingdoms located in the confluence of South and South East Asia. Commercial factors and geostrategic consideration were paramount elements that informed the British policy toward the erstwhile independent states such as Ahom (now called Assam), Cooch Behar, Cachar (Kachar), Manipur, Tripura (Tipperah) etc., located in the present North East region of India.

The first half of the 18th century and early part of the 19th century witnessed constant wars between Manipur and Burma. During the reign of Pamheiba, alias Garibniwaz (1714–54), Manipur as a regional power reached its zenith. It was during his reign that Manipuri forces defeated the Burmese army in 1725, 1735, 1738, 1739, and 1749 (Sanajaoba 2005: xliv), thereby containing Burmese expansion and intrusion towards states of Assam, Cachar and Manipur. However, in the post-Pamheiba period, the power equation was tilted in favour of Burma,

SITUATING MANIPUR IN THE GEOPOLITICS

which subsequently led to the Burmese devastation of Manipur in 1755–58, 1769 and 1819–26. With the decline of Manipur's power as a regional actor, Burma came in to fill up the power vacuum. Both external and internal factors were responsible for this change in power configuration. First, from the middle of the 18th century to early part of the 19th century, there was constant competition for colonial possessions and market in South and South East Asia among the British, French and Portuguese. In order to prevent British expansionism, the French and Portuguese supplied tactical weapons and guns to the Burmese who were opposing the British intrusion in its sphere of influence. Second, the rise of Alaungpaya from the ordinary ranks to the highest position of ruler led to the establishment of a strong Konbaung Dynasty by consolidating the human and material resources of a greater, stronger and enlarged Burma. Conversely, the abdication of King Pamheiba, followed by almost ritualistic palace intrigues and fratricidal wars for the throne, along with the restive situation in the Manipur Hills, occurrence of natural calamities such as floods and epidemics of all kinds (Sanajaoba 2005, xliv–vi) during the same period led to the decline and weakening of Manipur's power and position.

It was against this backdrop of shifting power equation and constant Burmese invasion of Manipur that Raja Gourshyam of Manipur concluded the Anglo-Manipur defence treaty in 1762. An overview of Anglo-Manipur relation from 1762 to 1891 throws significant light on the strategic importance of both Manipur state and the British Empire. Manipur needed to maintain a friendly diplomatic relation with the British to protect her sovereignty against the frequent Burmese invasion. For the British, alliance with Manipur was essential to consolidate, protect and advance their imperial interests, both political and commercial, in Assam, Burma and in greater South East Asia. In the British perspective, a stronger and stable Manipur was inevitable to counter the Burmese expansion towards the British sphere of influence such as Assam, Cachar and the Jaintia Hills. British calculation was proven true when the Burmese invasion and occupation of Manipur in 1819 led to the former's influence and domination over Assam, Jaintia Hills and Cachar, which were in the British sphere of influence. As a result, the British declared war against Burma on 4 March 1824. It was a convergence of interest between Manipur and British against the common enemy (Burma) that the Manipur Levy, of soldiers 500-strong, under Gambheer Singh and Nara Singh fought the invading Burmese along with British soldiers. The defeat of Burma in the war led to the signing of the Treaty of Yandaboo on 24 February 1826 between the British and Burmese authorities.

The strategic significance of Manipur was borne out by the fact that both British and Manipur soldiers even took joint expeditions such as the Burmese expedition in 1825, Naga Hills expedition of 1879 and Third Anglo-Burmese War of 1885–86. In the Third Anglo-Burmese War (1885–86), Burma was defeated and came under British control. The British perspective on the political status of Manipur was essentially to create a buffer state between the British Indian and the Burmese empires in order to enhance the interests of the British Indian Empire (Dena 1991: 9). Writing against the backdrop of European powers' occupation of Third World countries, prominent British historian Eric Hobsbawm opined that the independence of Third World countries mainly rested

> either on their convenience as buffer-states (as in Siam – now Thailand – which divided the British and French zones in Southeast Asia, or Afghanistan, which separated Britain and Russia), on the inability of rival imperial powers to agree on a formula for division, or on their sheer size.
>
> (Hobsbawm 2002: 57)

In this context, it can be argued here that Manipur lost its significance of being a buffer zone between British India and Burma. Ultimately, the British also put Manipur under their control as a consequence of the Anglo-Manipuri War of 1891. This war removed the lone independent country between British India and British Burma; by virtue of its defeat in the war, Manipur had become part of the British Empire consisting of the whole of South Asia, Burma and Malaya in South East Asia. The onset of World War II, and Japan's expansion in the Asia-Pacific region and occupation of countries in South East Asia, had only reinforced the strategic importance of Manipur.

Japanese geopolitics and South East Asia

The growth of Japanese geopolitics right from its inception is influenced by German *geopolitik* – Karl Haushofer's ideas were central to the Japanese geopolitical stream. However, Japanese geopolitics was not solely derived from German *geopolitik* and Haushofer's ideas. There were several trends of geopolitical thoughts and movements in Japan: first, there was a geopolitical school of the Imperial University of Kyoto, directed by Saneshige Komaki; second, a group comprised of faithful followers of Haushofer or the German-type geopolitical school; third, there was the Japan Association of Geopolitics (Nihon Chiseigaku Kyokai) (Takeuchi 1980, 1994) and finally, the members of Hidemaro Konoe's 'brains trust' (Fukushima 1997). Apart from these schools, Japanese geographers of early 20th century indicated little interest in German geopolitics. This was attributed to the contrasting positions of Germany and Japan during the period. Under the Weimar Republic, German geopolitics demonstrated a certain chauvinistic and patriotic character with reference to its own state and German-related lands as well as potential territories (*Lebensraum*) and potential enemy countries.

Japan's political position as a victorious nation of World War I, in possession of colonies such as Korea, Formosa (Taiwan) and a number of Pacific islands, differed considerably from Weimar Germany, suffering under the restriction of the Treaty of Versailles. Consequently, the specific political geography produced in Weimar Germany was considered inapplicable to Japan. This understanding of German *geopolitik* got a jolt when the Nazis succeeded in transgressing the terms of the Treaty of Versailles and commenced to flaunt a new slogan, the 'New European Order'. The development in Germany produced a consequential impact in Japanese geopolitics. Directly or indirectly, this stimulated Japanese leaders to invent the 'New Order in East Asia', which later developed into the 'Greater East Asia Co-Prosperity Sphere' (Dodds and Atkinson 2000: 77–78).

The USA constituted a major determining factor in the case of Japanese geopolitics and its subsequent expansion in the Asia-Pacific region. Surrounded by the mighty USA in the east, and China in the west, which was already under shared domination of several European imperial powers along with the USA, Japan quickly adopted a policy of expansionism. The geographical position of Japan was highly conducive to the acceptance of Karl Haushofer's doctrine of pan-regions (Abdel-Malek 1977). Once the doctrines of pan-regions were embraced by Japanese rulers, Japanese geopolitics specialised in area studies of specific countries of the Greater East Asia Co-Prosperity Sphere. Specialised studies were made for different areas and countries such as South East Asia, China, North America, Europe, South Asia, Siberia, Australia, Africa, Polar region and the Pacific Islands.

The growth of militarism in Japanese society during the 1930s – in the imperialist expansion of Japan and the course of the war in China, and Japan's economic needs and the ideology of co-prosperity – led to Japanese expansion in South East Asia. Amongst the more noteworthy features of South East Asia were, first, raw materials such as rice, rubber, coal, natural gas and other minerals that the region itself offered to the Japanese; second, the realities of the colonial position, which, in contrast to appearances of virtual omnipotence, was marked in all instances by a fundamentally rickety network of collaborative ties with local peoples; and third, the absence of any co-ordinated resistance to the Japanese advance (Tarling 1999: 2). Japanese expansion into the region was greatly favoured by the fallout of war in Europe. In May–June 1940, when the Netherlands and France fell to Germany, Japan signed an agreement with the Phibun Songkhram Government in Siam and also began to demand special privileges to land forces in French Indochina, which the Vichy regime of France granted in August 1940. This enabled Japan to extend and consolidate its territorial position in the region, since it had succeeded in obtaining supplies of rice, rubber, coal and other minerals from Indochina. By the end of July 1941, Japan had effectively occupied Indochina, and the army and navy were preparing for operations in South East Asia. Meanwhile, the USA was attempting to block Japan's advance in the region with a combination of negotiations and embargoes.

The period of expansion through diplomatic means ended soon after mid-October when Prince Fumimaro Konoe was replaced as premier by General Hideki Tojo, the Minister of War, who had previously served as chief of staff with the occupation force in China. Feeling the pressure of the economic blockade, particularly as regards oil supplies, determined not to lose international status and mindful that the USA would be likely to assist Britain and the Netherlands in the defence of their colonies, Tojo's government decided at the start of November on an early military strike. Ultimately, Japan invaded South East Asia in December 1941. During the night of December 7–8, Pearl Harbor, Malaya, the Philippines, and Hong Kong were attacked, and on December 8–9, the USA, Britain and the Netherlands declared war on Japan (Tarling 1999: 2).

Japanese troops quickly overran the whole of South East Asia. On 2 January 1942, Japanese troops captured Manila and Cavite. British and Commonwealth troops were unable to make an effective stand in the Malayan peninsula; Kuala Lumpur was captured by troops of General Yamashita's 25th Army on 11 January, and Fortress Singapore came under siege on 31 January. Towards the end of the same month, a two-pronged invasion of Burma was mounted from Thailand, which, having revised its relationship with Japan in the form of a ten-year alliance on 21 December, declared war on the Allies on 25 January. The climax of the blitzkrieg came with the fall of Singapore on 15 February. Secure in the air, at sea and on land, controlling the major strategic point in the region and divested of effective enemies, Japan could now proceed to mop up residual colonial resistance. The Battle of the Java Sea (27

February–1 March 1942) opened up the Dutch East Indies to the Japanese, who, having captured Batavia on 6 March, virtually completed their occupation of Dutch possession by early May. Meanwhile, the British had evacuated Rangoon on 2 May; the conquest of Burma culminated with the seizure of Mandalay on 2 May, while the campaign in the Philippines ended with the fall of Corregidor on 6 May (Tarling 1999: 3).

Engaging the World War II:
The battle of Imphal

The Japanese occupation of South East Asia had converted Manipur once again into a buffer zone between Japan and British India. The event had brought the war to the doorstep of the British Empire and Manipur remained the last bastion of the Allied Powers' counter-attack. In view of the strategic vitality and urgency to consolidate and launch an offensive, Britain had initiated construction and widening of the ImphalDimapur, ImphalTiddim and ImphalTamu roads from the later part of 1942 in order to ensure speedy movement of troops and other logistic supplies. Besides, Allied Powers had also started development and construction of Koirengei and Tulihal airports and one temporary airport near Pallel. On the other hand, after the conquest of Burma in the early part of 1942, the Japanese were planning for the next move whether to defend what they had conquered or to push on in India.

In 1943, certain disturbing events and reports began to cause concern in the Japanese High Command and led to the revision of their strategy. In the north, the Chinese Army were reorganising and developing with American assistance to press for an early Allied offensive to reopen the Burma Road. In Manipur, the British were reported to be developing a base and making roads eastwards and southwards from that place. Such events clearly indicated the impending Allied offensive. The best option left before the Japanese was to forestall the attack by destroying the base from which the British would launch their attack (Evans and Brett-James 1962: 54–57). It was in this atmosphere that a decision was taken in September 1943 to issue orders to the 15th Army to prepare plans for the invasion of Manipur and the capture of Imphal. General Mutaguchi, with his senior commanders, went ahead to make the detailed plans for what was termed Operation 'U-Go' (Evans and Brett-James 1962: 59). This operation was to be executed by the 15th, 31st and 33rd Divisions and the best part of the 1st Division Indian National Army under the overall command of General Mutaguchi.

The capturing of Imphal, the capital of Manipur, had become so decisive that General Mutaguchi wanted to complete the entire operation in one month, which would allow the Japanese Army a breathing space and convenient base for a defensive and offensive strategy that the British were playing at the moment. In view of this urgency, 33rd Division had to advance towards Imphal on 7 March 1944 from Tiddim and Tamu, and to smash the British 17th Division and 20th Division, the Japanese 15th Division had to start advancing towards northwest Imphal through Ukhrul district of Manipur, while the Japanese 31st Division had to advance directly to Kohima on 15 March 1944. The task assigned to 15th and 31st Divisions was to capture Imphal and Kohima and to prevent British reinforcement.

The faith of the entire operation depended on the swift capturing of the TamuImphal and TiddimImphal roads and ultimately in capturing Imphal itself to ensure the supply of food and other logistics to the soldiers. This could enable the Japanese to consolidate their position and, ultimately, further advance towards British India. At the same time, the British 20th Division on the Chindwin front, 23rd Division and 254 Tank Brigade in Imphal valley and 17th Division around Tiddim were preparing to engage the Japanese troops. It is not wrong to emphasise that British and Japanese troops were engaged in one of the bloodiest and decisive battles in Imphal. The faith of the Japanese position in South East Asia was highly dependent on the outcome of the battle at Imphal. This can be gleaned from the Special Order of the Day issued by General Mutaguchi:

> This operation will engage the attention of the whole world and is eagerly awaited by 100,000,000 of our countrymen. By its very decisive nature, its success will have a profound effect upon the course of the war and may even lead to its conclusion. Our mission is thus of the greatest importance and we must expend every energy and talent in the achievement of our goal.
>
> (quoted in Evans and Brett-James 1962: 111)

Among the important battles in Manipur, mention can be made of the Battle of Sangshak and the Tank Battle around Bishenpur. By April 1944, the Japanese were on the verge of capturing Imphal, but the British troops with support from the Royal Air Force, Indian Air Force and American Air Force withstood the Japanese offensive. By June 1944, General Slim's Fourteenth Army successfully withstood the Japanese offensive and launched a massive counter-attack, and by the end of June 1944 the Japanese were defeated.

Conclusion

The story of the Battle of Imphal and strategy adopted by both imperial powers revealed the geo-strategic significance of Manipur's location. It was the intrusion of British imperialism in the region called North East India that the strategic importance of Manipur was systematically exploited to advance British imperial interest. The British had always used Manipur both as buffer and transit point. The attention of imperial powers to a country or a region was not only drawn by its resources but also by the geo-strategic implication of the country or the region. The location of Manipur in the confluence of South and South East Asia in addition to its geography of having a fertile valley surrounded by nine hill ranges was temptation enough to any imperial power. The events surrounding World War II in the region had reinforced the vital implications of Manipur as a zone of strategic importance. The defeat of Japan and its failure to capture Imphal during World War II had thrown into light the importance of Manipur in the realm of global geopolitics. The British imperial exploitation of Manipur in particular, and the North East region in general, as resource base, buffer zone and transit point is still relevant in the contemporary situation where China and India are emerging as major contending economic and military powers.

References

Abdel-Malek, A. 1997. 'Geopolitics and National Movements: An Essay on the Dialectics of Imperialism', *Antipode* 9(1): 28–36.

Agnew, John. 2003. *Geopolitics: Re-visioning World Politics*. London and New York: Routledge.

Agnew, T. and S. Corbridge. 1995. *Mastering Space: Hegemony, Territory and International Political Economy*. London: Routledge.

Bell, M., R. A. Butlin and M. Heffernan. 1995. *Geography and Imperialism, 1820–1940*. Manchester: Manchester University Press.

Chaube, S. K. 1999. *Hill Politics in Northeast India*. Patna: Orient Longman Ltd.

Dena, Lal. 1991. History of Modern Manipur, 1826–1949, Delhi: Orbit Publishers.

Dodds, Klaus and David Atkinson (eds). 1988. *Geopolitical Traditions: A Century of Geopolitical Thought*. London: Routledge.

Fukushima, Y. 1997. 'Japanese Geopolitics and its Background: What Is the Real Legacy of the Past?', *Political Geography*, 16: 407–21.

Evans, Geoffrey and Antony Brett-James. 1962. *Imphal, a Flower on Lofty Heights.* London: Macmillan.

Herrmann, D.G. 1996. *The Arming of Europe and the Making of the First World War.* Princeton: Princeton University Press.

Heffernan, Michael. 2000. 'On the Origins of European Geopolitics, 1890–1920', in Klaus Dodds and David Atkinson (eds), *Geopolitical Traditions: A Century of Geopolitical Thought.* London: Routledge.

Heffernan, M. J. 1998. *The Meaning of Europe: Geography and Geopolitics.* London: Arnold.

Hobsbawm, Eric. 2002 [1987]. *The Age of Empire, 1875–1914.* London: Abacus.

Massie, Robert K. 1991. *Dreadnought: Britain, Germany and the Coming of the Great War.* New York: Ballantine Books.

Sanajaoba, Naorem (ed.). 2005. *Manipur, Past and Present, Vol. IV: The Ordeals and Heritage of a Civilization.* New Delhi: Mittal Publications.

Sondern, F. 1941. 'The Thousand Scientists behind Hitler', *Reader's Digest,* 38(7): 44–48.

Takeuchi, K. 1980. 'Geopolitics and Geography in Japan: Re-examined', *Hitotsubashi Journal of Social Studies,* 12: 14–24.

———. 1994. 'The Impact of the Japanese Imperial Tradition and Western Imperialism on modern Japanese Geography', in A. Godlewska and N. Smith (eds), *Geography and Europe: Critical Studies in the History of Geography.* Oxford: Blackwell.

———. 2000. 'Japanese Geopolitics in the 1930s and 1940s', in Klaus Dodds and David Atkinson (eds), *Geopolitical Traditions: A Century of Geopolitical Thought.* London: Routledge.

Tarling, Nicholas. 1999. *The Cambridge History of Southeast Asia, Vol. 4.* Cambridge: Cambridge University Press.

10

CONSOLIDATION OF BRITISH 'INDIRECT RULE' IN MANIPUR

Naorem Malemsanba Meetei

This chapter examines the events and processes that went into the formation of the 'modern' princely state of Manipur, which was characterised by the assertion of the sovereign to define subject population within a fixed boundary for the purpose of regular administration. Roughly, the period between the signing of the Anglo-Manipuri Mutual Defence Treaty, 1762, and the year 1947 is taken under consideration for the purpose of the study. Sustenance of a system of 'indirect rule' by the British was primarily responsible for the formation of a modern princely state of Manipur. The mechanism for the expansion and consolidation of British power in Manipur was achieved through the signing of various legal documents such as 'Treaties' between the British and Manipur. In addition to the signing of treaties, there were several other attempts responsible for the consolidation of British power in Manipur, which included the establishment of political agency by the British in Manipur, British's involvement in the settling of succession disputes, fixing of boundaries etc. The native institutions, ranks and hierarchies were accommodated and engaged through a new domain politics. The focus of the chapter is to delineate colonial encounter which resulted in the formation of the modern princely state of Manipur. Put differently, the chapter seeks to expedite the assertion of power by the British as a monolithic and extraterritorial power on which the power at Kangla (the seat of sovereign power of Manipur) derived or depended (for) its legitimacy to rule.

Emergence of a monolithic and extraterritorial power

Barbara Ramusack emphasised the significance of legal documents – ranging from treaties to *sanad* s to proclamations and letters of understanding – for the creation and maintenance of the British indirect system of rule, otherwise termed as 'treaty system' (2004: 51). Such a perspective holds true in the case of Manipur, too, although initially the willingness to join hands with the British proceeded from the Manipuris. Within the fold of the treaty system were factors such as seeking to achieve dominance in succession disputes to establish a superior position and gain support in military confrontation with other regional states and so on. These factors can be described as 'multiple reasons' (ibid.: 49) for allying with the East India Company. On the part of the British, strategic and commercial necessities were the driving forces to ally with Manipur. Incidentally, these processes, wherein both the stakeholders looked for their own advantages, favoured the British and ultimately resulted in the emergence of it as a monolithic and extraterritorial power. British power can be termed as monolithic in the sense that it was characterised by rigidity and total uniformity, which were manifested in various spheres, such as legal, political (including foreign affairs/external relations) and the economic. And it was an extraterritorial power in the sense that although the British did not occupy Manipur, it remained as a source of power for Manipur through the agency of the political agent, a British officer appointed by the Crown, who at will could interfere in the internal affairs of Manipur.

Michael Fisher has defined indirect rule in India as the exercise of determinative and exclusive political control by one corporate body over a nominally sovereign state, a control recognised by both sides (1998: 6). The fundamental legal document responsible for the creation and maintenance of the British system of indirect rule in Manipur – the Anglo-Manipuri Mutual Defence Treaty – was signed on 14 September 1762 (documents reproduced in Sanajaoba 1988: 472–73). With the signing of the treaty, Manipur entered into formal relationship with the East India Company. The treaty was signed by Haridas Gassain on behalf of Bhagyachandra (Jai Singh), the Maharaja of Manipur and by Harry Verelst, Chief of Chittagong Factory, on behalf of the East India Company. The circumstances leading to the signing of the treaty can best be explained by the political uncertainty facing Manipur in the second half of the 18th century.

Manipur was constantly and repeatedly overrun by the Burmese, and to make the situation worse, in 1748, denying the legitimate claim of the eldest son, Shyam Shai, Maharaja Garibniwaz abdicated the throne in favour of his son, Ajit Shai, who was in turn dethroned by his younger brother, Bharat Shai, These circumstances drew the attention of the Company whose territorial control in India had been expanded steadily since the middle of the 18th century. Ajit Shai, who took refuge at the

CONSOLIDATION OF BRITISH 'INDIRECT RULE'

Cachar Court, sought the intervention of the British. Knowing the plan of Ajit Shai, Bhagyachandra (Jai Singh) also immediately sent his lawyer Haridas Gossain to meet the British officials.

Bhagyachandra was aware of the fact that Manipuris lacked firearms and modern weapons and understood that his frontier was not secure until and unless he was supported by a superior power. On the part of the British, political and commercial considerations were the motivating factors.[1] Not only could such instability endanger the delicate frontier between India and Burma but the Company also felt the threat particularly in the context of balance of power strategies that saw a stable frontier in the North East Frontier of India as the only guarantee against the looming threat of Burmese advance. Restriction of Burmese influence from a strategic location such as Manipur or the North East Frontier would enable British merchants and traders to have direct trade with Chinese merchants. Such considerations prevailed over the British to intervene in Manipur. Considering the abovementioned factors, the Anglo-Manipuri Mutual Defence Treaty was signed between Manipur and the East India Company. Although essentially a defence alliance, on the whole, the treaty ensured the British a safe base in Manipur from which they could further embark upon their imperial policy in South East Asia.

However, the signing of the treaty did not bring about any positive developments as the Burmese continued to overrun Manipur especially after the death of Raja Bheigyachandra in 1799. The Burmese occupied Manipur for seven years (1819–26), popularly referred to as the *Chahi Taret Khuntakpa* (Seven Years' Devastation), which signified the highwater mark of Burmese domination over Manipur and the North East Frontier. The British officials once again felt the necessity of strengthening their alliance with the ruling prince of Manipur, who had lately fled to Cachar, in order to drive out the Burmese and also to defend effectively the North Eastern Frontier (Pemberton 2000: 46). The British calculation was based on the insight that Manipur with a stable and strong government would act as buffer state between Burma and the British.

In 1823, before the First Anglo-Burmese War, negotiations between Manipur under the leadership of Gambhir Singh and David Scott, the Agent to the Governor-General, was started. In 1825, the Manipur Levy under the command of Gambhir Singh co-operated with the British troops under the command of Lieutenant R. B. Pemberton in driving the Burmese out of Cachar and Manipur. By 1826, the Manipur Levy and British troops under the command of Captain Grant assaulted the Burmese in the Kabaw Valley and occupied it. Subsequently, the Treaty of Yandaboo was concluded on 24 February 1826, between the British and

149

the Raja of Ava (Burma). The treaty had a clause pertaining to Manipur: 'With regard to Munnipore ([sic] Manipur), it is stipulated that, should Gumbheer Singh desire to return to that country, he shall be recognised by the King of Ava as Rajah thereof' (Article no. 3 of the Treaty of Yandaboo, 1826; document reproduced in Sanajaoba 1993: 17). Though the treaty recognised Gambhir Singh's claim to the throne of Manipur, the constitutional position of Manipur vis-à-vis the British was, however, not clearly mentioned. Alexander Mackenzie writes, 'Manipur . . . though independent is at the same time a protected or dependent state' (1993: 151).

What is to be noted here is the use of the term 'protected state' by the British, which later on is taken as the basis for establishing 'indirect rule'. Moreover, intervention in the internal politics of the state was projected as protection of the ally. As part of British interventions, two separate treaties that would define their policy towards Manipur were concluded: first, the Anglo-Manipuri Treaty of 1833, which was signed between Raja Gambhir Sigh and Commissioner F. J. Grant on 18 April 1833; and second, the Agreement regarding the Kabaw Valley on 9 January 1834. These treaties reflected the colonial policy with respect to territory and sovereignty of Manipur and were in accordance with the Company's special logic that viewed 'sovereignty as territorially circumscribable or that which was territorially bounded' (Rai 2004: 27–28). It can also be understood as what Peter Robb termed as 'fixing boundaries' with 'increasing restricted sovereignty' (2007: 130). What was an issue was sovereignty itself as it reflected the authority over the populations that were inscribed within the boundary.

In developing paramountcy as an instrument for legitimation, the British official took readily to the notion of Manipur as a territory bounded by physical and cultural features. The boundaries of the princely state of Manipur became frozen at varying stages in state formation. The present 'fixed' and 'visible' boundary of Manipur was relatively recent as it was demarcated to suit the administrative conveniences of the British. The idea of fixed and visible boundary is closely related to what Robb says of the 'scientific frontier with strategic and defensive consideration' in deciding just where the definite line should be (ibid.: 131).

Following such logic, the British, as far as the agreement signed in 1833 was concerned, agreed to give the Raja of Manipur the adjoining areas of Jiri River and the western bend of the Barak River that would be the western boundary of Manipur. On the other hand, the Raja agreed to remove his *thana* from Chandrapur (Cachar) to the eastern bank of the Jiri River (Anglo-Manipuri Treaty 1833; document reproduced in

Sanajaoba 1993: 19–20). By the same token, the agreement regarding the Kabaw Valley on 9 January 1834 between the British and Burma, without even consulting Manipur, transferred the Kabaw Valley from Manipur so as to demarcate the eastern boundary of Manipur.[2] In similar efforts, in 1872, the northern boundary between Manipur and the Naga Hills district of Assam was fixed and pillars were erected with some alterations to the Biggs – Gordon line (Mackenzie 1993: 122–23). The eastern boundary, after the Kabaw Valley was leased out to Burma in 1834, was later fixed by the Boundary Commission led by Colonel Johnstone in 1881, and again from the Kangal post to the Tinzin was demarcated by Colonel Maxwell and Captain Mac Nabb in 1896 and permanent boundary pillars erected at the cost of Rs 2,564, half of which was borne by Manipur (*Manipur Administrative Report* (hereafter, *MAR*) 1896–97: 1). And the southern boundary was fixed through the Boundary Commission consisting of B.S. Carey, the Political Officer, and A. Porteus, Officiating Political Agent in Manipur in 1894 (*MAR* 1899–1900: 2). Thus, by the end of the 19th century, Manipur's political boundary was more or less internationally recognised and settled.

The treaties signed in the process of carving out a modern princely state of Manipur were crucial for the indication of the relation between Manipur and the British. Such agreements, which were based on the logic of sovereignty bounded territory, indicate how far the British influenced/interfered in the politics of Manipur. The demarcations suited the administrative convenience of the British at the cost of the wishes of the native people and created an indelible bitterness in the minds of the Maharaja and his people (Kabui 1993: 35–36). The British claimed a monolithic and extraterritorial means from which the ruler of Manipur would continue to derive his or her authority to rule. There was little or no room for opposition or objection from the Manipuris since the British exercised the de facto rule over the North East as the 'paramount power'[3].

Political agency: consolidation of British indirect rule

Another issue that we need to explore related to the expansion and consolidation of the British Empire is the issue of appointing a political agent who was responsible for translating policies and documents into practice by involving himself in the internal administration of Manipur. In order to consolidate their power, the British advanced many arguments that reflected the features of colonial policy especially on the question of sovereignty, political succession and territory. As a part of maintaining the existing relationship with Manipur, William Bentinck (in a Minute dated 7 February 1835) argued, 'The preservation of the friendly intercourse and as a medium of the communication with the Manipur Government... and with the Burmese authorities on that frontier and more especially to prevent border feuds and disturbances . . . it may be necessary to retain an officer in the character of political agent in that quarter' (quoted in Mackenzie 1993: 153). William Bentinck again, in his Minute of 25 March 1833, argued, 'if the British troops should be placed in it, we can hardly doubt that the feeling of security to the inhabitants of Manipur generally would be greatly increased by the permanent residence of British official' (Mackenzie 1993: 151). The British logic of intervention is clear in what William McCulloch says;

> The establishment of good order and the maintenance of authority in this country can be effected only by the British Government. In a country which, like this, owes its existence and owns that it does so, to the British. I humbly conceive, to be paramount and capable of effecting this . . . towards the effecting of good order and maintenance of authority in stationing of British troops in Manipur would be most effective means.
>
> (1857: 23)

Arguments such as the establishment of good order and political stability in the North Eastern frontier guided the colonial policy towards Manipur. The British decided to appoint Lieutenant George Gordon in 1835 as political agent in Manipur.

The establishment of the office of the British Political Agency in Manipur in 1835 – supported by official arguments such as fulfilment of limited objects like maintaining friendly relationship with Manipur and, if required, with Burmese authorities, and preventing the disturbances in the frontier area – was one of the most significant political developments in Manipur. In the later part of the 20th century, the office of the Political Agency became an instrument for direct and harsher interference in the affairs of the princely states like Manipur under the guise meticulously popularised 'indirect rule' of the British.

As informed by Ramusack, 'helping in the process of settling the succession disputes and giving recognition to the *gaddi* in any other princely state in India' (2004: 49), the British asserted its legitimacy as the source of power in Manipur. Invoking the authority of paramountcy and usage, the British gradually claimed that no succession, whether or not adoption was involved, would be valid without their assent. On the one hand,

CONSOLIDATION OF BRITISH 'INDIRECT RULE'

the colonial power assured the preservation of princely dynasties; on the other hand, it however retained a stringent capacity to either recognise or de-recognise the dynastic successions. Therefore, despite the imageries of having put under an indirect rule of the colonial power, the state of Manipur as kingdom began to receive powerful exertion of colonial pressure and interference in her daily performances.

The period witnessed consolidation of the British position in Manipur through the activities of its political agents. So as to have the kind of 'political stability' that the British wanted to have in the frontier area in 1834, after the death of Gambhir Singh, Nar Singh was recognised as Raja on settling the succession dispute. Political Agent Gordon warned the rebel princes that they were liable to be removed into Bengal if their proceedings were such as to create disturbances in Cachar or on the borders of Manipur (Mackenzie 1993: 155). In 1850, Raja Nar Singh was succeeded by Devendra Singh, who, on the recommendation of Political Agent McCulloch, was recognised as Raja by the British Government. Again on 13 July 1850, Chandrakirti became the king of Manipur and made a courtesy call to the political agent on whose recommendation the British Government formally recognised him as the Raja of Manipur. McCulloch also strongly advocated to the British Government for a more formal acknowledgement of the Raja. Endorsing his proposal, the British Government of India, in its letter on 3 October 1851, thus instructed McCulloch 'to make a public avowal of the determination of the British Government to uphold the present Raja and to resist and punish any parties attempting here after to dispossess him' (ibid.). At the same time, the Court of Directors of the East India Company, in a dispatch on 5 May 1852, also confirmed that the political agent was both a protector and a guide to the Raja. In the problematic parlance of the colonial power, the political agent was obligated to conduct a regular surveillance over the possible atrocious activities of the King against his subjects. However, in needy and tumultuous times of kings, political agents had been able to garner acknowledgment and support from the kings. The importance of the political agent in Manipur can be understood from the communication sent by the Raja to the Governor-General on 18 August 1861:

> Manipur was ruined by the Burmese but the British Government's European officer having been stationed at Manipur to settle all affairs of the Burmese frontiers, the people of my territory dwell in peace and without any fear. There is an order of the Government to the effect that no prince would create rebellion and commit slaughter. From this order, as well as from

the presence of a political officer, the people of this country feel more confident than before, that no misfortune may befall this place . . . The inhabitants of Bengal, Naga, Burma and Manipur are trading to different places for safety, but if there be no political agent in Manipur, the people will not thereof, from fear, be able to enjoy peace and tranquility.

(*MAR* 1891–92: 8)

Such information cements my argument that the ruler of Manipur depended on the British, which through the political agent became the source of power. Thus, the intervention in the succession of disputes through the invocation of the paramount power and the usage by the British established indirect rule in Manipur. In other words, the British had acted as a monolithic and extraterritorial power from which a ruler of Manipur would derive the legitimacy to rule over Manipur. The Treaty of Yandaboo in 1826 gave Gambhir Singh the legitimacy to rule over Manipur.

Invocation of double allegiances and ritual representations

The Anglo-Manipuri War of 1891 marks the beginning of a new relation between Manipur and the British. As a consequence of the defeat in the war, the British Government of India had forfeited the sovereignty of Manipur while transferring it to the British crown.

The nature of power transfer was such that while it established the overarching authority over the state of Manipur the authority of the native ruler whom the Governor-General in council may select was still protected. Major Maxwell suggested that the five-year-old Churachand Singh, son of Chaobiyaima and great-grandson of Raja Nar Singh, should be the Raja. The Government of India confirmed and selected Churachand Singh as the ruler of Manipur which was notified in the *Gazette of India*, dated 18 September 1891. In the sanad given to him, it was mentioned that the Chiefship of Manipur state and the title and the salute would be hereditary and would be descent in the direct line, provided that in each case the succession was approved by the Government of India (Government of India 1891a). Further the permanence of the grant, according to the sanad,

was to depend upon the ready fulfilment of all orders given by the British government with regard to the administration of your

CONSOLIDATION OF BRITISH 'INDIRECT RULE'

territories, the control of hill tribes depended upon Manipur, the composition of the armed forces of the state, and any other matters in which the British Government may be pleased to intervene.

(Government of India 1891b: 1–2)

The British Government appointed Major Maxwell as Political Agent of Manipur and Superintendent of State. After his formal investiture to the gaddi of Manipur with an eleven-gun salute, the young Raja Churachand Singh was sent for education to Mayo College, Ajmer, and he later joined the imperial cadet corps at Dehradun in 1901 (Sever 1985: 324). Such arrangement was basically following the logic the British held after the Revolt of 1857 in India that the subjects of princely states owed a 'double allegiance' to their rulers and to the British Crown. This position was clearly enunciated in the Viceroy's telegraph to the Secretary of State on 28 May 1891 regarding the murder of British officials during the 'palace rebellion' in 1890 in Manipur. The telegraph stated:

It is essential to our [the British] position in India that the subjects of the native state should understand that the murder of British officers renders the murderers and their abettors liable to punishment of death, whatever orders they may have received from the authorities of the state concerned.

(Government of India 1930: 17–18)

By denying the validity of the defence put forward that the subjects in this case were obeying the orders of state officials, the British were articulating the principle of 'double allegiances', which the state subjects should owe to their ruler as well as to the British Crown.

The colonial avenues of interventions were generated intentionally, which became even more appropriate in the name of an underaged King, Maharaja Churachand Singh.

The colonial power enjoyed a commendable influence in the appointment of royal officials in the post-1891 political affairs of Manipur. One hallmark of colonialism was that it re-enforced feudal institutions and acted swiftly whenever there was substantial possibility for rebellion from the native people, including the princes. The trap of the indirect rule was evident from the fact that here was already a growing mass mobilisation against feudal and monarchical institutions in the state. The mobilisation went on to directly challenge the imperial strategic association with the monarchs. It is interesting that the British continued to

155

extoll the princes as 'natural leaders' and as 'faithful feudatories' after 1857, inaugurated a series of ritual representations in which the British proclaimed the breadth of their imperial enterprise and sought to reaffirm ties with loyal clients through the dispensation of honours *(Ramusack 2004: 124)*.

One such trend was evidently emerging when the then Political Agent gifted Chandrakirti Singh a dress of honour, sword and belt (Dun 1992: 47). His eight chief officials received *khillut* s (robes of honour sanctified by being touched to the body of the patron and then presented to a client). The recognition and honour were given as an acknowledgement from the British for showing the proof of native loyalty to the British power. One significant proof was the successful military expedition to Kohima and second, for the help in rescuing European officials in Kabaw Valley during the outbreak of the Third Anglo-Burmese War. Again acknowledging military loyalty the British Government rewarded the then Raja with the title of Knight Commander and presented him with 500 Victoria muskets and 12 sporting rifles. His officials, Bolaram, Thangal and Gokhul, also received khilluts in recognition of their services (Dun 1992: 50). Further, formulation of hierarchy and ranks in the British system of governance could be visible and actual as evidenced by the 11-gun salute given on the investiture ceremony for Raja Churachand on 29 April 1892, and His Highness the Raja's presence at the Delhi Durbars of 1903 and 1911 (Government of India 1932). These were the most significant ritual arenas for the articulation of British ideas about their relationship with Manipur, which legitimised the processes that provided the consolidation of British power. These ceremonies were designed to reaffirm British superiority.

Conclusion

Partha Chatterjee observes that the chief characteristics of colonial power include controlling and managing the 'public domain' or 'material domain' of the colonised world (2001: 6). These characteristics are revealed in the case of the British's dealing with Manipur. For instance, the administration of the state remained in the hands of the British though the administrative work was done in the name of the Raja. Moreover, the authority of the king was isolated only in the realms of culture and religion. In order to legitimise their rule over the princely state, and in turn become a monolithic and extra-territorial power from which the native rulers would continue to draw power, the British advanced many ideologies. The colonial ideology as enforced through control and subjugation gave a powerful

CONSOLIDATION OF BRITISH 'INDIRECT RULE'

blow to the idea of protecting and respecting the territorially and actual sovereignty of Manipur. The roping in of a political agent and associate rooting of colonial administrative structures had sufficiently interfered in the native politics and governance, largely impacting upon the ideas of community and shared living. Indirect rule as popularised by the colonial discourse did not actually abrogate the harsher and subjugating characters of the Empire in any sense. One such aspect of the subjugation was the instance of territorial shrinkage of Manipur in several phases of colonial rule. The history and memory of the shrinkage have not evaporated over the years as the colonial and post-colonial times continue to witness resurrection of political aspiration to recover what was lost during and after the colonialism. Such memories have come to constitute a major site of the political of the past, present and future.

Notes

1 Article nos. 1, 2, 3, 4, 5 and 9 of the Treaty of 1762 indicate the political considerations of the British and Article nos. 6 and 7 indicate the economic factors for the signing of the Treaty by the British. See Sanajaoba (1988).

2 Kabaw Valley is a flatland lying west of the Chindwin (Ningthee) River and contiguous to the territory of Manipur on the east. The valley became part of the kingdom of Manipur in the year 1485 CE following the first ever recorded boundary agreement in the history of Manipur between Meidingngu Kiyamba, King of Manipur and Chaofa Khekkhomba, King of Pong. Since then, the valley was well included in Manipur until it was leased to Burma by the British Government in 1834 with a grant of a stipend of 500 sicca rupees per annum to Manipur. Even after India's independence in 1947, the Government of India continued to pay the amount to Manipur till its merger with the Indian Union in 1949.

3 The British evolved two key concepts of suzerainty and paramountcy. A suzerain power had superior sovereignty or control over states that possessed limited sovereign rights. The British officials who had served under Lord Wellesley began to use the word 'paramount' to describe their perceived position in India. Edward Thompson has claimed that the first formal articulation of paramountcy as a doctrine occurred in a letter from David Ochterlony, Resident at Delhi, to Charles Metcalf in 1820, and that the latter was the first to use it to justify intervention during a succession dispute at Bharatpur in 1825. See Ramusack (2004: 55).

References

Chatterjee, Partha. 2001. *The Nation and Its Fragments: Colonial and Postcolonial Histories*. Delhi: Oxford University Press.

Dun, E. W. 1992. *Gazetteer of Manipur*. Delhi: Manas Publications.

Fisher, Michael. 1998. *Indirect Rule in India: Residents and the Residency System: 1764–1858*. Delhi: Oxford University Press.

Government of India. 1891a. *Sanad of the Governor General in Council 1891*. Signed by H. M. Durrand, Secretary to the Government of India, Simla, 18 September 1891.

———. 1891b. *Chief and Leading Officials and Personages in Manipur*. File no. R-1/S-B/103: 1–2. Imphal: Manipur State Archive.

———. 1891c. *Gazette of India*. No.1862E dated 18 September 1891.

———. 1892. *Gazette of India*. No.1862E dated 18 March 1892.

———. 1930. *Report of the Indian States Committee, 1928–29*. Imphal: Manipur State Archives.

Kabui, Gangumei. 1993 [1988]. 'The Lost Territory of Manipur: Cession of Kabaw Valley', in Naorem Sanajaoba (ed.), *Manipur, Past and Present: The Heritage and Ordeals of a Civilization, Vol. 1*. Delhi: Mittal Publications.

Mackenzie, Alexander. 1993. *The North East Frontier of India*. Delhi: Mittal Publications.

Manipur Administrative Report. 1891–92. Government of Manipur, Imphal: Manipur State Archives.

Manipur Administrative Report. 1896–97. Government of Manipur, Imphal: Manipur State Archives.

Manipur Administrative Report. 1899–1900. Government of Manipur, Imphal: Manipur State Archives.

McCulloch, William. 1857. *Account of the Valley of Munnipore and of the Hill Tribes: With a Comparative Vocabulary of the Munnipore and Other Languages, Selections from the Records of the Government of India (Foreign Department)*. Calcutta: Foreign Department.

Pemberton, R. B. 2000. *The Eastern Frontier of India*. Delhi: Mittal Publications.

Rai, Mridu. 2004. *Hindu Rulers, Muslim Subject, Islam, Rights and the History of Kashmir*. New Delhi: Permanent Black.

Ramusack, Barbara N. 2004. *The Indian Princes and Their States*. Cambridge: Cambridge University Press.

Robb, Peter. 2007. *Liberalism, Modernity and the Nation Empire: Identity and India*. Delhi: Oxford University Press.

Sanajaoba, Naorem. 1993. *Manipur Treaties and Documents: 1110–1971, Vol. 1.1*. Delhi: Mittal Publications.

Sanajaoba, Naorem (ed.). 1988. *Manipur, Past and Present: The Heritage and Ordeals of a Civilization, Vol. 1.1*. Delhi: Mittal Publications.

Sever, Adrian. 1985. *Documents and Speeches of the Indian Princely States, Vol. 2*. Delhi: B.R. Publishing.

11

INTERROGATING INTO THE POLITICAL STATUS OF MANIPUR

Kangujam Sanatomba

An important issue that is central to the understanding of the conflict situation prevailing in Manipur is the question pertaining to whether Manipur was independent in 1947. Such a question would entail a dispassionate study of how the advent of British imperialism in the North East region generated far-reaching implications on the political status of Manipur. It, therefore, becomes increasingly indispensable to ascertain as to whether there was any significant impact on the sovereign status of Manipur following its historic encounter with the British.

Certain quarters hold the view that Manipur was not a truly independent state in 1947 (H. B. Singh 1988: 130). The Standstill Agreement and the Instrument of Accession signed on 11 August 1947 were taken as the focal points of their argument and emphasised that Manipur became a part of the Dominion of India on account of signing the two documents. According to this school of thought, Manipur during that period had already formed an integral part of India and the signing of the Merger Agreement in 1949 was a mere ceremonial formality. They further claim that native states in the Indian subcontinent were given only the option to join either the Dominion of India or Pakistan, and the availability of a third option that guaranteed the independent existence of the native states was ruled out. Such an understanding, therefore, cannot acknowledge the existence of a sovereign Manipur that was independent of India.

The chapter begs to differ with the above school of thought and suggests that Manipur sustained its independent sovereign status notwithstanding the execution of the Instrument and the Agreement. In order to substantiate such an understanding, there is the necessity to move beyond the fading days of British imperialism and analyse the nature of relationship

KANGUJAM SANATOMBA

between Manipur and the British in the formative years and subsequent historical developments which ultimately led to Manipur losing its sovereign status. As a framework of analysis, the chapter adopts a politico-legal approach, wherein legal treaties and documents are taken as the units of analysis and a political reading is rendered as discursively discerned.

An Asiatic power in alliance

The Anglo-Manipuri War of 1891 and subsequent trials and convictions of royal dignitaries of Manipur generated far-reaching debate on the political status of Manipur that had existed prior to the war. According to the British Government, Manipur was a 'subordinate and protected state', which owed submission to the paramount power and that its forcible resistance to a lawful order constituted the act of waging war, treason, rebellion etc. (Sanajaoba 1993: 307). Further, it has been stated that the Government of India (hereafter, GoI) had in Manipur the unquestioned right to remove any person whose presence in the state might seem objectionable. Moreover, the British authorities had the right to summon durbars for the purpose of declaring their decisions. The Governor-General in Council was of the view that the British officers had the right to take proper steps for forcible apprehension of Prince Bir Tikendrajit, who was the *Senapati* [*sic*, the army General], and any armed and violent resistance towards a police officer armed with a magistrate's warrant in British India constituted an act of rebellion. The Governor-General in Council, therefore, held that the accused persons were liable to be tried for 'waging war against the Queen' (ibid.: 308).

Certain implications can be derived from the previous statements. First, Manipur was regarded as a subordinate and protected state. Second, the British paramount power apparently had the right to intervene or interfere into the internal affairs of Manipur. Third, any attempt to resist with violence the British authority constituted as treason and rebellion and was, therefore, liable to be tried accordingly. How far the British declaration on Manipur was justified will be clear only if we make a critical study of the treaties that the two powers had compacted and keenly observe the British policy towards Manipur.

Here, it may be recalled that the Treaty of Yandaboo, 1826 had extended recognition to the sovereign status of Manipur. This treaty still remained in force at the time when the British intervened into the internal affairs of Manipur in 1891. Though Manipur was not a signatory to the treaty, the same had never been abrogated by the British or the Burmese. Rather, the treaty was reaffirmed by the Government of India Act, 1858, which stipulated that all the treaties made by the Government of the English East

160

INTERROGATING INTO THE POLITICAL STATUS

India Company should be binding on the British Crown (M.I. Singh 1986: 30). This indicated that the sovereignty of Manipur had remained intact till its defeat in the Anglo-Manipuri War of 1891. Therefore, the British did not have the legitimate authority to entertain the application of Surchandra for regaining the throne of Manipur and to secure the arrest of Tikendrajit. The change of rulers in Manipur either through peaceful means or violent revolt was purely an internal affair of Manipur. The British Government had no right to exercise its jurisdiction over Manipur as no state can claim jurisdiction over another under the Law of Nations (ibid.: 31).

Two more treaties were signed between the British and Manipur in 1833 and 1834, respectively. While the former dealt with the boundary of Manipur, the latter dealt with the Kabaw Valley. Both the treaties did not affect the sovereign status of Manipur. A careful examination of the wording of these two agreements shows that there is nothing in them that affects any condition of 'owing allegiance' to the British or which prejudices the State of Manipur as an independent kingdom' (Parratt and Parratt 1992: 187). Besides, there was no evidence at all that Manipur ever entered into a formal agreement which gave it the status of a protected state (ibid.: 188). No doubt, the presence of a political agent in Manipur after 1835, as a representative of the GoI, was a factor of discouraging external aggression as well as preserving the internal stability of Manipur to a certain degree. However, the incidental rendering of the claim of Manipur to be a protected state is highly contentious as the protection that the British had extended to Chandrakirti was not extended to Sur-chandra when the latter was forced to abdicate the throne. John Parratt and Saroj Parratt thus opined that the protection given by the British to Manipur was not in perpetuity on account of the fact that the British did not agree to protect all Manipuri rajas therefrom (ibid.: 189).

Manomohon Ghose, the Bengali barrister who defended Kulachandra and Tikendrajit in their trials, made a brilliant contribution to the debate relating to whether or not Manipur was a sovereign independent king-dom in 1891. According to him, the royal dignitaries of Manipur could not be guilty of waging war against the British Government since they did not owe allegiance to the British Government by residing in its terri-tory (Sanajaoba 1993: 262). Therefore, Manipur being an 'alien' country, neither the English laws nor the Indian Penal Code could be invoked.

Manipur was never acquired by the British either through conquest or by a treaty till 1891. Although certain amount of protection was prom-ised to Manipur on certain conditions, Manipur paid no tribute to the British. The kingdom of Manipur was governed by its own laws with

KANGUJAM SANATOMBA

the raja of Manipur exercising sovereignty over his subjects. However, the British Government occasionally interfered in the internal management of the kingdom. Now, the question remains: do such acts of interference destroy the character of Manipur as a sovereign state? In order to clarify this doubt, Ghose cited the following paragraph from relevant sources of International Law:

> The sovereignty of a particular state is not impaired by its occasional obedience to the commands of other states, or even the habitual influences exercised by them over its councils. It is only when this obedience, or this influence assumes the form of express compact, that the sovereignty of the state inferior in power is legally affected by its connection with the other. Treaties of equal alliance freely contracted between independent states do not impair their sovereignty. Treaties of unequal alliance, guarantee, mediation, and protection may have the effect of limiting and qualifying the sovereignty according to the stipulation of the treaties.
>
> (quoted in Sanajaoba 1993: 263)

Ghose further pointed out that there was no express reservation, by treaty or 'compact of allegiance' due to the sovereign of England from the ruler of Manipur (ibid.: 264). Since there was no such declaration of allegiance on the part of any ruler of Manipur to Her Majesty, occasional interference into the management of the internal affairs of Manipur by the British did not create such allegiance to make Manipur liable to be tried for treason. Manipur was not a British territory but an *Asiatic power in alliance*. The way the British dealt with Manipur was on a footing of its being a sovereign power in alliance and not as owing any allegiance to the Queen, such as might be due from some of the native states in India (ibid.: 266).

That Manipur was an independent state as on 24 March 1891 was fairly demonstrated by the official conduct of the British authorities when they tried to secure the arrest of the Manipur prince. J. W. Quinton, the Chief Commissioner of Assam, having failed to arrest the prince through holding a durbar approached the king and asked him to either surrender the prince or give a written authority to arrest him. The mode of arrest undertaken by the British officers did not demonstrate even the slightest procedure to indicate that Manipur was a Subordinate State. A formal request for a written authority from the king was absolutely unnecessary for securing the arrest of an objectionable person in a Protected State.

INTERROGATING INTO THE POLITICAL STATUS

As Manomohon Ghose said, 'The mode of arrest proposed by the Chief Commissioner was perfectly in keeping with the sovereign and independent character of Manipur' (Sanajaoba 1993: 268).

A subordinate native state

The distinctiveness of the political status of Manipur lies in the fact that it was not annexed into the British Empire after its defeat in the Anglo-Manipuri War of 1891. It is also interesting to point out that Manipur was the last native state in the entire Indian subcontinent to succumb to British imperialism. The greatness of the Manipuri legendaries who attained martyrdom in the War of 1891 was the stiff resistance, political as well as military, they offered against the British in defence of the sovereign independence of Manipur.

After the war, Manipur became a '*Sanad* State'. A sanad is a patent, an authority in writing, from the ruling power to hold a land or an office for a period which the ruling power may be pleased to grant. In other words, sanad is a form of engagement or an acknowledgement of concession or authority or privileges generally coupled with conditions proceeding from the paramount power (Government of India 1950: 21). The Governor-General in Council selected five-year-old Churachand, son of Chowbiyaima, to be the Chief (King) of Manipur State. He was also granted the title of Raja of Manipur and given an eleven-gun salute. The sanad granted to Churachand laid down that the chiefship should be hereditary under the law of primogeniture and each succession should be recognised and approved by the GoI (Sanajaoba 1993: 309). Under the sanad, the Chief would continue in office so long as he readily fulfilled the orders given to him by the GoI. In this regard, it has been rightly observed that the sanad provided for complete subordination of Manipur State under the GoI and Manipur practically became a vassal state (M. I. Singh 1986: 45–46).

During the non-age of Churachand Singh, the administration of Manipur was entrusted to the British officers under the direct control of the Chief Commissioner of Assam. The regency administration was reintroduced and the native rule re-established primarily with a design to suit the exigencies of British imperial interests. The political agent and the superintendent were given full power to introduce any form of reforms considered beneficial for the British. However, as a matter of policy, the British/GoI did not undertake major reforms during the regency administration (Dena 2008: 46). This enabled Manipur to retain a distinct political character quite different from that of British India.

163

However, after Churachand Singh formally took charge of Manipur State on 15 May 1907, he had to administer the state in accordance with the Rules for the Management of the Manipur State sanctioned by the GoI. The Manipur Durbar was reconstituted to assist the Raja in the administration of the State, which consisted of the king as the president and a vice president who was an English ICS (Indian Civil Service) officer selected by the Assam Government. There were also six Durbar members appointed by the GoI on the recommendation of the raja and the political agent and were removable by an order of the government (Dena 2008: 59). In the new administrative set-up, the raja occupied a subordinate position. Enormous financial power was vested with the vice president. The real executive and legislative powers were concentrated in the hands of the political agent who was the de facto head of the state. He could interfere in the day-to-day functioning of the Durbar. Key powers being taken over or controlled by the paramount British power, the raja of Manipur had no sovereign power (Dena 2008: 58).

Although native rule was reinstalled in Manipur, the paternalistic character of the new administration and the sanad eroded the sovereignty of Manipur to a large extent. The post-1891 Manipur was a *Subordinate Native State* under the suzerainty of the British Government and it continued as such until the passing of the Indian Independence Act, 1947 (R. M. Singh 2000: 9).

The constitutional transition

With the conclusion of World War II, the prospect of British withdrawal from the Indian subcontinent became imminent. The lapse of British paramountcy would naturally mean the reversion of the native states to their erstwhile sovereign status. Such a prospect made the rulers as well as the subjects of the native states, such as Manipur, restive and apprehensive. Moreover, popular movements demanding the establishment of a responsible government were fast gaining momentum in the state. In what can be regarded as a significant break from the feudal tradition, Maharaja Bodhchandra on 21 September 1946 wrote to G. P. Stewart, the political agent of Manipur, requesting permission to make a declaration for introducing a responsible form of government in the state as per the instruction from the Chamber of Princes (Dena 2008: 130). Subsequently, on 12 December 1946, the Maharaja issued an order for setting up a Constitution Making Committee (CMC) to draft a constitution for Manipur, which was eventually constituted on 10 March 1947 consisting of 16 members. F. F. Pearson, President of the Manipur State

Durbar (PMSD), was the Chairman of the Committee. The Maharaja gave his assent to the Draft Constitution which later came to be known as the Manipur State Constitution Act (MSCA), 1947. On 26 July 1947, Manipur adopted the Constitution. The MSCA, when it was finally adopted, formalised the transfer of powers from the Maharaja to the elected representatives of the people. The new constitution envisaged a partially democratic government with the Maharaja as a mere constitutional head. The real powers were duly vested with the State Assembly. The MSCA was a landmark political achievement of the Manipuri people.

In the meantime, the Manipur State Durbar was transformed into Manipur State Council on 1 July 1947 to suit the changing political situation. Accordingly, the members of the Manipur State Durbar were rechristened as ministers in the Manipur State Council and the president of Manipur State Durbar came to be called the chief minister. In this way, F. F. Pearson became the first Chief Minister of Manipur and held the said post from 1 July to 14 August 1947 (Maipaksana 1995: 121).

In the midst of this development, a series of discussions were held between the chief minister and the Maharaja on the modalities of forming a new Interim Council. The Interim Council was a temporary political arrangement to be in force between the transfer of power and until such time that the new constitutional structure was ready for operation. After hectic negotiations, a notification was issued by the Manipur State Council on 28 July 1947 on the order of the Maharaja in which the service of the Council was terminated with effect from 8 a.m. on 14 August 1947 and the first list of four ministers of the new Council was announced. It was also mentioned that the names of one minister from the valley and two from the hill areas would be announced later on.

The Rules for the Administration of the Manipur State were revised in order to provide the basic legal framework for the governance of Manipur and it became operative on 1 July 1947. The revised Rules provided for an Interim Manipur State Council consisting of a chief minister and six other ministers who were appointed by, and responsible to, the Maharaja. However, owing to strong public protest over the mode of constituting the Interim Council, a final list of the Council was declared by an order of the Maharaja on 13 August 1947 with M. K. Priyobarta as the chief minister. The interim ministry started to function from 14 August and lasted till 7 October 1948.

Meanwhile, the Manipur State Constitution Act was already in force. Accordingly, election to the Manipur State Legislative Assembly (Manipur Parliament) as envisaged in the Act took place in the second half of 1948. Elections in the valley were held on 11 and 30 June 1948 and in the hills on 26 and 27 July 1948. The total number of seats in the Legislative Assembly was 53. The elections were held on the basis of Universal Adult Franchise. It is significant to note that this was the first democratic election to be held on the basis of Adult Franchise in the entire Indian subcontinent. Election was held in free India only in 1952. Moreover, the significance of the election of 1948 lies in the fact that both the hills and the valley equally participated in the said election. On the basis of this election, a popular ministry with M. K. Priyabarta Singh as the chief minister was installed.

The lapse of British suzerainty in Manipur

The Indian Independence Act, 1947, was passed by the British Parliament to formally put an end to British colonialism in the Indian subcontinent. Under the Act, two independent dominions known as India and Pakistan were set up with effect from 15 August 1947. Along with that, Manipur also became technically and legally independent from the British Crown by virtue of Section 7(1)(b) of the Act. The suzerainty of the British Crown over Manipur lapsed with effect from 15 August 1947. It states:

> The suzerainty of His Majesty over the Indian States lapses, and with it, all the treaties and agreements in force at the date of passing of this Act between His Majesty and the rulers of Indian States, all functions exercisable by His Majesty at that date towards Indian States or the rulers thereof, and all powers, rights, authority or jurisdiction exercisable by His Majesty at that date in or in relation to Indian States by treaty, grant, usage, sufferance or otherwise.
>
> (Section 7(1)(b), Indian Independence Act, 1947)

There is a proviso in the same Section, which states that notwithstanding anything contained in this section, all earlier agreements relating to customs, transit, communications, posts and telegraphs, or other like matters would continue to be given effect until denounced by the ruler of the Indian states on the one hand, or by the Dominion concerned on the other, or superseded by subsequent agreements.

However, the proviso to Section 7(1)(b) of the Indian Independence Act, 1947, does not implicitly or explicitly affect the independence of the native states. In other words, this proviso does not limit or contradict

Sub-section (1), Clause (b), of Section (7). It only allows the continuation of the states' relations with the Dominions on a few subjects such as posts and telegraph and communications. There is nothing in this proviso that prevents the sovereign existence of the native states. Besides, it has no binding character as the same could be abrogated at will by either of the two parties concerned. Therefore, the independence of Manipur remained intact notwithstanding the inclusion of the said proviso in the Independence Act.

On 12 May 1947, the Cabinet Mission presented the Memorandum on States' Treaties and Paramountcy to His Highness, the Chancellor of the Chamber of Princes. Paragraph 5 of the Memorandum states the following:

> His Majesty's Government will cease to exercise the power of paramountcy. This means that the rights of the States which flow from their relationship to the Crown will no longer exist and that all the rights surrendered by the States to the paramount power return to the States.
>
> (quoted in Y. M. Singh 2009: vii, Appendix II)

Confirming the independence of the native states, Lord Mountbatten declared on 25 July 1947 to the representative of Indian states thus:'Now, the Indian Independence Act releases the states from all their obligations to the Crown. The states have complete freedom – technically and legally they are independent' (quoted in Sanajaoba 1996: 71).

Reaffirming the same position Mohammed Ali Jinnah also made the following statement:

> Constitutionally and legally the Indian states will be independent sovereign states on the termination of paramountcy and they will be free to decide for themselves any course they like to adopt . . . it is open to the states to join Hindustan Constituent Assembly or the Pakistan Constituent Assembly or decide to remain independent.
>
> (ibid.: 72)

The instrument of accession: a fraudulent exercise

It is also worthwhile to point out that more than 500 native states also became independent, technically and legally, as per Section 7(1)(b) of the Indian Independence Act, 1947. The Act, while granting independence to the native states, did not prevent them from acceding to the new Dominions. Sub-section (4) of Section (2) of the Act thus states: 'Nothing in this section shall be construed as preventing the accession of Indian states to either of the new Dominions.' But this does not necessarily imply that the accession was compulsory. Rather, it merely provides room for accession to those who would like to opt for it. That the accession was not compulsory was revealed by the Government of Pakistan in its complaint lodged to the United Nations on the Kashmir issue. Paragraph 10 of the 'Particulars of Pakistan's Case' states:

> In accordance with the agreed scheme of partition and the Indian Independence Act, 1947, Indian States were under no compulsion to accede to either of the two Dominions. Notwithstanding this clear provision the Government of India by a combination of threats and cajolery forced a number of States into acceding to the Indian Dominion.
>
> (Government of Pakistan 1948)

However, the Dominion of India undertook various steps towards effecting integration of native states with the Dominion of India by promulgating the India (Provisional Constitution) Order, 1947, by enacting the Extra-Provincial Jurisdiction Act, 1947 and by amending the Government of India Act, 1935 (R. M. Singh 2000: 15).

Prior to independence, Sardar Vallabhbhai Patel invited the princes to accede to the Dominion of India on three subjects, namely, defence, external affairs and communications. Lord Mountbatten was entrusted with the task of conducting negotiations with the rulers of native states. On 25 July 1947, he urged the rulers of the native states to accede to the Indian Dominion on three subjects exclusively and not beyond (ibid.: 21). He further stated that either the internal autonomy or independence of the states would be protected. Accordingly, by 15 August 1947, most of the native states (except Hyderabad, Kashmir and Junagarh) had acceded to the Dominion of India by signing the Instrument of Accession (hereafter, the Instrument). The Maharaja of Manipur also signed the Instrument on 11 August 1947 and, thus supposedly acceded the three main subjects to the Indian Dominion.

The legality of the Instrument will be dealt with later, but assuming that it is valid for the time being, the assumption behind the very 'act' of signing such an Instrument deserves to be understood. If the native states were not independent or were not separate political entities, the necessity for executing the instrument would not have arisen. The fact of giving the option

INTERROGATING INTO THE POLITICAL STATUS

to join either of the two Dominions or remain independent underscored the sovereign status of the native states like Manipur. Clause (8) of the Instrument clearly envisages that nothing in the said Instrument affects the continuance of the Maharaja's 'sovereignty' in and over the state. Therefore, from the juridical point of view, the Instrument of Accession signed between the Maharaja of Manipur and the GoI was in the nature of a bilateral treaty of international status concluded between two sovereign states.

Fallacy of sovereignty claim under the instrument of accession

The pertinent question is whether or not the signing of the Instrument of Accession by the Maharaja of Manipur on 11 August 1947 deprived Manipur of its sovereign status. Such a question has become increasingly relevant mainly on account of divergent interpretations of the act of signing the Instrument. Besides, there seems to be a serious lacuna inherent in the argument that claims to sustain the sovereignty of Manipur notwithstanding the signing of the Instrument of Accession. It is, therefore, pertinent to interrogate into how Manipur could still remain sovereign even after executing the Instrument by which key powers were supposedly ceded to the Dominion of India.

The Instrument of Accession provided for the cession of three subjects, namely, defence, external affairs and communications, by Manipur to the Indian Dominion. This is often interpreted by certain informed quarters as not implying the transfer of Manipur's sovereignty to the Dominion of India by citing Clauses (7) and (8) of the Instrument which are given below:

> Clause 7: Nothing in this Instrument shall be deemed to commit me in any way to acceptance of any future constitution of India or to fetter my discretion to enter into arrangements with the Government of India under any such future constitution.
> Clause 8: Nothing in this Instrument affects the continuance of my sovereignty in and over the state or, saves as provided by or under this Instrument, the exercise of any powers, authority and rights now enjoyed by me as Ruler of this State or the validity of any law at present in force in this State.

These two clauses are often cited to drive home the point that sovereignty still remained with Manipur. They are considered as the 'escape clauses' which enabled Manipur to absolve itself from any obligation arising from the Instrument. In this regard, it is worthwhile to recall the '16th

May Statement of the Cabinet Mission' issued in 1946: 'The states will retain subjects and powers other than those ceded to the Union'. This provision is also often invoked to substantiate the claim that Manipur retained its sovereignty even after the signing of the Instrument.

However, the earlier stated arguments lack substantive understanding of what constitutes sovereignty. Far from succeeding in reclaiming the sovereign status of Manipur, such arguments unwittingly land oneself into the trap of accepting the subservient political status of Manipur. The notion of sovereignty implies the supreme authority of the state in both internal and external spheres. Internally, it establishes supremacy of the state over all individuals and associations; externally, it upholds independence of the state from the control of or interference by any other state. Sovereignty is generally defined in terms of its absoluteness, inalienability and indivisibility. Once sovereignty is limited by any superior power or is transferred to another authority or divided/shared between two entities, a state can no longer claim to remain a sovereign entity.

In the light of this understanding, it is difficult to imagine how Manipur would qualify to be a sovereign state in the absence of such vital powers such as defence, external affairs and communication. Matters like defence and external affairs constitute the external spheres of sovereignty which Manipur was deprived of under the Instrument of Accession. Even the so-called internal autonomy was seriously undermined under the framework of the Instrument. As such, the understanding that Manipur was a sovereign state regardless of the Instrument of Accession is fraught with serious theoretical misconceptions.

Critiquing the critique of critics

A highly misplaced understanding with regard to the Instrument of Accession is that it had become invalid after the adoption of the Indian Independence Act, 1947. Such an understanding is rooted in the wrong interpretation of Section 7(1)(b) of the Act, which states that all treaties or agreements in force at the date of passing of this Act between the rulers of the Indian states and the British Crown also lapsed with the lapse of British suzerainty over the Indian states. Put simply, any kind of treaty or agreement concluded between the native states and the British suzerain power had been superseded by the said provision of the Act.

However, the above understanding (or rather the critique of the Instrument of Accession) suffers from certain legal and historical fallacies. First, Section 7(1)(b) of the Indian Independence Act, 1947, mentions only about agreements, treaties and the like and the term 'instrument' cannot

INTERROGATING INTO THE POLITICAL STATUS

be found in the said provision. As such, the Instrument (if it were a legally valid document) did not lapse with the lapse of British suzerainty nor was it superseded by the Act. Second, Section 7(1)(b) refers only to the agreement and treaties concluded between the British Crown and the rulers of the native states. It does not even slightly refer to any kind of political or legal transaction reached between the native states and the Dominion of India. Third, contrary to the understanding that the Act supersedes the Instrument of Accession signed on 15 August 1947, Sub-section (4) of Section (2) of the Indian Independence Act, 1947, rather leaves the options open for the accession of the native states to either of the two independent Dominions of Pakistan or India. Fourth, an instrument is a legal transaction which once entered cannot be revoked by the acceding party on the grounds that it no longer wants to remain in the state of being acceded. Therefore, the Instrument of Accession, if transacted following proper legal procedures, remains an irrevocable legal document. The Act cannot invalidate nor supersede the Instrument. Last, the understanding of the Instrument being superseded by the Act implies that it was valid up to the moment before the adoption of the Act on 15 August, since it became invalid only after the said date. Such an understanding, instead of critiquing the legality of the Instrument, sustains the validity of the same from 11 August 1947, the day on which it was signed, to 15 August, the day on which the Act was adopted. In other words, the above understanding invariably accepts the historicity of the transaction of the said Instrument without any historical awareness of its occurrence. Therefore, a fresh attempt to offer a more informed critique of the Instrument of Accession is rendered highly crucial to sustain the independent political status of Manipur after the lapse of British suzerainty.

Legality, historicity and the politics of secrecy

Most of the scholars seem to attach more importance to the Merger Agreement than the Instrument of Accession. This is primarily on account of the understanding that Manipur was integrated into the Indian Union following the signing of the Merger Agreement in 1949. However, undue obsession with the issue of merger leaves the issue of the accession (Instrument of Accession) without giving it the fair treatment it deserves. Any effort to establish the exact political status of Manipur should entail a clear interpretation of the Instrument. In other words, an attempt to understand the validity of the Merger Agreement without enquiring into the implications of the Instrument of Accession would always remain a wasteful exercise. In fact, the ground for integration was already prepared by the Instrument, while the signing of the Merger Agreement was simply a ceremonial formality that merely consummated the process of integration already initiated with the execution of the Instrument. Therefore, re-evaluation of the Instrument has become increasingly indispensable for understanding the political status of Manipur in the post-suzerainty period.

A paragraph of the Instrument of Accession reads thus: 'I . . . Ruler of . . . in the exercise of my sovereignty in and over my said state do hereby execute this my Instrument of Accession and . . . ' This statement indicates that the Maharaja had apparently executed the Instrument in his capacity as a sovereign ruler of a sovereign state. But the question remains whether the Maharaja was vested with the sovereign authority to execute such a political transaction. At least two points may be stated in this regard. First, Manipur was not a sovereign entity as on 11 August 1947. It regained its independence and sovereignty only on 15 August 1947 like all the princely states and the two Dominions, namely India and Pakistan. Hence, Manipur could not enter into such an Instrument, which assumed the form of an international treaty transacted between two sovereign states. Only a sovereign state can execute such an Instrument. Second, as on 11 August 1947, the ruler of Manipur was not a sovereign ruler. Even after Independence, the Maharaja had become a mere constitutional head of the state with all the powers and responsibilities transferred to the Manipur State Council since 1 July 1947. The Maharaja of Manipur, in his inaugural address of the first Manipur State Assembly session held on 18 September 1948, had said the following words:

> I now bring to the notice of the people that I had transferred my powers and responsibilities other than those of a Constitutional Ruler of the State Council since 1st July, 1947 before the lapse of British paramountcy and since then, I have already remained as a Constitutional Ruler.
>
> (H. B. Singh, 1988: 317)

Furthermore, Section 9(b) of the Manipur State Constitution Act, 1947, would certainly dispel any doubt about the titular status of the Maharaja, which was expressedly stated thus: 'The Maharaja means His Highness, the Maharaja of Manipur, the constitutional head of the state.' The Maharaja in his capacity as the constitutional ruler could not execute the Instrument without proper authorisation and constitutional endorsement. This was simply on account of the fact that he was not a sovereign ruler and that Manipur was not a sovereign state then. Therefore, the act of signing

INTERROGATING INTO THE POLITICAL STATUS

the Instrument of Accession on 11 August 1947 by the Maharaja could not be considered an Act of the State. Hence, the Instrument was deemed null and void right from the moment it was executed.

Now, another question that requires due attention is: could Manipur enter into the Instrument of Accession with the 'Dominion of India' on '11 July 1947'? The answer is an absolute 'No'. The Dominion of India came into existence only on 15 August 1947 with the adoption of the Indian Independence Act, 1947. Section 1 Clause (1) of the Independence Act states thus: 'As from the fifteenth day of August, nineteen hundred and forty-seven, two independent Dominions shall be set up in India, to be known respectively as India and Pakistan.'

The Maharaja signed the Instrument of Accession on 11 August 1947, four days before the Dominion of India was set up. It is highly inconceivable that the Maharaja should accede to something that was yet to be born. For example, the Indian Dominion had never existed on or before 11 August 1947. Being so, it can be aptly said that the Maharaja acceded to a political non-entity. Therefore, it can be claimed that the Instrument was never executed in actuality. It was simply pre-judicial to execute the Instrument between two political entities which were yet to be born. The story of the Instrument of Accession was a mere political fiction scripted and enacted by the Indian leaders to secure the integration of the native states.

Yet another issue which is closely associated with the question of legality or illegality of the Instrument of Accession is the authenticity of the document. A clause of the India (Provisional Constitution) Order, 1947 was promulgated by the Governor-General on 14 August 1947 by amending the Government of India Act, 1935. After the amendment, the Subsection (1) of Section 6 of the Act provided thus: 'An Indian state shall be deemed to have acceded to the Dominion if the Governor-General has signified his acceptance of an Instrument of Accession executed by the ruler thereof.' In the light of this provision, it is necessary to ascertain whether or not the Instrument carries the signature of the Governor-General (Lord Mountbatten).

The original copies of the Standstill Agreement and the Instrument of Accession signed by Maharaja Bodhchandra are still marked 'Secret' and are currently with the Ministry of Home, Government of India, in File Number F/375/48-Public (H. B. Singh 1988: 70). So far, the GoI has not given access to these two important documents relating to Manipur. The question is: why? In order to make the Instrument effective (assuming that it is valid), it is mandatory or statutory for the then Governor-General of India to append his signature on the Instrument 'within 31 March 1948' as per Sub-section (5) of Section 9 of the Indian Independence Act, 1947. In the absence of his signature, the Instrument has no legality and validity. In this regard, it may be recalled that as per a news item in *The Sangai Express*, dated 23 October 2009, the Humanist Party had written to the Home Ministry to provide a photo copy of the Instrument way back in 2008. But the Home Ministry has till date refused to provide the same. The classified status of the Instrument leaves ample scope to question the authenticity of the document.

The Standstill Agreement: unauthorised transfer of paramountcy

On the day of signing of the Instrument of Accession on 11 August 1947, the Maharaja also signed the Standstill Agreement. The Agreement provided for the time being all agreements as to matter of common concerns existing then between the Crown and any native states, such as between the Dominion of India and the native states, until new agreements on this behalf were made. By signing the Standstill Agreement, Manipur surrendered 18 subjects like air communications, currency, external affairs, post telegraphs and telephones, etc., to the Dominion of India and thereby apparently depriving herself of the independence granted under the Indian Independence Act. Thus, the Standstill Agreement was an agreement by which paramountcy over Manipur was supposedly transferred from the British Crown to the Dominion of India.

In this regard, informed circles have attempted to defend the independent sovereign status of Manipur by citing Clause (3) of the Standstill Agreement which states thus: 'Nothing in this Agreement includes the exercise of any paramountcy functions.' It is claimed that this particular clause had enabled Manipur to retain its sovereignty. But as stated in the case of the Instrument of Accession, it is problematic to sustain the claim of sovereignty under the Standstill Agreement as well after surrendering key subjects like external affairs, currency and air communications to the Indian Dominion. The internal as well as the external dimensions of sovereignty were seriously jeopardised under the Agreement.

It is also claimed that the Independence Act had superseded the said Agreement. This line of argument, though factually correct, implicitly acknowledges the validity and legality of the Agreement till 15 August 1947. Logically, this would imply that Manipur had remained under the suzerainty or paramountcy of the Dominion of India from 11 August to 15 August 1947. Such a conclusion has the tendency to undermine the distinctiveness of the history of Manipur. Contestation of the validity of the said Agreement, therefore, has to be made on more appropriate and concrete grounds.

Sometimes, it is misunderstood that the Dominion governments were the rightful inheritors of the native states and that the paramountcy was transferred to the Dominion governments. Such line of understanding has been substantiated and strengthened by the existence of the Standstill Agreement which purportedly transferred paramountcy of the British Crown over Manipur to the Dominion of India. In this regard, Paragraph 2 of the Memorandum on States' Treaties and Paramountcy, which formed part of the Cabinet Mission Plan, needs to be recalled. It states:'But the British Government could not and will not in any circumstances transfer paramountcy to an Indian Government' (Y.M. Singh 2009: vi). Reiterating the position of the Cabinet Mission Plan, 1946, Prime Minister C.R. Attlee issued a letter of instruction to Lord Mountbatten in March 1947 wherein he states, 'His Majesty's Government does not intend to hand over their (native states) powers and obligations under paramountcy to any successor Government' (Sanajaoba 1996: 70). Therefore, the signing of the Standstill Agreement was not supported by any statute, Act or law passed by the British Parliament.

Moreover, Manipur was still under British suzerainty at the time of signing of the said Agreement and the Dominion of India was yet to be born. It is, therefore, highly inconceivable that Manipur had agreed to transfer British paramountcy over to the Dominion of India without the knowledge and consent of the British parliament. The transfer of paramountcy, if any, could only be effected by a special imperial legislation enacted by the British Parliament. It is also pertinent to point out that the Agreement was merely a temporary arrangement and did not possess any permanent binding character. The Standstill Agreement is neither a Treaty of Accession nor a Merger Agreement. In case Manipur failed to accede to the Dominion of India within a reasonable timeframe, the Standstill Agreement naturally became redundant. And since the signing of the Instrument of Accession has been a failed exercise, as explained above, the Standstill Agreement has no implications on the political status of Manipur.

Was Manipur a part of British India?

Sovereign or not, if Manipur was not a separate political entity, the need to execute the Instrument of Accession would not have arisen at all. The act of acceding to the Dominion of India definitely underscored the pre-existing historical reality of Manipur as a separate political entity. By signing or executing the Instrument, Manipur supposedly ceded to the Dominion of India the sovereignty over certain subjects. Before that, sovereignty over defence, foreign affairs and communication remained with Manipur. It is said that Manipur became a part of the Dominion of India by virtue of executing the Instrument. From this, it can be inferred that before the execution of the said Instrument, Manipur remained as a separate political entity (assuming that the Instrument is a legally valid document). This is further corroborated by the fact of invoking the Extra-Provincial Jurisdiction over the native states by the Dominion of India.

It is crucial to clarify that the native states were not part of British India. In fact, British India means all territories comprised within the Governors' Provinces and the Chief Commissioners' Provinces. Section 311(1) of the Government of India Act, 1935 as originally enacted, defined 'Indian state' (*sic*, native state) as including any territory, whether described as a state, an estate, a *jagir*, or otherwise, belonging to or under the suzerainty of a ruler who is under the suzerainty of Her Majesty, and not part of British India (R. M. Singh 2000: 12).

From this, it becomes clear that native states did not form part of British India. As a matter of fact, the native states were under the suzerainty, and not under the paramountcy, of the British Crown (not under that of British India). British India was under the British paramountcy (not suzerainty). Besides, the native states were under the control of the Viceroy as the representative of the Crown, while British India was under the control of the Governor-General although the same person might hold the two posts simultaneously. Therefore, British India and native states were two separate political entities. Here lies the distinctiveness of the native states, which was clearly reflected in the Indian Independence Act, 1947. The two Dominions of India and the native states were given separate treatment implying recognition of their distinctive political characters.

It was precisely because of this fact that the Extra-Provincial Jurisdiction Act was enacted to interfere into the working of the native states by British India. The promulgation of this Act would have been rendered redundant if the native states were not separate political entities. The implication of this Act points to the fact that the native states like Manipur were not a part of British India and, by extension, the Indian Dominion.

The issue of joining the Constituent Assembly

There has been a controversy surrounding the issue on whether or not Manipur joined the Constituent Assembly of India and participated in the making of the Indian Constitution. Certain informed quarters have

INTERROGATING INTO THE POLITICAL STATUS

held the view that Manipur did join the Constituent Assembly of India by entering into an agreement with the Governor of Assam on 1 July 1947 (Y. M. Singh 2009: 61). The agreement entered into between the Governor of Assam and the Manipur State Durbar mainly pertained to joining of the Constituent Assembly of India by Manipur and acceptance of G. S. Guha, a foreigner, as the representative of the state in the Constituent Assembly.

However, the issue of Manipur joining the Constituent Assembly of India is highly problematic on account of the fact that the 1st July Agreement became inoperative beyond 15 August 1947 by the logic implied in Section 7(1)(b) of the Indian Independence Act, 1947. The said agreement becomes null and void with the lapse of British suzerainty on 15 August 1947. As stated earlier, according to Section 7(1)(b) of the Act, the suzerainty of Her Majesty over the rulers of the Indian states lapsed, and with it all the treaties and agreements in force prior to the date of the passing of this Act. Manipur had to enter into a new agreement with the Indian Dominion in order to join the Constituent Assembly of India. Unfortunately, however, no such agreement was concluded between Manipur and the Dominion of India.

Moreover, the representation of Manipur by Guha in the Constituent Assembly of India was also highly contentious and problematic as Guha was neither a 'citizen' of Manipur nor a Manipuri national, which contravened the established democratic principle of representation since no 'alien' could represent an independent nation or a State. The proxy representation of Manipur by Guha lacked democratic basis and legal binding on the state of Manipur. Representation of an independent country by a foreign national in the Constituent Assembly of another country is absolutely inconceivable. If the representation was made by deputing a genuine representative (for example, a local Manipuri) duly elected by the people of Manipur in the Constituent Assembly of India, the controversy centring on the issue of Manipur joining the Constituent Assembly of India would not have emerged.

The core of the contestation is that the Indian Independence Act had superseded whatever agreements had been concluded prior to 15 August 1947. Therefore, the ground on which Manipur joined the Constituent Assembly has been rendered highly contested. Second, the representation of Manipur by Guha was not in harmony with democratic principles of representation. These are some of the reasons why some sections claim that Manipur was not party to the Indian Constitution-making process.

Conclusion

The distinctiveness of Manipur's historical realities lies in the preservation of its political status as an independent kingdom state throughout its existence despite occasional disruptions by external forces. The advent of British colonialism brought about far-reaching changes in the political history of Manipur. Under the indirect British rule, Manipur evolved into a multi-ethnic modern state. The first encounter with the British was formalised with the conclusion of a Mutual Trade and Defense Treaty in 1762. Although the Treaty placed the British on a more advantageous position, it still remained as a treaty contracted between two equal powers.

As far as the Treaty of Yandaboo is concerned, Manipur was not a signatory to the treaty. This fact puts a serious question on the credibility of the state as a sovereign entity. Nevertheless, it deserves to be pointed out that the Burmese occupation army was driven out from the soil of Manipur by the Manipuris themselves under the command of Gambhir Singh. Though the Manipuris had the logistic support of the British, it had no bearing on the status of Manipur. However, the Treaty of Yandaboo is significant for it conferred 'recognition' to the independent sovereign status of Manipur. With the termination of Burmese occupation, the sovereignty of Manipur was automatically restored. In this context, therefore, the treaty comes more as an occasion that recognises the sovereignty of Manipur, not restoration per se, as many would argue. Manipur would remain sovereign with or without the conclusion of the Treaty of Yandaboo.

That Manipur was an independent kingdom state in 1891 is aptly proved by the mutual declaration of war by Manipur and the British Empire against each other. For example, the act of declaring war underscored the fact that Manipur was an independent kingdom state. The necessity of declaring war upon Manipur on the part of the British would not have arisen if Manipur were a British territory or if Manipur were under British control. Similarly, Manipur would not have declared war on the British Empire if it were not a sovereign political entity. Only sovereign states have the capacity to declare war and make peace. Hence, the act of declaring war against each other in 1891 points to the attributes of the sovereign political status of Manipur.

Another significant aspect of the distinctiveness of the historical realities of Manipur was the non-annexation of Manipur into the British Empire even after its defeat in the Anglo-Manipuri War of 1891. Besides,

INTERROGATING INTO THE POLITICAL STATUS

Manipur was permitted to re-establish its native rule under the supervision of the British. In spite of the overwhelming control of the British and resultant erosion of its internal autonomy to a great extent, Manipur could retain a semblance of self-governance and self-administration. In fact, Manipur remained as a subordinate native state under the suzerainty of the British Crown and retained its identity of being a distinct political entity till October 1949.

With the lapse of British suzerainty following the adoption of the Indian Independence Act on 15 August 1947, Manipur regained its sovereign independence. Manipur became independent, legally and technically, notwithstanding the signing of the Instrument of Accession on 11 August 1947. Contrary to what many would argue, the option to accede either to the Dominion of India and Dominion of Pakistan was not compulsory but purely voluntary, and nowhere in the Indian Independence Act, 1947 does it state that the native states should accede to either of the two Dominions. The claim that Manipur signed the Instrument of Accession on 11 August 1947 and, therefore, had acceded to the Dominion of India, holds no water as the Dominion of India was born only on 15 August 1947. Moreover, it can be argued that the GoI would not have forced the Merger Agreement on Manipur in 1949 had it felt the representation of Manipur by Guha in the Constituent Assembly as valid beyond 15 August 1947.

References

Dena, Lal. 2008. *British Policy towards Manipur (1762–1947)*. Imphal: Nogeen.

Government of India. 1950. *White Paper on Indian States*. Delhi: Ministry of States.

Government of Pakistan. 1948. *Document III – Particulars of Pakistan's Case*. Enclosed in the text of letter dated January 15, 1948 (S/646) from the Minister of Foreign Affairs of Pakistan addressed to the Secretary General of the U.N. concerning the situation in Jammu and Kashmir under the title *Pakistan's Reply and Counter-claim*.

Maipaksana, Rajkumar. 1995. 'Constitutional Development of Manipur in a Nutshell', in People's Democratic Movement (ed.), *Annexation of Manipur, 1949*. Imphal: People's Democratic Movement.

Parratt, John and Saroj Parratt. 1992. *Queen Empress v/s Tikendrajit, Prince of Manipur: The Anglo-Manipuri Conflict of 1891*. Delhi: Vikas Publishing House.

Sanajaoba, Noarem (ed.). 1993. *Manipur Treaties & Documents (1110–1971), Volume One*. New Delhi: Mittal Publications.

Sanajaoba, Noarem. 1996. *Right of the Oppressed Nations (and Peoples)*. New Delhi: Omsons.

Singh, H. Bhuban. 1988. *The Merger of Manipur*. Imphal: Pritam Haobam.

Singh, M. Ibohal. 1986. *Constitutional & Legal History of Manipur*. Imphal: Samurou Lakpa Mayai Lambi Law College.

Singh, Rajkumar Manisana. 2000. *A Short Constitutional History of Manipur (1891–1972)*. Imphal: Usha Devi.

Singh, Y. Mohendro. 2009. *The Status of Manipur (1823–1947)*. Yumnam Leikai, Imphal. Published By Yumnam Indira Devi.

12

CHRISTIAN MISSIONARIES AND COLONIALISM IN THE HILLS OF MANIPUR

Lianboi Vaiphei

Contrary to the chronology of colonial events in other parts of India, in the case of Manipur, Christian missionaries came prior to the establishment of colonialism. In fact, they can be regarded as the forbearers or agents of colonialism. The coming of the Christian missionaries not only influenced native cultures in the hills but also was responsible for creating the perception of identity associated with territory. However, the natives of the hills made a clear distinction between the proselytising efforts of the Christian missionaries and the political aspect of British colonialism. These distinctions, in fact, shaped the responses of the hill natives against the two seemingly different entities and thereby brought about a distinct discourse on colonial history in the hills of Manipur. In the light of the above understanding, this chapter seeks to study not on what has led to the interface of the traditional cultures with the coming of the Christian missionaries but rather to make an attempt to analyse the different responses of cultures with the political agent of colonialism and its consequent influences in the making of contemporary Manipur.

Natives of the hills of Manipur

The topography of Manipur is such that the hills surround the valley. The hills are a part of the Eastern Himalayas and the Chin Hills of Myanmar in South East Asia. This explains why the hills of Manipur are an extension of the hills of Assam but overlap with the neighbouring Chin Hills of Myanmar in the east. The hills occupy 90 per cent of the total land area of present-day Manipur (Singh 1997: 15). The hills are the abode of several different communities having different dialects, customs and worldviews.

The similarities of the different ethnic communities are not as smooth-flowing as the terrain of the hills. They do not have any similarities or striking closeness with their immediate neighbours, yet share close characteristics with people of the Far East. For example, the communities living in the southern parts of Manipur share close characteristics with those ethnic communities living in the Chin Hills. At present, the Government of Manipur has recognised 33 ethnic communities, under the list of Scheduled Castes and Tribes, which reside within the political boundary of the state.[1]

During the British colonial administration, different ethnic communities were classified under two main generic groups, namely, the Nagas and the Kuki-Chins. Both the terms, 'Kuki' and 'Naga', have interesting elements of similarities as they belong to the same racial family (Mongoloid) and speak dialects that come under the Sino-Tibetan family of languages. While the term 'Naga' has been propagated and internalised and has been constituted in the identity formation, the term 'Kuki' as a generic term is infringed with contentions as well as contested for being legitimised as an identity.

The reason why the generic term 'Kuki' could not be internalised requires an understanding of the different communities of tribes that have been clubbed and classified as Kuki. 'Kuki' is not a self-proclaimed term but rather one that has been exogenously used by the British for the purpose of governmentality. Tribes such as Aimol, Anal, Chiru, Chothe, Kom, and Purum, which share many cultural affinities, traits and norms with the other ethnic communities, were classified as Kukis by British ethnographers (Hodson 1984). However, of late, they have been absorbed within the political identity of the Naga. Besides, there are also certain contentions among some ethnic communities to retain their unique identity rather than being clubbed with a conglomeration of ethnic communities.

Contemporary identity formation in the hills of Manipur remains contentious and political and there is always a strong undercurrent of the colonial legacy wherein colonial ethnographies are taken as sources of authenticity. The terms Naga and Kuki are fluid identities propagated to serve one's political goal and can be taken to be relative as well as dynamic as cultural affiliations undergo changes as dictated by the exigency of time. However, one cannot ignore the process of religious socialisation which is responsible for the solidification of distinct identities with not only strong cultural but also political implications. In such contexts, discussion of the role played by Christian missionaries carries weight especially in the context of hill communities of Manipur.

182

Call of the 'Christ': civilising mission of the Christian missionaries

In order to implement imperialistic designs, the British masqueraded as the benevolent civiliser, and used Christian missionaries – who were to spread the 'good word' – among the unsuspecting natives. Such a policy was followed in the case of the North East Frontier of Bengal, especially in the hill areas. It provided a convenient justification for carrying out the 'white man's burden', the defining characteristic of British colonialism. In addition to the ideological justification of the white's man burden, it also legitimised the British Empire as they were on a civilizing mission to civilise the savages who led barbaric lifestyles. 'Savages' was a clichéd term that the British coloniser used to describe the natives whom they wanted to colonise. In fact, the very concept of savage is a creation of the West, which is in binary opposition to how they viewed themselves. As Edward Said puts it, for the British, the Oriental or the natives belonged to 'a much inferior world, a place of backwardness, irrationality, and wildness' and were, therefore, characterised as being emotional and static, as opposed to the West – the principled, Occident, therefore, lived in a superior world that was progressive, rational and civil. In such a definition of the 'self' vis-à-vis the other, the British justified their civilising mission as the white man's burden, and rationalised their 'destiny to rule' over the others – the savages and the barbarians (Said 1995). Within this understanding, the hill natives of the North East Frontier of Bengal living in the societies of the remote hills as a village republic based on kinship and clan who practised head-hunting, but who, nevertheless, were fierce lovers of freedom and independence, were termed as savages.

The coming of the Christian missionaries in the hills of Manipur is closely related with the political happenings in the south adjoining the Lushai Hills. The Battle of Plassey, 1757, saw the British colonial rulers extending their empire beyond Bengal to the plains of Assam, into the North East Frontier Region. The eastern border of the British Empire stretched to present-day Silchar, located on the foothills of the Lushai Hills adjacent to Manipur. The Lushais used to assert political hegemony by raiding any neighbouring villages that they perceived as a threat. Incidentally, the Lushais came in contact with the British, who had established their empire in close proximity to the native kingdom. However, the Lushai chiefs were oblivious to such developments. In 1871, after Silchar came under the suzerainty of the British Empire, the Lushais raided the tea gardens in Silchar and were reprimanded by the British with two military expeditions in the Lushai Hills (Ropui 2010). The expedition saw lots of bloodshed and revolt against the Britishers. Eventually, they established forts in various places including Aijal (present-day Aizawl) that eventually was annexed to British India in 1895 (ibid.).

The periodic raids conducted by the Lushais, especially in the tea gardens of Silchar, not only alarmed the British but also were perceived as a challenge to their supremacy. It was felt that the rationale of legitimising their colonial expansion could be achieved by propagating the message of Christ through Christian missionaries (the 'white man's burden'). The Lushais were regarded to be the quintessential 'unevangelised' tribes who were in need of salvation from their barbaric practices. Meanwhile, similar ploys were undertaken and the Christian missionaries were given the responsibility to discover different natives – who were isolated from the outside world – in the North East Frontier to preach salvation through Christ. In this way, Christian missionaries were regarded as the pioneers who discovered the natives. In similar fashion, St. John Dalmas discovered the natives in Assam and beyond Furloug (Moore 1901: 59–60). John Dalmas was a Christian missionary working in Bengal. He was familiar with the different natives and their habitats, which were in the vicinity of Bengal, and reported about those who were bereft of 'salvation'.

Based on such reports, Robert Arthington commissioned 13 missionaries in 1890. Arthington, a self-motivated individual living in Leeds, England, had a strong desire to work among the 'unevangelised' tribes in different parts of the world. He had set up the Arthington's Private Mission from his own fund (being a millionaire himself), a society which was better known as the Arthington Aborigines Mission. Out of the 13 missionaries, three missionaries – William Pettigrew, J. H. Lorraine and F. W. Savidge – were asked to concentrate on the hills of North East India. Pettigrew proceeded to Manipur while Lorraine and Savidge went to the then Lushai Hills (present-day Mizoram) (Dena 1985). Arthington, whose sole interest was sending a mission for Christ, was oblivious to the colonial designs in this part of the world.

Lorraine and Savidge, being whites, were received with suspicion in Aizawl as fellow colonisers had undertaken expeditions there. Gradually, they began to recognise that the missionaries were different. For example, they did not demand that the natives carry them as well as their goods unlike the colonial administrators. Besides, they wanted to live among the natives and had a friendly attitude, which the natives recognised, so much so that they called them *sap riangvaia*, meaning 'the poor whites' (Dena 1985). A friendly relation was thus developed. At first, the missionaries took keen interest in understanding the native culture, sought to letter native alphabets and gradually began preaching the teachings of Christ.

CHRISTIAN MISSIONARIES AND COLONIALISM

The changes that the Christian missionaries brought about echoed throughout the Lushai Hills including the southern hills of Manipur. One of the profound changes was the introduction of Western education and modern medicine. The faith healing, along with the introduction of modern medicine, enhanced penetration of the work of the Christian missionaries into the interiors of the hills and their vicinity as other village chiefs invited them to preach there as well. On the other hand, the introduction of Western education provoked curiosity for learning (to read and write), for example, among the Vaipheis and other natives.

In due course, the three missionaries who were commissioned to work in the North East Frontier struggled to fulfil their missions. Although, the Christian missionaries had first gone to the valley of Manipur, they were forbidden by the then Maharaja. In the hills of Manipur, Pettigrew worked among the Thadou-Kukis and Tangkhul-Nagas in the Sadar Hills and the northern regions of Manipur. The work of Lorraine and Savidge spread across the Lushai Hills to the southern hills and its vicinity in the present-day Churachandpur district of Manipur. The coming of the Christian missionaries had a deep impact among the ethnic communities in the hills than in the rest of Manipur. This religious socialisation changed the worldview of the ethnic communities at large. The all-pervasive change affected the social fabric because the work of the missionaries did not just concentrate on changing the belief system but also other areas of their life.

Christianising the cultures of the natives

Values and norms based on the belief system are major components of the culture of every society. The coming of the Christian missionaries and the acceptance of the Christian faith as a belief system has often led to the common perception that the dominant Western tradition has subjugated the local native cultures and belief systems. Assuming such a proposition will be an oversimplification and it would be like overlooking the forest for the trees. Nevertheless, there has been a conscious attempt to Christianise the cultures as a consequence of accepting the belief system, and this has happened without any friction. A frictionless process in terms of accepting an alien faith has been possible because the Christian missionaries delved into the private domain of the 'self' beyond the public sphere among the ethnic communities of the hills in Manipur.

In order to tame the untamed savages through the message of Christ, Christian missionaries focused on understanding the socio-cultural milieu of the natives. A systematic approach was adopted to read the social psyche of these savages and efforts were made to study the constituent elements of the native belief system so as to determine the influencing factors of their worldviews. In other words, in order to understand what constitutes the 'untamed' characteristics of the society, the missionaries delved not only into the public realm but also into the private domain of the society, for the understanding was that finding out what constituted the 'self' would reveal their belief system and associated practices that had prevailed in the hills since time immemorial. The traditional belief system of the indigenous society was based on how to quench the deep-seated fear that the people have about the different 'evil spirits'. The fear of these spirits led to a kind of reverence and, therefore, compulsion to worship them through sacrifices of animals and others, acts that are characteristic of animism. The sacrificing of animals would be undertaken by the local traditional priests on behalf of the individual lest the wrath of these spirits be invoked thereby causing misfortune through ill health on individuals or the society at large. Here we find a 'self' deeply entrenched in fear, and whose normal existence hinged upon collective efforts to ward off evil spirits and misfortunes.

A familiar reading of such characteristics induced the Christian missionaries to rely on modern science, such as medicine, and to undertake developmental works to isolate the 'self' from the clutches of orthodoxy in general and counter the ancient belief system. For example, delving in the private domain of the natives demanded they should taste the fruits of development through knowledge of both literature and the medical sciences. The knowledge of medical sciences helped them to understand that diseases were not a manifestation of the spirits' wrath but ailments which could be cured. Besides, the lettering of the local languages brought knowledge within their grasp as they could analyse and reflect on life through the help of literature. Christianity was viewed with curiosity due to the commendable work by the Christian missionaries and this religion was eagerly received by the people in the neighbouring villages.

In the case of the southern hills of Manipur, it was not British colonialism that brought Christianity but rather the local natives themselves who wanted to adopt Christianity. For example, it was the Chief of Senvon Village (in present-day Churachandpur District), Kamkholen Singson, who invited Watkin R. Roberts to share the 'good news', when he had accompanied Dr Peter Fraser to the Lushai Hills. The chief had requested: 'Sir, come yourself, and tell us about this book and your God' (quoted in Dena 1985). Although Roberts was a dispenser and more of a private helper to Dr Fraser rather than a Christian missionary in the true sense of the word, he accepted the invitation and started the mission work in the land offered by the chief of Senvon Village.

Thus, began the works of the Christian missionaries in Manipur. This was soon followed with the establishment of the Indo-Burma Thadou-Kuki Pioneer Mission in 1910, which was later on renamed the North East India General Mission (NEIGM). On the other hand, Pettigrew could establish a pioneering mission in the northern part of Manipur, mainly the Ukhrul district among the Tangkhuls. The NEIGM could initiate an undenominational pioneer mission in the south, after the first three converts, namely, Vanzika, Thangchhingpuia and Sawma, became the mission workers. The new converts helped in penetrating into the neighbouring regions such as North Cachar, Tamu (Myanmar) and Tripura. It was only a matter of time that the Christian missionaries would establish a new Christian community among the ethnic communities throughout the hills of Manipur (Lloyd 1984: 18).

Besides medicines and literature, the Christian missionaries undertook social welfare schemes to uplift the society. For example, vocational education was introduced, which emphasised on teaching weaving skills, needlework and many such activities that would help in contributing towards meeting the cost of education, especially that of the girls. Introduction of vocational education changed the patriarchal society's attitude, taboo and their prejudice against women's education. Inasmuch as a livelihood alternative was given to the women, education also played an important role in restructuring societal norms and outlook, as well as the subordinate status of women in relation to men were also reversed. Therefore, the evangelisation of the natives by the Christian missionaries occurred without much resistance as they did not solely concentrate on religious discourse but infringed into the secular side of the public sphere like education, literary translation and medical science. The fruits of development penetrated into the interiors through the work of the missionaries as they became the interface of the progress that the world had made.

At the same time, Christianisation of the hill natives produced an interesting assimilation and symbiosis of the traditional native culture with Western culture and Christian belief system, which the missionaries propagated. The natives of the hills, hitherto isolated from the outside world, became acquainted with the norms of Western cultures. Modernity made inroads through Western education and gradually brought about changes even in the sphere of stereotyped gender roles. Moreover, traditional status accorded by birth, such as the role of village chieftainship, began to be challenged by the newly educated elite. However, even after Christianisation, the traditional concept of community and group feelings prevalent in each of the ethnic communities became more prominent and defined with one's search for identity.

The concept of identity formation has retained all traditional customs and practices such as the social rituals that are associated with marriage, childbirth and funerals. In fact, many of the pre-Christian traditions have been assimilated into the Christian faith that only a true sociologist can identify the different layers of the traditional customs that are imbedded into the present practices followed as Christian culture. Therefore, contrary to popular perception, the traditional beliefs and value systems of the native ethnic communities have not been fully replaced by the Western cultures that Christianity brought in. Rather, one witnesses a symmetric assimilation of the traditional belief system with that of the Christian faith, perhaps owing to the fact that Christianity as a belief system does not have a culture of its own. The very fact that this system of faith has travelled from its place of origin in Asia to Europe and been adopted across different cultures has shown its adaptability as well as how each of these cultures has assimilated according to the faith. That is the reason why colonial Britain relied upon the Christian missionaries to legitimise colonial administration in colonies around the world.

Response of the natives

The ethnic communities in the hills of Manipur had their first brush with the Christian missionaries and later on with the British colonial rulers. The friendly response that had been accorded by the natives to the missionaries did not assume any legitimacy for colonial rule as had been accepted in Manipur. The hills came under the direct administration of the British in 1891 after the defeat of Manipur in Anglo-Manipuri war. The defeat in the 1891 war led to administrative division of the hills and valley of Manipur. With the assertive colonial intervention at the political realm, there was a simultaneous growth in the preaching of Christianity in Manipur, particularly in the hills.

The situation was exploited by the British who left no stone unturned to impose their economic suzerainty. They spread their administration even to the hills through the introduction of taxes, and each household had to pay an annual tax of Rs 3 to the colonial rulers. This move was resented and strongly opposed by the local natives of the hills, especially the different tribes that come under the generic name of Kuki.

The introduction of the tax system in the hills had far deeper consequences than it was ever imagined. The imposition of tax equalised every household within a common bracket, be it a commoner or the

CHRISTIAN MISSIONARIES AND COLONIALISM

village chief. In other words, the tax system took away the traditional rights enjoyed by the village chief who earlier had the sole authority of taxing the village households. Opposition to this form of taxation led to the Kuki Rebellion of 1917. The Rebellion, also known as the Chassad Rebellion, began in Chassad Village, located in present-day Ukhrul District of Manipur, when its village chief refused to pay the tax imposed on them.

The Kuki Rebellion is also known as Zougaal as it was fought by different ethnic groups, including the Zou, for two long years against the colonial rulers. The Rebellion saw strong resistance from the natives against the white men. The author's grandfather, who was a *lambu* during those days, was called to resolve the conflict. *Lambu*s were the local educated elite who were employed as political intermediaries between the natives and the colonial rulers. The Kuki Rebellion marks an important event as it was an armed resistance, with which the natives of the hills had struggled against British colonialism. It was also the last anti-colonial struggle in Manipur. The colonial agenda of the British rulers riding on the works of Christian missionaries to legitimise their imperial agenda, which had been successfully implemented, did not translate into easy subordination of the natives contrary to popular perceptions and expectations. This was because the hill natives had a strong sense of political independence and resisted any kind of subjugation. Even though they had embraced the works of the Christian missionaries, they continued to defy attempts at submission by the British. Christianisation of the natives did not make penetration by colonial rulers in the hills easier than during the pre-Christian period. Primordial beliefs and values such as respecting the land and people had strong roots in the cultural psyche of the people. Moreover, Christian belief did not in an absolute way dilute the cultural sense of their being and identity even after Christianity had been largely followed by the hill people in Manipur.

Conclusion

Every society responds to alien rule in different ways. In the case of the hills in Manipur, imperial British used Christian missionaries to legitimise their rule. However, popular perceptions that Christianisation would make the local natives more hospitable to the colonial rulers were proved wrong as evident in the Chassad Rebellion. Christian missionaries absorbed the prevalent social and cultural practices of the natives and helped evolve an amalgamation of local pre-Christian cultures with Christian values. However, Western education that was introduced later on by the Christian missionaries became an instrument of consciousness among the converts. For instance, it made them more alert and aware about the need to assert their identities in a new pattern. Nevertheless, it would be wrong to single out this factor as solely responsible for creating a strong sense of political independence. The sense of political autonomy as often seen to be flagged off by the Christian communities as distinct group has its origin in their ascribed sense of identity since time immemorial. The idea of being distinct also comes from the fact that there had been numerous people's resistances against colonial politics in the past. The influence of the Christian missionaries has only been internalised in terms of constituting an identity that is largely politicised, for example, that of a Christian identity.

Note

1 As per the list of Scheduled Castes and Scheduled Tribes Lists (Modification) Order, 1956, Part X–Manipur, published by the Government of India, the recognised tribes include: Aimol, Anal, Angami, Chiru, Chothe, Gangte, Hmar, Kabui, Kacha Naga, Koirao, Koireng, Kom, Lamkang, Lushai, Mao, Maram, Maring, Monsang, Moyon, Paite, Purum, Ralte, Sema, Simte, Salhte, Tangkhul, Thadou, Vaiphei, Zou, Poumai, Tarao, Kharam and any Kuki tribes.

References

Dena, Lal. 1985. *Colonialism and Christianity.* New Delhi: Mittal Publications.

Hodson, T. C. 1984 [1911].*The Naga Tribes of Manipur.* Delhi: Low Price Publications.

Lloyd, J. Merion. 1984. *On Every High Hill.* Aizawl: Synod Publication Board.

Moore, P. H. 1901. *20 Years in Assam or Less from My Journal.* Calcutta.

Ropui, Thukna. 2010. 'Impact of the Missionaries in the Mizo Life', *Amazing Deep: The Gospel Centenary in South West Manipur, 1910–2010.* Delhi: Hmar Christian Fellowship.

Said, Edward W. 1995 [1978]. *Orientalism: Western Conceptions of the Orient.* London: Penguin.

Singh, A. K. Sunder Kumar. 1997. 'Distribution Pattern of Population in Manipur: A Geographical Analysis', *Journal of Geographical Society of Manipur,* 1(1): 15–30.

Part IV

POST-EMPIRE MANIPUR, ORGANISATIONAL POLITICS, AND FRONTIER

13

ORGANISATIONAL POLITICS IN 20TH-CENTURY MANIPUR

Trajectories and footprints

Arambam Noni

The first half of the 20th century in Manipur is significant as it was characterised by various socio-economic and political developments. The period witnessed the alteration of political status of Manipur and reconfiguration of power relation along with the consolidation of British imperialism. The major fallout on civil life was the sophistication of a mixed sphere of influence created by feudalism and imperial administrative arrangements. The British adopted a more strategic approach in colonising Manipur and it kept the State (Manipur) under its suzerainty and did not opt for complete annexation. The strategic ways of effecting political hegemony produced acute hardship for the dispossessed class which prompted simultaneous response in the form of people's defiance. The political articulation of an autonomous Manipuri identity had gained its prominence particularly among the ruling elites. The initial decades of the 20th century were largely characterised by bitter memories of the Anglo-Manipuri War of 1891. The retributive feeling amongst the populace against the alien regime was further aggravated with the spread of cholera, small pox etc. In addition, the economic condition of Manipur began to witness crisis of a very modern kind in the wake of extensive economic exploitation of local daily subsistence commodities. The increase in the export of rice became evident with the British India's 1920 notification to remove restrictions on interprovincial movement of rice. The poor peasants began to lose their basic livelihood as they were dispossessed of their agricultural products leading to severe impoverishment. On the other hand, the British regime introduced several exploitative tax regimes in Manipur. The taxation designs reflected the empire's connivance with the 'native' feudal elements as it seemed to have barely affected the interest of the ruling class.

193

The history of colonial exploitations and its administrative arrangements had strong impact on the popular history of Manipur. A discussion on the history of contemporary people's movement and the rise of organisational politics in Manipur can be done in the light of growing complexes of political dynamics in Manipur. The chapter attempts to discuss the colonial history and movement for democratisation in Manipur, particularly with reference to the first half of the 20th century. Under the garb of imperial self-proclaimed civilising mission and imageries of individualism as something inherited from the European Enlightenment tradition, the British regime had rather produced complexes of colonial subjectivity in the form of anti-people tax regimes and myriad other policies that suited the interest of the regime. Some of the important tax strictures include *chandan senkhai, wakhei shel, yairek sentry*, and codes of *mangba–sengba*, etc. The abolition of lallup was only to be replaced by more rigorous taxation systems such as housing tax both in the hills and the valley. Under the dual authority of the British and titular king, the public had to shoulder various atrocious taxation on road, forest, water, and even on ritual practices and entertainment.

Reflective of colonial manipulation, the proverbial 'divide and rule' policy began to ethnicise Manipur when the hills and valley were subjected to separate administrative arrangements. The imperial policies and its coercions were in turn aggravating a ground for mass politics and assertion as a result of which led to the emergence of organisational politics in Manipur. An interesting feature of Manipuri social thinking towards the third decade of the 20th century was the emergence of a class with formal acquaintances with English education. The English literate class started to dominate the modern Manipuri social awakening. The period between 1920 and 1930 is largely overdriven by literary movements and predominantly liberal intellectual positioning. The period characterised a growing blending of political awakening and mass resentment, which subsequently led to the emergence of political organisations and demand for the democratisation of Manipur. This chapter discusses the emergence of political organisations, quest for democracy, anti-colonial assertion, and complexes associated with Manipur's controversial integration with the Indian union.

The making of a common history

The people's movement in the early 20th century was not guided by any organised or established party. The strength of the resistance was provided by a highly aggrieved populace. The first *Nupi Lan* of 1904 is a case in point; it was the assertion of the people against the resuscitation of lallup, albeit in different form and context, and colonial exploitation. The system of lallup, which prevailed in Manipur, was acknowledged by the authorities themselves to be radically bad but without any credible commitment to extinguish such a system permanently or be threatened by it. One of the primary reasons for the delay in abolition of the system was that officials attached to the lallup would be deprived of their perquisites. The system was only a modified form of slavery system, as under its operation none of the inhabitants were free to go where they chose in the valley, and were utterly prohibited from leaving it without a pass from the authorities. Lallup was theoretically labour for a fixed number of days a month, which generally was mandatory whenever the labourers were needed by the regime. The gravity of the issue was such that the then Maharaja Chandra Kirti had ordered that slaves should remain the property of their owners under all circumstances (Singh 2006: 13–15). The following years after the first *Nupi Lan* began to witness people's resistance in various forms. The Thoubal resistance of 1909 against oppressive labour systems, the Kuki Rebellion of 1917 against colonial imposition and several other resistances defined Manipur's occupied history. The resistances challenged the oppressive systems, including that of the Empire. The pothang system, which dictated free labour from the masses in the name of providing logistic support to the royal family and the imperialists, and for public purposes like road repairing, construction of river embankments, etc., became the cause of strong mass uprising. The villagers of Thoubal refused to comply with the orders of the State Darbar that dictated the villagers to repair a local school. The Darbar enforced a fine of Rs 10 in case of non-compliance, which the villagers resolved to defy. Responding to the popular movements, the state Darbar had shown its interest to protect the interest of the Rajkumars, Brahmins, security officials and religious heads. The move was widely criticised as 'class legislation'. The British regime and Monarchy worked together to put into effect an exploitative class regime. In the case of lallup and pothang systems, the higher echelons and royal families were generally exempted and given preferential treatment at the cost of mass hardships.

In the aftermath of the first *Nupi Lan*, there were multiple social and economic upheavals in Manipur due to the increasing agrarian complications. The British regime encouraged the export of rice from the State, which created a shortage of food grains. In addition, the taxation system of the British Empire included prohibitory dictates to deprive people from using forest products, fines for cattle trespasses, cycle tax, road tax, vehicle tax, hunting norms, water tax, fishing tax etc. The exploitative policies had alienated the common people and gradually led to general discontentment. The fragments and legacies of people's resistances to the colonial administration gradually evolved into the making of organisational politics and subsequent demand for democratisation in Manipur.

Organisational politics and quest for democracy

The advent of colonialism began to bring home new contours of social formation. A newly educated class was beginning to emerge as the imperialist and the missionaries were in need of clerical employees and theologically informed natives. Loosely locating itself beyond what the imperialist had planned, the educated class began to intervene and pose perspectives on the conditions confronting Manipuri society. The imperial design to produce clerical staff for colonial administration and missionary works could not entirely limit the growing interventionist concerns among the emerging educated class of people in Manipur. The social background of the emerging literate class was mainly urban middle class. Increasingly, they began to comment on the Empire's subjects and feudal oppressions. The period also coincided with a strong movement to reclaim Manipuri literary heritage and culture. The period 1920–1930s witnessed the emergence of several news agencies and literary productions. The period was marked by the establishment of important print media houses such as *Yakairol, Lalit Manjiri Patrika, Deinik Manipur Patrika, Manipur Matam,* etc. An important dynamics of the newly emerging literate class was that it was not fully able to operate beyond the ambit of colonial and palatial scheme of things as their education was largely supported by the palace. The collaborative tendency between the emerging social class and the palace was well reflected when the Monarch had enjoyed extensive say over the political developments in Manipur, particularly in the social and cultural realm.

In 1934, the Nikhil Hindu Manipuri Mahasabha (NHMM) was formed. The outreach of the organisation had been extensive as some of its annual sessions were organised in Cachar and Mandalay of Burma. Manipuri participant members from Dacca, Tripura and Assam had extensively conveyed their concern and solidarity. The initial responses came mainly from the educated urban middle class, government employees and community representatives. The first conference was presided over by Maharaja Churachand Singh. The maiden session dealt with the socioeconomic problems in Manipur. The initial years of the NHMM had no actual scope for critical questioning of the feudal, imperial and monarchic practices, perhaps for the reason that the leadership was dominated by state

ORGANISATIONAL POLITICS IN MANIPUR

officials. Thus, the initial years of NHMM activity remained confined to the field of education, cultural interface, language preservation, reclaiming Hinduism, and consolidation of Manipuri ethno-identity. In other words, religion and State continued to work hand in hand, which means colonialism was also actually not rejected in its entirety. It was so perhaps due to the nature of organisational composition and royal influences. Initially, the NHMM appreciated the British contribution of English education. The Maharaja at several occasions called upon the participants to be optimistic about the British Government.

Towards the fourth session of the Mahasabha, politics in Manipur started to take a radical turn as the question of establishing a Legislative Council was placed before the Monarch. This period also coincided with the heightening of Brahminical exploitations such as outcasting of people who failed to live up to the expectations of casteism. The emergence of Hijam Irabot can be located in the context of severing ties between the people and the Monarch. Irabot threw up critical debates on the issue of colonisation of Manipur and feudal practices. Irabot began to question the use of imported clothes and salt. Irabot explicated the extensive export of local food grains as the main source of Manipur's poverty and economic complexes. In the early 1930s, Manipur was reported to have exported only two items against 21 items of import (Irabot 1993: 1432–35). A response to the economic and political practices of British India was beginning to take firmer root among the literate class and directly affected the population. The Chinga session of 1938 resolved to defy the Monarchy and went on to drop the word 'Hindu' from its name. One of the important reasons that necessitated the dropping of the word was the scandalous attitude of the Brahmins of imposing fines and hardships on the people in the name of mangba–sengba. A significant dimension of the Chinga session was the widening worldview of the Mahasabha to become an inclusive platform. The Mahasabha with its inclusive worldview can be said to have attempted to redefine and reconstitute the idea of a broader Manipuri identity that was to become a ground for the future imagination of Manipuri peoplehood. The Monarchy having sensed the emerging radicalism of the Mahasabha opted for stronger surveillance on the activists. The dropping of the word 'Hindu' testified to the onset of a new trajectory in the politics of Manipur. The influence of the Monarchy almost came to an end.

Hijam Irabot provided a strong leadership to the emerging current of organisational movements. Under his leadership, the organisation gradually began to succeed in politicising available popular discontent. The charismatic Irabot drew the interest of several organisations such as the Mahila

Sanmelani, Praja Sanmelani and Chhatra Federation. The Chhatra Federation is recorded to have demanded for the installation of responsible Government, sufficient supply of basic consumption items – kerosene, paper, textbooks, and reduction of school fees. In this way, there was a growing contestation between the British suzerain and organisations in Manipur along with a growing demand for responsible government. As a result, the colonial agents and Monarchy began to acknowledge the need for reforms in the state. The reforms were carried out through the abolition of all grants for religious prayers, abolition of temple allowances and Monarch's allowances, and slashing down of palace staff (Singh 1998: 135). The historical Chinga session was followed by another significant sociopolitical movement, popularly remembered as the second *Nupi Lan*.

The *Nupi Lan* of 12 December 1939 laid a successful legacy of people's struggle against colonialism while hailing the democratic concerns and freedom of the oppressed (Dena 2008: 110). The significance also lies with the fact that women led the movement for which it is fondly remembered as Women's War. The women of Manipur also received strong support primarily from the peasantry and urban middle class including the Mahasabha. Against the backdrop of the 1939 resistance, the concern for democracy and demand for instituting a responsible government through adult franchise had become clear. Interestingly, the period also witnessed widening worldview of the people's movement in Manipur, which went on to express solidarity for people's movements elsewhere particularly in the post–World War II period. On 20 May 1947, the Manipur Praja Sangha (MPS) and the Chhatra Federation jointly organised the '"Sheikh Abdullah Divas Pallan" which vehemently criticized the repressive policies of the Dogra King in Kashmir' (Singh 1998: 203). The immediate years after the Second World War can be described as an intensified phase in the history of political parties in Manipur. The parties had a distinctive class support base and operational strongholds. The Manipur Krishak Sabha (MKS) was predominantly rural based, whereas the MPS is perceived to be an urban counterpart of the former and the Manipur State Congress which was mainly constituted by the urban elites. Politics in Manipur during this period was polarised on the two strands of ideology visualised by the MKS and MPS on the one hand, and the MSC on the other. The binary in the political ideological formation was to remain a strong reason for contestation in the history of democratic movements in Manipur.

The political turmoil in the state was reflective of the political changes taking place across the British Indian Empire due to the impending British departure. The enormous changes brought about by the Second

ORGANISATIONAL POLITICS IN MANIPUR

World War necessitated a radical socio-political programme in Manipur particularly under the leadership of Hijam Irabot. In Manipur, Irabot tried to galvanise the masses by reorganising the mass fronts such as the Mahila Sanmelani, Praja Sanmelani, Praja Mandal, Krishi Sanmelani, as well as students. The political positioning on ideological basis became stronger with the emergence of a communist dimension in Manipuri politics. The parties with socialist leanings were linked with Irabot. The Krishak Sabha and the Praja Sangha represented the social axis in Manipur. Their political perspectives were non-elitist and supported the cause of the poor. Irabot finally joined the Communist party of India in 1943 when he was fully acquainted with communist ideology in Sylhet jail. His communist politics finally made him an outlawed underground from the colonial juridical point of view. Irabot dreamt of a peasant revolution in the South East Asian region.

The activities of the political organisations had increased tremendously. In April 1946, a joint meeting of the Nikhil Manipuri Mahasabha and Praja Mandal was held at Wangkhei. The meeting made certain important political resolutions. It resolved to protest against Prof. Coupland's plan of forming an independent North-Eastern Frontier Province. It was argued that the proposal was an act of continuation of imperialism and pleaded to make Manipur a free nation within a free India. The Krishi Sanmelani, which later on became the Krishak Sabha, began to play a crucial role in the history of Manipur people's struggle for socio-economic and constitutional changes between 1946 and 1952. The second conference of the Krishi Sanmelani, which was held at Nambol on 16 May 1946, unanimously elected Irabot as its president. The significance of the conference was that it demanded installation of a full responsible government in Manipur, including the setting up of Panchayats at the local level, etc. (Singh 2006: 179).

In a significant development, the leaders of both the Praja Mandal and the Praja Sanmelani held a joint meeting on 21 August 1946 and floated the Praja Sangha by merging the two organisations. R. K. Bhubansana and Irabot were made the president and the general secretary, respectively. The first general body meeting of the Praja Sangha held on 1 September 1946 resolved to support the popular demands of the various organisations for a quick installation of a responsible government in Manipur. The meeting also decided to urge for the formation of a committee representing different organisations in the state for ascertaining the views of the people on the nature and type of a 'Legislative Assembly' that they wanted for Manipur. The growing strength of the Praja Sangha and the Krishak Sabha alarmed the elite leaders of

199

the Mahasabha who were determined to outwit the two organisations in the struggle for power.

Due to the evident ideological differences, there were attempts to isolate Irabot from the political landscape of Manipur. The tussle became distinctive when pro-Mahasabha students initiated to explore the feasibility of forming a united party to enhance the struggle for democracy in Manipur on 4 October 1946. The October conference decided to form a single party by merging all the organisations and appointed three representatives each from the Mahasabha and the Praja Sangha, two from the Krishak Sabha, two from the organisers of the conference, and five from the general public to constitute the working committee of the new organisation. Not surprisingly, when the Praja Sangha and the Krishak Sabha selected Irabot as one of their representatives, a section of delegates of the conference arbitrarily rejected him on the ground of his association with the communist movement in the region. Sensing the undemocratic nature and duplicity of the conference, the representatives of the two organisations, excepting R. K. Bhubansana of the Praja Sangha, walked out of the conference. The remaining members including Bhubansana formed the Manipur State Congress (MSC) with Bhubansana and Khoimacha appointed as president and the secretary respectively. The stage was set for intense struggle for capturing political power in Manipur.

The formation of the MSC through political machination 'set in trend a culture of grasping for power and personal aggrandizement, through cynical and undemocratic manipulation, which has bedevilled Manipuri politics ever since' (Parrat 2005: 96). The history of 20th-century political organisations reflect a phase of ideological contestation on the questions of democracy, departure of colonial regime, relations with India and proportionality of community representation, etc. The debate and differences can be argued as the reflection of the ideological dynamics that was inherent in the making and unmaking of Manipur.

Representation, democracy and complexes

The impending departure of the British had heightened the demand for responsible government. Almost succumbing to the growing popular movement, on 12 December 1946, the Maharaja of Manipur issued an order for setting up a Constitution-making committee with F. F. Pearson, president of the Manipur State Darbar (PMSD), as its chairman. The Committee was to consist of: three Durbar members including the PMSD; one member from the Judicial Department; one nominee of the king; one representative to be deputed by each of the five tehsils in the

ORGANISATIONAL POLITICS IN MANIPUR

valley; one representative to be deputed by each of the five hill areas, particularly Ukhrul, Mao, Tamenglong, and Churachandpur. The composition of the Committee was meticulously arranged to serve the interests of both the hills and valley. For the best predictable reasons, the interest of the palace was to be ensured in any case. Sensing the manipulative designs of the Monarch, the Praja Sangha registered their voice against the ambiguous proceedings of constitutional committee. On 12 January 1947, a public meeting was held under the leadership of the Sangha, which resolved to demand a constitutional committee duly elected on the basis of universal franchise with sufficient democratic participation from the hills and valley. The Government did not acknowledge the resistance and went on to conduct the elections to constitute the constitutional committee which was boycotted by the Praja Sangha and the Krishak Sabha. The members of the MSC dominated the committee and were in the good books of the Maharaja. As for the Hills, the PMSD nominated five members, viz., i) A. Daiho, ii) R. Suisa, iii) Teba Kilong, iv) T. C. Tiankham, and v) Thangopao Kipgen, as members of the committee. Finally, a 16-member committee including five nominees from the Durbar with a nominee of the Monarch was formally inaugurated on 3 March 1947. The king and the MSC largely influenced the constitutional development in Manipur. Due to the conspiring collusion of the British and the Congress Party, the institution of the interim government was considered to be not in actual favour of the popular demand which included the demand for compulsory primary education, reduction of school fees, lands to peasants, etc. The induction of Darbar members in the new council and institution of the partly elected and partly nominated interim Government ran short of popular expectations.

The Praja Sangha and Krishak Sabha were the two main organisations which were ideologically driven against feudalism and monarchy. Spelling out the reasons for their protest, Irabot exposed the undemocratic process of forming the Constitution Making Committee in his presidential address at the third annual conference of the Praja Sangha held at Khurai from 16 to 17 March 1947. Realising the urgency of the situation, the colonial officials decided to convert the Manipur State Darbar into Manipur State Council on 1 July 1947. On 4 July, F. F. Pearson wrote to the Raja while recommending that the new council was to be headed by a chief minister and representatives from different communities, particularly the Manipuri Muslims and members from the hills. As a result of the continuous pressure on the British officials and the Monarch, Irabot and his associates were assured of proper representation of members from the hills and valley in the proposed interim Government. The task of the Constitution Making Committee was completed in July 1947, two months before the scheduled date of submission. The recommendation of the Committee visualised elections with full adult franchise to a Legislative Assembly, with no required qualification for voting either in terms of land ownership or education. On 23 November 1947, the Government announced its acceptance to introduce the draft constitution consequent upon which there began the preparation for the upcoming election.

The Manipur Constitution Act 1947, in the words of John Parratt, 'was a remarkably enlightened and liberal piece of legislation. . . . It provided, for the first time on the Indian sub-continent, for a legislature to be elected by full adult franchise under a constitutional monarchy' (Parrat 2005: 10). The Constitution (1947) visualised an elected Legislative Assembly having a term of three years. The proposed legislature was to consist of 30 seats for valley areas, 18 seats for the hills and three seats for the Muslim communities. Besides, there was provision for two seats representing education and commerce respectively, which were to be elected by a limited franchise. The plurality reflected in the spirit of the constitution was largely due to the incessant people's movement.

Electioneering and alliances

In the wake of the forthcoming elections in Manipur, and formation of new political parties, attempts to forge alliances and electoral campaigns had increased enormously. The period coincided with the ever increasing penetration of the ideas and practices of the Indian National Congress (INC) as it began to take keen interest in the political activities of the princely states. The penetration of the INC can be seen as a reflection of the then ongoing nationalist campaign for India's freedom. The mainstream Indian nationalists' campaign did not necessarily result in the production of a similar trajectory of freedom movement in Manipur. There was a growing attempt by the Indian nationalists to effect a dominant historiography in the present South Asian region. The increasing interest of the Indian nationalists, particularly led by INC, in the formerly independent kingdom states lacked content and spirit in terms of producing a democratic people's experience. This lack can be explicated in the context of the controversies and contestations that began to unfold once the British departed. In other words, Manipur was hardly a comfortable zone, particularly as it was viewed as a 'border State' by the Indian nationalists and their imagination (Menon 1961: 289).

Amidst the above intricacies of political developments, the political forces began to prepare for the forthcoming elections in Manipur. The

ORGANISATIONAL POLITICS IN MANIPUR

MSC and INC went on to constitute a very similar kind of political articulation. On the other hand, Hijam Irabot, along with M. K. Shimray of Tangkhullong, Lunneh of Kuki National Assembly, Kakhangai of Kabui Association, and some organisations from the valley, tried to form a United Front to fight the election. The plan did not materialise. The Praja Sangha and Krishak Sabha garnered strong support from the valley and hills, which included Tankhulong, Kuki National Assembly, Kabui Association, Khulmi Union and the Mizo Union, and the Meitei Marup and Nongok Apunba Marup from the valley. The alliance produced leaders like Shimray and Irabot. In the meantime, another political party, the Praja Shanti Party (PSP), emerged in the political spectrum of Manipur immediately before the Assembly elections. It was widely believed that Maharaja Bodh Chandra floated the PSP and, not surprisingly, the party was pro-royalist and fiercely anti-Congress and anti-merger (Parrat 2005: 101). From 11 June to 27 July 1948, elections were held for 53 assembly seats, out of which 30 were meant for the valley, 18 for the hills, 3 for the Muslims and 2 for the distinguished professionals. The election produced a hung Assembly as no single party could get absolute or simple majority. In the election, the Krishak Sabha won 6 seats, the Manipur State Congress won 14 seats, the PSP won 12 seats and 18 seats were won by representatives of the hill area of Manipur. The election outcome was a shattering blow to the State Congress' grand design of wresting power in collaboration with the Indian National Congress.

A coalition government led by the PSP which was supported by the Krishak Sabha and the Hill representatives came into existence. Maharaja Bodh Chandra, with M. K. Priyobarta Singh as the chief minister, formally inaugurated the first ever (partially) democratically elected Assembly on 18 October 1948. At the same time, the Government of India appointed Priyobarta Singh as 'Dewan' – formerly Dominion Agent – of Manipur to look after the treaty obligation between Manipur and India. The long quest for democratisation of Manipur was finally seeded only to be lost in the midst? of the 1949 militarism of Indian nationalists, who did not ensure a democratic and consensual option to those who were hitherto unfamiliar and alien to their integrationist imaginations. On 21 September 1949, Manipur was undemocratically merged with India in Shillong; this was officially declared on 15 October 1949 notwithstanding the autonomy of the then elected State Assembly in Manipur. The issues over ManipurIndia 'merger' continue to predominantly cast its shadow over the contemporary political discourses and popular movements.

Conclusion

The history of early 20th-century Manipur encourages historians and social readers for it was a long era of critical movements, women's assertions, gradual emergence of organisational politics and attempts to nurture democratic political traditions in Manipur with the departure of British colonialism. The years 1947 and 1948 signify the making of a new democratic Manipur whereas the forced merger of Manipur with India in 1949 marked the beginning of a new era of complexity. Prior to the 1949 political incident, the political relationship between Manipur and India was characterised by the Instrument of Accession and the Standstill Agreement on 11 August 1947.[1] Under the Instrument of Accession, Defence, External Affairs and Communication were to be looked after by the Government of India. It would be uncritical to conclusively abandon the issues surrounding the nature of India's relationship with Manipur as some writers have narrowly studied the context and content of the Instrument of Accession, the Standstill Agreement and the subsequent coercion in 1949 as a complex academic subject. The existing academic positioning from some quarters on the pre-merger democratic sovereign status of Manipur as 'controversial' is too little and impotent as it fails to capture the narratives and epistemic claims that recollects the same historical junctures as the basis to their ideas of resistance and emancipation.

What can be learnt is that the history is important perhaps not for the numerous events and dates it produces but for the potential implications, legacies and materials of interpretative sources that it leaves behind. Interestingly, when it comes to the issue of reclaiming, it is expected to have its own internal complexes and external coercions.

Note

1 From a legal perspective, the Article 7 of the Instrument of Accession leaves ample ground for future political choices as it reads: 'Nothing in this Instrument shall be deemed to commit me (the Maharaja of Manipur) in any way to acceptance of any future constitution of India or to fetter any discretion to enter into arrangements with Government of India under any such future constitution' (PDM 1995: 4). The Article 8 of the same Instrument, Article 3 of the Standstill Agreement and section 7(b) of the Indian Independence Act, 1947, also carry the same spirit.

References

Dena, Lal. 2008. *British Policy towards Manipur: 1762–1947*. Imphal: Nongeen Publications.

Irabot, Hijam. 1993. 'Meiteigi Maru Oiba Awatpa', *Lalit Manjuri Patrika*, 12, 1 July.

Menon, V. P. 1961. *The Story of the Integration of Indian States*. Madras: Orient Longman.

Parrat, John. 2005. *Wounded Land: Politics and Identity in Modern Manipur*. New Delhi: Mittal Publications.

Peoples' Democratic Movement (PDM). 1995. *Annexation of Manipur 1949*. Imphal: Peoples' Democratic Movement.

Singh, K. M. 2006. *Nupi Lan* (Women's War of Manipur). Imphal: Iboyaima Printers.

Singh, N. Lokendra. 1998. *Unquiet Valley: Society, Economy and Politics in Manipur, 1891–1950*. New Delhi: Mittal Publications.

14

POLEMICS OF THE MANIPUR MERGER AGREEMENT, 1949

Kangujam Sanatomba

> The merger was a political decision forced on Manipur through the Maharaja, by the Government of India to merge into the Dominion of India, in the wake of rising Indian nationalism after India's independence which had echoed in the political life of Manipur during the period.
>
> (Kamei 1995: 94)

Revisiting the historical events that took place in the post-1947 period has become increasingly indispensable for identification of the core issue of the prevailing conflict in Manipur. The chain of events and the circumstances surrounding the signing of the Manipur Merger Agreement at Shillong between the Maharaja of Manipur and the Indian authorities on 21 September 1949 needs to be studied in order to discern the finer nuances underlying the politics of resistance. In fact, the Merger Agreement has become the bone of contention between the insurgent groups of Manipur and the Government of India. For the Government of India, the merger issue is a closed chapter. Likewise, many scholars have also taken the merger issue for granted without subjecting it to any critical study. But major insurgent groups and responsible non-state actors like the Revolutionary People's Front (RPF) and the United National Liberation Front (UNLF) have always cited the Merger Agreement as the root cause of the prevailing conflict in Manipur. In this chapter, therefore, an attempt shall be made to describe the historical trajectories leading to the signing of the Agreement. Besides, the Manipur Merger Agreement, 1949 will be examined to understand the polemics surrounding the merger issue.

The Shillong conspiracy

Even ahead of the transfer of power on 15 August 15 1947, it became quite obvious that the native states would naturally revert to their erstwhile independent status with the lapse of British suzerainty. Paradoxically, the Indian leaders did not entertain the idea of independence of the native states owing chiefly to India's security reason (Singh 2005: 28). The Indian leaders wanted the relations then existing between the British Crown and Manipur to be continued as between Manipur and the Dominion of India. That was why Manipur was made to sign the Standstill Agreement and the Instrument of Accession on 11 August 1947. Moreover, an agreement was reached between the Governor of Assam and the Manipur State Durbar on 1 July 1 1947. Another agreement was also concluded between the Governor of Assam and the Maharaja of Manipur on 2 July 1947. The 1st July Agreement (Singh 2009, Appendix xxviii–xxix) pertained to Manipur joining the Constituent Assembly of India and acceptance of G. S. Guha as the representative of Manipur in the Constituent Assembly. And the 2nd July Agreement (Singh 2009: xxx–xxxi) was concerned with the stationing of the Dominion Agent in Manipur to aid and advise the Manipur administration.

This was necessitated on account of the fact that the political agent would cease to exist from 15 August 1947 and unless an officer of the Indian Dominion was appointed to take the place of the political agent, there would be no relation between Manipur and the Dominion of India. The Dominion Agent was to look after the relations of the Indian Dominion and the Manipur State. He was intended to safeguard the interests of the Government of India with the power to report any matter of importance to the Government of India (Singh 1995: 66). The Governor of Assam as the agent of the Government of India in that area appointed the Dominion Agent who was to have the same power and functions enjoyed by the political agent prior to 15 August 1947.

G. P. Stewart, the then political agent of Manipur, became the first Dominion Agent in Manipur. When he left Manipur in September 1947, Debeswar Sarmah was appointed the Dominion Agent. However, he resigned and quietly left Manipur without even informing the Maharaja. This resulted in the absence of a Dominion Agent or any other Indian officer in Manipur for a brief period. But when Sir Akbar Hydari, the Governor of Assam, came to know of the election held in Manipur and of the new responsible government to be sworn in shortly, he decided to appoint a Dewan to take the place of the Dominion Agent. The Governor of Assam abolished the post of the Dominion Agent with effect from such date as the popular ministry would take office. Akbar Hydari's letter to the Maharaja of Manipur stated that the Dewan was to simply watch the treaty obligations between Manipur and the Indian Dominion (Singh 1988: 90). The Maharaja after initial resistance yielded to the pressure exerted by the Governor and accordingly issued an Order on 29 November 1948 whereby M. K. Priyobrata was appointed to carry on the duties of the Dewan with respect to watching the relation between Manipur and the Dominion Government. Priyobrata also simultaneously held the post of the Chief Minister of Manipur.

Later, on 10 April 1949, the Government of India sent a telegraphic message to Maharaja Bodhchandra intimating him about the appointment of Major General Rawal Amar Singh as the Dewan of Manipur (Singh 1988: 95–96). The letter also stated the powers of the Dewan:

> First, the administration of Manipur shall be carried on under the general superintendence, guidance and control of the Dewan.
>
> Second, the Dewan shall hold direct charge of the portfolios of (*a*) law and order, (*b*) administration of hill tracts, (*c*) state forces, and (*d*) relations with the Government of India.
>
> Third, the distribution of portfolios shall be subject to confirmation by the Dewan.

Accordingly, the Maharaja of Manipur appointed Major General Rawal Amar Singh as the Dewan of Manipur through an Order on 16 April 1949. Amar Singh assumed the charge of Dewanship on 18 April 1949. The appointment of the Dewan was the first direct interference into the internal administration of Manipur by the Dominion of India. It was a political move initiated by the Indian Government that ultimately culminated in the conclusion of the controversial Merger Agreement.

The appointment of the Dewan did not evoke any reaction from any quarter on account of the fact that it was not done within the purview of the Manipur State Constitution Act, 1947. However, the appointment of the Dewan was a glaring example of violating the sovereignty of Manipur. In due course of time, the Dewan came into serious conflict with the Maharaja owing to the former's overwhelming authority in the administrative matters of Manipur. As the conflict got heightened, the Governor of Assam summoned Maharaja Bodhchandra to Shillong on the pretext of discussing for clarification of pending cases and for exchange of views on administrative matters of the state (Singh 1988: 101). In fact, the purpose was to resolve the simmering tension generated due to the excessive power exercised by the Dewan.

Maharaja Bodhchandra along with his associates reached Shillong on 17 September 1949 and put up at the Redland bungalow. The next day, the Maharaja was told to sign the Merger Agreement. Bodhchandra conveyed his inability to sign the Agreement without the consultation of his Council of Ministers. He also stated that being merely a constitutional head, he lacked the authority to enter into such an agreement. He, therefore, requested the Governor to let him return to Manipur to elicit the approval of his government and his people on the matter (Singh 1988: 106–7).

Faced with this dilemma, the Governor sent a telegram to Sardar Vallabhbhai Patel seeking permission to detain Maharaja Bodhchandra by force if necessary at Shillong (Singh 1988: 109). Thereafter, the Maharaja was put under strict surveillances with many CID men swarming the Rajpari area. The strength of the Jat Regiment, which was already stationed in the area since 17 September, was increased from one section to two sections. It was the intention of the Government of India to prevent the Maharaja, forcibly if necessary, from leaving Shillong before signing the Merger Agreement. In fact, the Maharaja was virtually kept under house arrest and subject to intense psychological torture. Ultimately, the Maharaja broke down and signed the merger document on 21 September 1949. On the Indian side, the Agreement was signed by V. P. Menon, Advisor to the Government of India, Ministry of States.

According to the terms of the Manipur Merger Agreement, the Maharaja of Manipur ceded to the Dominion Government full and exclusive authority, jurisdiction and powers for and in relation to the governance of the state (Singh 1988: 328–32). Besides, he also agreed to transfer the administration of the state to the Indian Dominion with effect from 15 October 1949. Consequent upon the signing of the Agreement, the Government of India promulgated the Manipur (Administration) Order, 1949 on 15 October 1949 and took over the state of Manipur. By the said Order, a Chief Commissioner was appointed by the Central Government as the head of administration of Manipur. Moreover, the pre-existing Council of Ministers and the State Assembly of Manipur were dissolved. Rawal Amar Singh was appointed as the Chief Commissioner of Manipur and the entire administration of the state was taken over by him. On 22 January 1950, C. Rajagopalachari, the Governor-General of India, issued an order titled 'The States Merger (Chief Commissioner's Provinces) Order, 1950' whereby each of the states of Manipur, Tripura and Vindhya Pradesh was made the Chief Commissioner's provinces. The Order came into force on 23 January 1950, and since then Manipur was formally integrated into the Indian Union.

Polemics of the Merger Agreement

The Manipur Merger Agreement, 1949, has become one of the most contested historical documents in contemporary Manipur. Many scholars have questioned the validity of the said document on various grounds. In this regard, it is pertinent to mention that the RPF and UNLF consider the Merger Agreement as illegal and unconstitutional. Therefore, it is highly crucial to examine the validity and the legality of the Agreement in light of the Manipur State Constitution Act, 1947, the International Laws and other relevant procedural norms duly recognised by democratic countries across the world.

The first important point of contestation often raised by informed quarters on the Merger Agreement is that the Maharaja was made to sign the Agreement under 'duress' and 'coercion'. This alone constitutes a serious allegation on account of the fact that any agreement or treaty whose conclusion was secured through application of force or threat is rendered invalid as per relevant provision of International Law. For example, Article 52 of the Vienna Convention on the Law of Treaties, 1969 provides:

> A treaty is void if its conclusion has been procured by the threat or use of force in violation of the principles of international law embodied in the charter of the United Nations.
>
> (United Nations 2005: 331)

Various claims point to the fact that the Maharaja was virtually kept under house arrest thereby subjecting him to tremendous psychological pressure. It has been revealed that the Government of Assam dispatched a section of the Jat Regiment (regular army) to the Redland bungalow. Two tents were pitched inside the Rajpari area within which the bungalow was located. The Maharaja and his team were holding up in the Redland bungalow.

The next day, i.e. 18 September 1949, police in plain clothes, most probably CID, followed the Maharaja wherever he went in a vehicle (Singh 1988: 103). The Maharaja refused to sign the Merger Agreement without consulting his Council of Ministers and conveyed his desire to return to Manipur to obtain the approval of the people. Rejecting such a reasonable proposal, Nari Rustomji, Advisor to the Governor of Assam, suggested that the Maharaja might as well finalise the merger issue during that current visit only, and further reminded that the Maharaja might not leave Shillong before signing the Agreement (Singh 1988: 106).

In the afternoon of 18 September 1949, the Governor wrote to the Maharaja that he had received instructions from the Ministry of States that the merger issue must be decided by 20 September 1949 at the latest (Singh 1988: 108). To this, the Maharaja replied that eliciting the opinion of the people in whom the sovereignty had been vested was necessary to render constitutional validity to the proposed line of action (Singh 1988:

109). Realising the futility of his attempt, the Governor sent a telegram to Sardar Patel seeking permission to detain the Maharaja by force at Shillong when the necessity arose. Thereafter, surveillances over the Maharaja got intensified with the CID men swarming the Rajpari area and the strength of the Jat Regiment being increased from one section to two sections. Besides, with all the communication lines remained cut off, the Maharaja was *ipso facto* under house arrest (Singh 1988: 109).

On 19 September 1949, the Maharaja wrote to the Governor that he would return home immediately. Replying to this letter, the Governor informed the Maharaja that very strict instructions were received from the Government of India that the negotiation must be completed before the Maharaja left Shillong. On 20 September 1949, a meeting to finalise the Merger Agreement was held at the Government House, Shillong. In what can be described as sheer display of military strength to intimidate the Maharaja, the entire battalion of the Jat Regiment was paraded within the Government House compound. A number of policemen were also scattered all around the area. In order to render maximum psychological impact on the Maharaja, the presence of the Inspector General of Police, Assam, in full uniform was ensured (Singh 1988: 113).

Ultimately, the Maharaja succumbed to the psychological torture, emotional blackmailing, prolonged detention and military threat. On 21 September 1949, the Maharaja signed the controversial Manipur Merger Agreement, 1949. From the above, it can be concluded that the whole events and circumstances leading to signing of the Agreement exhibited treachery of the worst kind. As the Maharaja vacillated, the case was referred to the States Ministry and the matter was placed before Sardar Patel. When the Governor of Assam expressed his apprehension regarding the Maharaja's reluctance to sign the Agreement, Sardar Patel said something like, 'Isn't there a Brigadier at Shillong?' (Rustomji 1971: 109). If we take into account the entire events and circumstances surrounding the signing of the Merger Agreement as stated earlier, its legality and validity are highly questionable.

The Merger Agreement and the Manipur State Constitution Act, 1947

Another important point of contestation is that the conclusion of the Merger Agreement violated the Manipur State Constitution Act, 1947. Before the signing of the Merger Agreement, Manipur had already adopted a written constitution of its own and a partially democratic government was already functioning. Under the new constitution and the new government, the Maharaja was a mere constitutional head with the real sovereign authority vested in the popular ministry. It is, therefore, significant to examine the power and status of the Maharaja under the Manipur Constitution Act, 1947.

Under Section 3 of the Manipur State Constitution Act, 1947, all rights, authority and jurisdiction which appertained or were incidental to the government of such territories were exercisable by the Maharaja subject to the provision of this Act. Section 8 of the said Act provided the Maharaja's prerogatives, which could not and should not extend to the legitimate interest of the state administration or a civil right sustainable in a court of law was involved. The executive authority of the state had been delegated to and vested in the Council of Ministers as per Section 10 of the said Act. Similarly, according to Section 26, the law making authority in the state was vested in the Maharaja in Council in collaboration with the State Assembly. A minute perusal of the above stated provisions would indicate beyond doubt that the real power was not vested with the Maharaja. Over and above, Section 9(b) of the Manipur State Constitution Act, 1947, would certainly dispel any doubt about the titular status of the Maharaja, which was expressedly stated thus: 'The Maharaja means His Highness, the Maharaja of Manipur, the constitutional head of the state'.

The Merger Agreement assumed the character of an international treaty for the simple fact that Manipur was a sovereign independent state before its integration with India. If Manipur was not an independent political entity, the necessity for concluding the Merger Agreement would not have arisen in the first place. According to Article 1 of the Merger Agreement, the Maharaja of Manipur ceded to the Dominion Government full and exclusive authority, jurisdiction and powers for and in relation to the governance of the state and agreed to transfer the administration of the state to the Dominion Government on 15 October 1949. This agreement was nothing but an accession treaty which envisaged transfer of sovereignty over state territory by owner state to another state through a bilateral agreement. The logic of accession of Manipur to India underscored the reality of Manipur being a sovereign state.

The Merger Agreement was signed by Vapal Pangunni Menon, Advisor to the Government of India on behalf and with the authority of the Governor-General of India, and Maharaja Bodhchandra Singh, the Maharaja of Manipur on behalf of himself, his heirs and successors. In the case of Menon, he was authorised by the Dominion Government to append his signature on the said Agreement and he did it not on his own behalf, but on behalf of the Governor-General of India. However, on the contrary, the Maharaja of Manipur was not authorised by his Council of Ministers to enter into such an agreement. The Maharaja lacked the capacity to enter into such a transaction and sign the Merger Agreement as he was neither an appointed plenipotentiary nor an authorised delegate of the Manipur Government (Khaidem 1995: 179). The Maharaja, without the concurrence of the State Assembly and without the consent of the Council of Ministers, in which the executive authority of the state was delegated and vested under the Manipur Constitution, did not have the authority to conclude the Merger Agreement. Significantly, the king knowingly or unknowingly signed the Merger Agreement on behalf of himself, his heirs and successors only and not on behalf of the people of Manipur or the Popular Ministry. This fact certainly left a room for the people of Manipur to reject or approve of his action, which greatly diminished the binding character of the said Agreement.

Thirdly, there had been numerous procedural lapses, which the Government of India chose to ignore in the process of transacting the Merger Agreement in 1949. For example, the RPF had claimed that the Merger Agreement could be valid only if it was signed by the plenipotentiary of Manipur as a high contracting party with the Indian Government only after fulfilling the following conditions (RPF 1999: 46):

1 Empowerment by the Manipur Cabinet
2 Signature by the Chief Minister (read Prime Minister)
3 Constitutional endorsement
4 Ratification by the National Assembly (read Parliament)
5 Enactment of a municipal law on the accession of the treaty, as it is being done in the Republic of India now or the British Parliament
6 Final endorsement by a popular referendum or a plebiscite in the event of altering the political status of the state

However, none of the above stated conditions was fulfilled in the process of concluding the Merger Agreement, thereby leaving ample scope for raising questions against the Agreement by dissenting groups.

Before 15 October 1949, Manipur was a sovereign country with a written constitution and a partially democratic government. The Manipur State Constitution Act, 1947, which was already in operation at the time of signing of the Merger Agreement, did not envisage anything that enabled or empowered the king or the government to effect accession to another State. In other words, there was no provision in the Constitution of Manipur for entering into a Merger Agreement. Therefore, if such an agreement was to be concluded at all with the Indian Dominion, the Constitution of Manipur required to be amended beforehand.

Constitutional amendment was never carried out in the case of Manipur as a consequence of which the signing of the Merger Agreement by the Maharaja had been rendered *ultra vires*.

Besides, the Manipur Merger Agreement, 1949 entered into between the Maharaja of Manipur and the Dominion Government of India was never ratified either by the Indian Parliament or by the Manipur State Assembly within an appropriate timeframe. As per relevant provision of International Law, a treaty without ratification has no binding on the high contracting parties. In his *International Law: A Treatise* (Volume 1), Oppenheim writes:

> Ratification is the term for the final confirmation given by the parties to an international treaty concluded by their representatives and is commonly used to include the exchange of documents embodying that confirmation. Although a treaty is concluded as soon as the mutual consent is manifest from acts of the duly authorized representatives, its binding force is, as a rule, suspended until ratification is given. The function of ratification is therefore; [*sic*] to make the treaty binding; if it is refused, the treaty falls to the ground in consequence.
>
> (Oppenheim 1905: 903)

In the absence of ratification by both the parties, the Merger Agreement lacked the binding character of a treaty. It was also not approved by the Council of Ministers. As such, integration of Manipur with India on the basis of the said Agreement was devoid of any legal sanction. There was no provision in the merger document that it would become operational once entered even without requiring confirmation by ratification. Failure to ratify the Agreement after conclusion of the same has rendered it operationally invalid.

One of the weaknesses of the Merger Agreement often cited by those who questioned its validity is that the same has never been subject to a plebiscite. It has been a universally accepted democratic norm to ascertain the will and opinion of the people concerned on issues which have far-reaching effect on their political future. A plebiscite is normally held to determine whether a people residing in a specific territory want to remain independent or join another country. Whenever there has been a controversy regarding the question of accession of one state to another such state, the issue can best be settled through the mechanism of a plebiscite, most probably under the supervision of a neutral third party like the United Nations. Likewise, any agreement involving the question of accession could become legally valid only if it has been finally endorsed by the people through a UN-supervised plebiscite. Despite this fact, a plebiscite was never held in the case of Manipur on the issue of its merger with the Dominion of India. This constitutes one of the most serious shortcomings inherent in the process of the merger. It is held in various quarters that the integration of Manipur with India was carried out without free and informed consent and prior consultation of the people of Manipur in whom the sovereignty was vested.

The Central Government of the Indian Dominion should have allowed Maharaja Bodhchandra to return to Manipur to consult his Council of Ministers and obtain the consent of his people. The Maharaja reminded the Indian authorities several times that he alone could not undertake such a transaction without consulting his government and the people in whom sovereignty resided. But the Indian Government rejected the Maharaja's plea and instead literally coerced him into signing the most controversial Agreement in the history of Manipur, thereby setting the stage for one of the most intractable conflicts in the North East. Had the Maharaja been allowed to obtain the consent of his Council of Ministers or his people, the existing controversy centring on the signing of the said Agreement would never have arisen. It was a mistake that the Government of India could have easily avoided.

The Indian Independence Act, 1947, and the merger issue

It is also worthwhile to examine the legality of the various orders issued by the Indian Government in the light of the Indian Independence Act, 1947. As stated earlier, two orders, namely, the Manipur (Administration) Order 1949 and the State's Merger (Chief Commissioner's Provinces) Order, 1950 were issued by M. K. Vellodi, Secretary to the Government of India, Ministry of States, and C. Rajagopalachari, the Governor-General of India, respectively, to consummate the process of integration. Here, the question is whether Vellodi had the power to make an order for dissolving the democratically elected Manipur State Assembly notwithstanding the signing of the Merger Agreement. Similarly, could the Governor-General of India, C. Rajagopalachari, issue the State's Merger (Chief Commissioner's Provinces) Order, 1950, on 22 January 1950? The moot question is: was the Governor-General endowed with the authority to promulgate such an order on the said date?

As per Section 9 of the Indian Independence Act, 1947, it remained the sole prerogative of the Governor-General to make any order. Therefore, the order issued in the name of Vellodi lacked constitutional validity. Besides, the State's Merger (Chief Commissioner's Provinces) Order made by the Governor-General on 22 January 1950 was also legally invalid as per Section 9(5) of the Indian Independence Act, 1947, which envisaged that no order shall be made by the Governor-General under that section after 31 March 1948. Therefore, the order made by the Governor-General of India on 22 January 1950 was well beyond the authority guaranteed to him by the Indian Independence Act, 1947.

Conclusion

From the preceding analysis, it is quite obvious that the Government of India had committed serious procedural lapses in the process of integrating the native state of Manipur. The Manipur Merger Agreement, 1949, was concluded in violation of certain democratic norms and relevant provision of international law. As stated earlier, the agreement was extracted under duress and coercion. The Maharaja did not have the constitutional authority to enter into such an agreement as he was during the moment of the signature merely a titular head of the state as per the provisions of the Manipur State Constitution Act, 1947. The Agreement was, the allegation continues, neither approved by his Council of Ministers nor ratified by the Manipur State Assembly, which had existed prior to the Agreement. A significant aspect of the whole drama of merger was that the nature of the said Agreement was in the form of a 'personal contract' between the Maharaja and the Government of India and, therefore, the Agreement does not reflect any imprint of treaty making between Manipur and India as they were distinct entities. The Maharaja did not sign the Agreement on behalf of the people or the Government of Manipur, but only on behalf of himself, his heirs and his successors. The weakness of the agreement lies also in the fact that the people of Manipur did not give consent in any form to the Merger Agreement as no referendum was held on that issue. Moreover, the dissolution of the democratically elected Manipur State Assembly and subsequent transformation of Manipur into a Chief Commissioner's province were in stark contravention to the provision of the Indian Independence Act, 1947.

As for the Dominion Agent or the Dewan, it was an extra-constitutional body which was appointed extra-judiciously without the free consent of the Manipur Government. There was no provision in the Manipur State Constitution with regard to the appointment of the Dewan; nor was any agreement reached between Manipur Government and the Indian Government to this effect. The 2nd July Agreement of 1947 cannot be cited in this context to justify the appointment of the Dewan for the simple fact that any agreement concluded between Manipur and the British India virtually became inoperative and non-functional after 15 August 1947. Conspicuously, the installation of Dewan did not have any legal basis as it was an act of superimposition of political authority upon Manipur by an alien power.

Serious procedural lapses committed by the Government of India in securing the signing of the Merger Agreement had prepared the ground for the emergence of conflict between India and Manipur. The Government of India should have acknowledged the fact that the Maharaja was a mere constitutional head and allowed him to return to Manipur for securing necessary approval from his Council of Ministers and obtain mandate of the people to initiate the process of merger in a constitutional and democratic manner. If Manipur was merged with India by adopting relevant procedural norms which are legally valid, the prevailing conflict could have been averted. As such, resolution of the current conflict should involve recognition of the lapses that were committed in the process of integration.

References

Kamei, Gangumei. 1995. 'Ethnic Responses to Merger: A Historical Perspective', in People's Democratic Movement, *Annexation of Manipur 1949*. Imphal: People's Democratic Movement.

Mani, Khaidem. 1995. 'The Manipur Merger Agreement & the Manipur State Constitution Act, 1947, Whether the Maharaja of Manipur Could Enter into the Manipur Merger Agreement – Whether Lawful or Not', in People's Democratic Movement, *Annexation of Manipur 1949*, 176–81. Imphal: People's Democratic Movement.

Singh, H. Bhubon. 1988. *The Merger of Manipur*. Imphal: Pritam Haobam.

Singh, Kh. Ibochou. 1995. 'Responsible Government under Manipur State Constitution Act, 1947: Extra Constitutional Powers of the Agent and the Dewan', in People's Democratic Movement, *Annexation of Manipur 1949*, 158–68. Imphal: People's Democratic Movement.

Singh, N. Joykumar. 2005. *Revolutionary Movement in Manipur*. New Delhi: Akansha Publishing House.

Singh, Y. Mohendro. 2009. *Status of Manipur: 1823–1947*. Imphal: Yumnam Indira Devi.

Oppenheim, Lassa. 1912 [1905]. *International Law: A Treatise, Volume 1 (Peace)*. London: Longmans, Green & Co.

Revolutionary People's Front (RPF). 1999. *Memorandum*. Manipur: RPF.

Rustomji, N. K. 1971. *Enchanted Frontiers*. London: Oxford University Press.

United Nations. 2005. 'Vienna Convention on the Law of Treaties, 1969', *Treaty Series* 1155.

15

CENTRALITY OF BODY POLITICS IN THOKACHANBA'S SCRIPT AND CULTURAL REVIVALISM IN MANIPUR

Naorem Malemsanba Meetei

The 20th-century princely state of Manipur witnessed a movement that emerged around reviving the traditional socio-cultural religious practices of *Sanamahism*[1] to reconstruct a new Manipuri identity which I describe as the *Laininghanba Eehou* (revivalist movement). It was started as a response to the Brahmin hegemony, Hindu proselytism of Meeteis and Christian missionary activities during the reign of Maharaja Churachand Singh (1891–1941). Naoriya Phulo formed the first revivalist organisation called *Apokpa Marup* (association of ancestors) on 12 April 1930. He began open defiance of Hinduism, the *Bamon* (Brahmin) hegemony and the institution of the Brahma Sabha. On account of his activities for the revivalism of *Sanamahi* religion and defying the rule of the Maharaja, on the advice of Panditraj Atombabu Sharma, Phulo and his close associates were declared as *mangba* (outcastes) in 1936. Due to the efforts of early revivalists (Nilabir 1991: 117), the Manipur State Meetei Marup (Manipur State Meetei Association) was formed on 14 May 1945 with Takhellambam Bokul and Ngashekpam Manikchand as the president and general secretary, respectively. With the endeavours of Thokachanba, Meetei associations like the Thougal Langal Marup (1954) and the Kangleipak Lamjing Marup (1962), later renamed Kangleipak Lamjing Thoushikon (Association of Pioneers of Kangleipak) in 1966, were formed in order to revive socio-cultural religious practices of the Sanamahi religion, which was associated with the people from time immemorial,[2] and to reconstruct a new Manipuri identity.

218

CENTRALITY OF BODY POLITICS

The Laininghanba Eehou aimed at: reconstructing or reshaping Manipuri identity through reviving the traditional cultural heritage of the people; doing research in ancient Manipur history, Manipuri language, script and other literature; and performing worship and chant of hymns in the mother tongue, i.e. Manipuri language (Kabui 1991:103). To revive the traditional socio-cultural practices, the revivalists generally discovered and produced the *Puya*s (sacred texts), and literatures that deal with various themes such as cosmology, genealogy, philosophy, script, religion, ritual, custom, tradition, religious song, and hymn and even colonial official accounts. Such rediscovering and reproduction of materials to revive the traditional socio-cultural practices could be what Eric Hobsbawm described as invention of tradition (Hobsbawm and Ranger 1983: 1). The movement gave strong emphasis for invention and construction of Meetei identity that was constituted on the basis of traditional socio-cultural practices of the people, which were sanctioned and prescribed by the Sanamahi religion. It was developed around the notion of defending the Sanamahi religion and traditional culture from outside cultural hegemony in the colonial and post-merger Manipur. The movement organised meetings, seminars, published books, circulated pamphlets etc., to renounce Hinduism, to discard all the theories of sanskritisation[3] of the name of 'their' land,[4] deities,[5] mountains,[6] rivers,[7] lakes,[8] etc., which were considered as *Laipham* (sacred worshipping place in accordance to Sanamahi religion) and the sanskritised history of *Kangleipak* (ancient name of Manipur) that linked modern Manipur to the Hindu epic Mahabharata, and described the *Kangleicha* (Manipuri) as descendants of epic hero Arjuna. The sanskritisation process of Vaishnavism, which I would better describe as Hinduisation of the Meeteis, particularly through Meetei Hindu scholars such as Panditraj Atombabu Sharma, L. Iboongohal Singh, R. K. Jhalajit, W. Yumjao, etc., depicted the sanskritised version of Manipur which used the term 'Manipur' while referring to their land, and showed the 'modern' Manipur as Manipur mentioned in the Hindu epic Mahabharata. Panditraj Atombabu Sharma, who was appointed to the Brahma Sabha and made court pandit in the 1930s, attempted to establish Vedic origins for Meetei culture and tradition. Such version of Manipur history also sanskritised the names of the kings of Manipur from *Pakhangba* (33–154 AD) to *Pamheiba* (1709–1748 AD) with *meeyan* (foreigner) originated names. The revivalists rejected the sanskritised version of Manipur history by referring to the *Puyas* because it misinformed the past and led to the systematic distortion of the Manipur 'reality' through fabrication and fraudulence by Meetei Hindu scholars (Chingtamlen 2007: 1). Moreover, the revivalists not only referred

219

to the *Puyas* but also the British colonial account for rejecting the term 'Manipur' to 'their' land and argued that the princely state of Manipur was never called 'Manipur' as late as the 18th century. For instance, they often argued that when the first treaty was signed between the representatives of the king of Manipur and the East India Company in 1762, the British recognised 'modern' Manipur as Meckley.

As a part of desanskritisation, the revivalists even cited the accounts of colonial officials as reference for the rejection of the sanskritized version of history of Manipur. E. W. Dun stated that the statements in support of the idea that the Hindu religion existed in the country (Manipur) at a very ancient period are highly contradictory and unsatisfactory (Dun 1975: 16). The desanskritisation campaigns of the revivalists used both *Puyas* and colonial accounts and claimed dichotomy between the socio-religious practices of the Meeteis and Hinduism so as to highlight the dichotomy between the 'spiritual domains' (Chatterjee 1993: 6) of the 'imagined' (Anderson 1983:16) Manipuri community and Hindu communities of India.

The desanskritisation process of *Laininghanba Eehou* attained new heights, especially in the 1970s, by successfully taking over traditional *lais* such as *Lainingthou Sanamahi, Hiyangthang Lairembi*[9] and *Laiphams* (place of worship) such as *Kongba Maru Laipham,*[10] *Mongba Hangba Umang,*[11] and *Nongpok Ningthou Laipham*[12] from *Bamon* (Brahmin) and emphasised to celebrate the traditional festivals dedicated to their traditional deities.[13] The revivalists' reaction against Hinduism,[14] or more so against the *'Bamon* hegemony'[15] in its spiritual domain, found expressions in matters concerned with re-conversion, popularisation of Meetei language and script, liberation of the Kangla fort and other cultural elements such as rituals, festivals, dress and so on. They invoked community sentiments to re-convert to Sanamahi religion and urged people to renounce[16] Hinduism as it was alleged that people were forcibly converted under the 'infamous' order of King Garibniwas who severely punished those who refused to convert. T. C. Hodson describes that 'religious dissent was treated with the same ruthless severity as meted out to political opponents and whole-sale banishment and execution drove the people into acceptance of the tenets of Hinduism' (Hudson 1984: 95).

Understanding the revivalist movement

In order to understand the movement, we need to understand its historical context. In the first half of the 20th century, Manipur witnessed socio-cultural, political and economic transformation due to the establishment

CENTRALITY OF BODY POLITICS

of British colonial rule and, similarly, in the second half of the 20th century, post-merger Manipur experienced transformation in various spheres. With the corresponding transformation, Manipur also experienced the various responses of the people, such as the first *Nupi Lan* of 1904 against colonial policy of forced labour and collective punishment upon the people; the anti-pothang movement (movement against forced labour) of 1910; the ThadouKuki rebellion of 1917–19 against forced conscription to the labour corps; the Bazaar boycott of 1920; the Zaliangrong movement of the 1930s; the second *Nupi Lan* of 1939–40 against the colonial economic policy and outsider's hegemony; and the sociopolitical awakening movements of the Manipuris under the leadership of Irabot for the establishment of democratic and secular institutions in Manipur. The revivalist movement could not be understood in isolation of these responses of the people but rather it was an integral part of the people's response to the changing situation that started with the establishment of British colonial rule.

My argument is that the *Laininghanba Eehou* and the people's response in the varying ways are part of the organised attempt of constructing 'we-self' or the formation of the 'imagined' Manipuri community in 20th-century Manipur. It was started as a response to the Brahmin hegemony, Hindu proselytism of Meeteis and Christian missionary activities during the reign of Maharaja Churachand (1891–1941) who was patronaged and encouraged by the British colonial rule. The movement started for the construction of 'alternative' imagined community that was free from perpetual subjugation and dominance of the Vaishnavism and hegemony of *Bamon*. In fact right from the beginning the revivalist movement attempted for the realisation of a collective self of the 'imagined' Manipuris and developed a notion that Manipuris were inferiors as they were discarding their traditional religion, culture, language and script. The revivalists advocated in reviving their religion, tradition, culture, language, and script so as to reconstitute a Manipuri identity redefined with distinct visible community markers discovered or invented. The movement though asserts 'collective identity or self through religio-cultural expression is very political and should not be treated as an exclusive affair that has no connection with politics of collective assertions' (Malemnganba 2004: 178). Adrian Hasting has emphasised that the history of religion can never be best understood within a box of its own and that it is particularly true in a society where religion, politics and culture so obviously interacted (Hasting: 1997: 2). My argument is that this was true in the prevailing situation in 20th-century Manipur where there was no distinct marker that separated culture from religion and other moral elements that constitute the markers of community identity. The movement invoked pre-Hinduised past not for the purpose of going back to the past but rather as an initiative with an agenda (Malemnganba 2004: 179). This essence for 'future agenda' is what has been described by Anthony D. Smith as 'to reconstruct out of received motifs a complete national trajectory in which continuity and identity with a distant past were the main characteristics' (Smith 1988: 196). Thus the notion of revivalism is not merely for the revivalism of socio-religious practices of Sanamahism but also linked to the political economy of the 'imagined' Manipur nation, i.e. the enactment of the 'spiritual domain' within the 'material domain' (Chatterjee 1993: 6). In other words the *Laininghanba Eehou* did not merely claim Manipuris' autonomy in the 'spiritual domain' but make use of this domain to perpetuate the cultural consciousness of difference and popularises the Manipuri identity vis-à-vis other identity. It was an attempt for collective assertion of the 'we-self' that culminated into the formation of 'imagined' Manipur community and continues in post-merger Manipur when the Indian state vigorously campaigns for the 'national' Indian culture. In other words, it reflects the integral component of the prevailing forms of identity formation.

My understanding of the revivalist movement as 'response' for the crystallisation of new Manipuri identity to the prevailing circumstances in 20th-century Manipur would be clearer if we analyse the ideology and activities of Thokachanba Meetei. This section focuses on the ideology and activities of Thokachanba Meetei in the crystallisation of Manipuri identity and struggle for an 'imagined' Manipuri nation. In response to the cultural hegemony of the British colonial rule and the Indian state that results in the destruction of local tradition, culture, language, scripts and identity in the name of an 'Indian national culture' he invented the notion of giving centrality to 'human body'. The movement for Manipuri language and *Kanglei* script[17] which are recognised by the Government of Manipur was very much central to the revivalist movement in Manipur. Maharaja Churachand on 15 May 1907 announced Manipuri language as official language of Manipur. In 1924 the University of Calcutta recognised Manipuri language for the matriculation examination (Administrative Report of the Manipur Political Agency, 1927–28). The king of Manipur's memo no. 249 dated 10 July 1931 approved the Manipur Durbar resolution on 20 May 1931 that the communities in the hills should be taught in Manipuri language. When the Manipur State Constitution Act, 1947, was adopted, it recognised Manipuri language and English as official languages of the state (Manipur Constitution Act 1947).

CENTRALITY OF BODY POLITICS

Simultaneously attempts were made to popularise the *Kanglei* scripts (*Meetei Mayek*). In the early 20th century English and Bengali scripts were used officially and thereby the *Kanglei* script was made obsolete. Different committees were formed to popularise and resolve the controversies and dispute relating to the *Kanglei* script. The first state-level conference on *Kanglei* script was held from 13 March 1958 to 15 February 1959 with 17 experts who recommended the *Kanglei* alphabets which read *Kok, Sam, Lai, Mit, Pa, Na, Chil, Til, Khou, Ngou, Thou, Wai, Yang, Huk, Un, Ee, Pham,* and *Atiya* and allied systems of writing to the Manipur government (Report of the Meetei Mayek Expert Committee, 1958).

The second state-level conference on *Kanglei* script was held from 12 February 1969 to 9 September 1969 at Imphal Polo ground by appointing 64 judges by a state-level joint committee which recommended to adopt the original 18 alphabets that were described in the *Wakoklon Thilen Salai Amailon Pukok Puya* produced and interpreted by Thokachanba Meetei and 9 derivatives of it, called *Lom Eeyek,* which were added so as to incorporate additional phonetic sounds present in modern-day *Manipuri* (Report of Meetei Mayek Expert Committee 1969).

The third state-level conference on *Kanglei* script in 1972 was shortly dissolved due to political crisis of the time and the fourth state-level conference on *Kanglei* script or 'Writers' Conference' held on 11 and 12 September 1976 endorsed the 18 alphabets and their allied systems of writing and urged the Government of Manipur to recognise the scripts (Report of Meetei Mayek Expert Committee 1976). Its pressure increased and following the discussion on the matter, the then chief minister Yangmaiso Seiza constituted a state-level expert committee under the nomenclature *Kanglei Eeyek Kanba Phamthou Lup,* which was formed on 16 November 1978 and held 24 sessions of the *Meetei Mayek* Expert Committee from 1 December 1978 to 31 July 1979 and recommended the 18 alphabets and 9 derivatives and other allied supplements (uses of *Lonsum, Cheitap, Cheikhei, Khudam, Cheising,* and original numerical figures) (Report of Meetei Mayek Expert Committee 1978). On 16 April 1980 the Government of Manipur accepted the report submitted by the *Meetei Mayek* Expert Committee[18] and on 19 January 1983 the Education Department of the Government of Manipur prescribed *Meetei Mayek Tamnaba Mapi Lairik* (text for learning Meetei scripts) as textbook for students of class VI. Thus there are continuous and sustained efforts on the part of the people for the popularisation of Manipuri language and *Kanglei* script.

NAOREM MALEMSANBA MEETEI

Centrality of body politics

These series of events just mentioned that raised various issues about Manipuri language and its scripts reflect the importance of the language and scripts in the revivalist movement in Manipur. Such consciousness of the significance of the language and script as an identity marker that symbolises unity in various ethnic communities in the context of Manipur was first started by *Kanglei Eeyek Lamyanba* (pioneer of Meitei scripts) Thokachanba Meetei who wanted to bring change in the outlook of the people towards the socio-culture of Manipur by reviving the traditional culture, language and script. He emphasised the essence of Manipuri language and its scripts as the distinct markers of Manipuri identity. This is what Peter Burke described about 'language as a community identity marker which reflects solidarities and conflicts, continuities and changes' (Burke and Porter 1995). Thokachanba discovered and interpreted *Wakoklon Thilel Salai Amailon Pukok Puya*[19] which deals with the cosmological and metaphysical backgrounds of the origin and phonetics of the *Kanglei* script and allied system of writing. He provided the whole philosophical interpretation of the origin, styles of the scripts and its phoneme. He argued for an organic relation or link between the *Kanglei* script and human body.

The centrality of the 'human body' in Thokachanba's argument provides a better and more complex understanding of the 'human body' in the history of socio-cultural, language and scripts revivalism in Manipur. His argument for the organic relation or link between the *Kanglei* scripts and its allied writing system to the human body essentialised the significance and importance of human body – the body that is to say, of the colonised – as a site of conflict and contest between colonial power and Manipuri identity politics. The responses of the cultural, language and script revivalism of Thokachanba Meetei was not merely signs of cultural essence but rather resonances of colonial and post-colonial encounters or it was part of the dialogue reverberating from certain political encounters. The centrality of the body provides an important illustration of what David Arnold in his analysis of Indian plague (1896–1900) describes as 'complex interplay of coercion, co-operation, resistance and hegemony in the colonial situation' (Arnold 1987: 90). The human body as informed in the west, colonial state was treated as a secular object, not as sacred territory and not as an integral to a wider community (Arnold 1987: 60). Or in other words Jean M. Langford in her study of 'reinvention' of Ayurveda in colonial and post-colonial times and with an argument that Ayurveda is a dialogically strategic sign evoked in political and cultural manoeuvres

224

CENTRALITY OF BODY POLITICS

(Langford 2002: 11) informs that the colonial policy was guided by the formulation of the body and person as isolated, solid and acted on rather than acting (Langford 2002: 12). David Arnold argues that colonial rule aspired to apprehend and exclusive control over the body of its subjects (Arnold 1987: 56). Brian Keith Axel argues colonial domination, perception, experience and governance enlist and transform both visibility and recognition in the dialectical production of an 'us' and 'them' by constituting between the invisibility of the sovereign whose effects were felt on the bodies and the distinctive visibility of the bodies of the colonised (Axel 2001: 41). The exercise of colonial power, thus, touched in many ways upon the issue of the colonised body which were subjected to 'insults and indignities' (Arnold 1987: 65) or could be described as what Brian Keith Axel calls 'enchantment of absolute humiliation' (Axel 2001: 41). And the modern Indian nation-state continues the colonial legacy, which subjected the human body to insult, indignity and humiliation of what Brian Keith Axel described as 'tortured body' (Axel 2001,131).

The body, however, was also profoundly symbolic of a wider and more enduring field of contention between indigenous and colonial perceptions, practices and concerns. Construction of the organic relation between the *Kanglei* scripts and human body by Thokachanba Meetei was generally based on the understanding of the body and person characterised by what Jean M. Langford in her study of 'reinvention' of Ayurveda describes as 'processes and patterns of relationships embedded in a particular cultural matrix' (Langford 2002: 11). It was the result of conceiving of the body as fluid and penetrable engaged in a continuous interchange with the social and natural environment of what Jean M. Langford terms as 'fluent bodies' (Langford 2002: 141). My argument, thus, follows that the centrality of the 'human body' in Thokachanba's construction and reinvention of the scripts was based on different understandings of the body and the issue of appropriating the body differently provides a platform for the contest or resistance.

Joseph S. Alter in his study of wrestler's body, identity and ideology argues how wrestling through the medium of human body provides a forum for social protest against stratification, which due to caste informs, that in order to make sense of a situation a person may interpret the significance of particular symbols in a novel way. And the significance of cultural production and reproduction depends at core to the manipulation and interpretation as the meaning or essence is the derivative of the interpretation and not intrinsic to the symbolic forms (Alter 1997: 21). What is crucial, however, is that the new interpretation is not pure invention but is rather the product of symbolic domination. The forms of ideological protest and counter-interpretation are encoded in the dominant symbols themselves. Domination defines the parameters of protest and interpretation or the dominant culture, so to say, at once produces and limits its own forms of counter-culture (Alter 1997: 22). To apply this argument to the Thokachanba's kind of revivalism one may say that an effective counter-interpretation or contest to the colonial hegemony, Brahma Sabha's concept of 'pure and impure' and Indian state's hegemony was necessarily couched in terms of 'human body'. Alter argues the 'human body' is the subject for the relationship between identity, culture and political anatomy (Alter 1997: 24).

Brian Keith Axel in his study of the Sikh diaspora, identity and the relation between the Sikh body and Sikh homeland informs that the transformation and translation of individuals into representative or representatives and human body like the masculinised body of *amritdhari*[20] for representation of a visible identity or collectivity points at which the politics of identity and homeland meets the politics of the body (Axel 2002: 35). The imagination of the nation as a bounded and discrete entity, mapped into geographic or demographic segments, is epistemically connected to the imagination of the body as a similarly bounded and discrete entity, principally visible through its anatomical structure. This assumption of the colonial and modern nation-state and counter understanding as I have said, however, provides 'human body' as a very powerful site for contest and source for identification. Thokachanba's argument for the organic relation between the *Kanglei* scripts to the human body provides the human body a site for contest and a source for identification of Manipuri and its homeland *Kangleipak*.

He explained that at the *talangmalang*, timeless state or antemundane naught or primordial indeterminate space, *Ama*, one without the second, evolved *Tingpanpa*, cosmos out of 'One' being the ultimate cause of the cosmos. *Ama* manifested as the qualified *Mapu* who was the absolute 'Being' qualified as male and female whole and *Sitapa* is the immortal, omnipresent, omniscient and omnipotent. *Mapu* again manifested as *Mapu's Ting*, absolute power and potentialities, through the astral counterpart of the cosmic body. The 18 heavenly bodies and heavenly phenomenon taken together are the animated seats of the *Ting* to govern the cosmic body. *Ama*, the absolute 'One', takes the astral form of *Thawaimichak Chayom Talep* (Great Bear) at the primordial time of the cosmic evolution. He also described and explained that the 18 seats of *Ama's* manifestation are parallely depicted in the *Taipangpanpa* (World of beings) of which the human body is the animated embodiment of the gigantic cosmos. The 18 seats of *Ama's* manifestation in the human anatomy are the 18 parts,

CENTRALITY OF BODY POLITICS

organs and segments of the human body where the 18 alphabetical figures are winded, contorted, plicated, wreathed and drawn from (Meetei 1961: 1–11). In other words the 18 *Kanglei* scripts and allied systems are incarnations of the *Ama*, the absolute 'One' through the animation in the human body (see Figure 15.1).

Figure 15.1 Taipangpanpa (World of beings)
Source: Meetei 1961.

Kok: The nomenclature of the first *Kanglei* script is *Kok*, meaning 'head'. In the human head the three vertical divisions represent the centres of thinking, feeling and willing and right one representing the forehead, the middle as the midbrain and the left as the hindbrain of occipital lobe. The crossing line running through upper right and lower left, the forehead, midbrain, and hindbrain is termed to be *Meiraching* (Meetei 1961: 13) (peak flame of wisdom), which enlightens the three faculties of mind that is thinking, feeling and willing. The wisdom of men is the gift of this light and human mind experiences spiritual entities at some certain stage of mental growth and development. When animated by divine, human head is called *Wakon* (reservoir of anything) and when depicted for phonological and morphological use the alphabet is called *Kok* (head).

Sam: Second nomenclature of the *Kanglei* script is *Sam* meaning 'hair'. The second animated abode for divine manifestation lies in the nerves of the human body which circulates blood. When thus animate the nerves are called *Singli* (Meetei 1961: 14) and the circulated blood gives soil or fertility to growth of hair over the head. The figure of the letter *Sam* is winded and drawn from the front of the hair commonly dressed.

Lai: Nomenclature *Lai* means 'forehead'. In the manuscript it had been described that the *Taipangpanpamapu* (Universal God) stays in the human forehead and human being lives as long as the God stays in his/her forehead (Meetei 1961: 15). Here within lies the seat of the 'third eye' of men – a spiritual centre of human psyche. The alphabetical figure of *Lai* is taken from the right vies of the lower forehead. The letter faces rightward being the end character indicating the direction to write, i.e. left to right.

Mit: Nomenclature *Mit* means eye. As stated earlier, the left and right ending letters are facing toward the right indicating the direction of writing. Similarly here it is also taken and drawn from the right view of the visual anatomy. The *Mitlis* (visual nerves) run through the *Luwailenphu* (midbrain) as seen in the figure and reach *Upham* (occipital lobe) in the hindbrain where lies at the centre of vision. A cross section is seen in the figure. The wrong-sided images of objects reflected through the eye lenses due to appearances from the opposite side are brought into a normal state at the cross section of the vertical line where visual nerves are crossing each other. In the manuscript 'man' is created in the *Mami* (image), which is reflected in the *Mitnaha* (eyerish) of *Salailel Sitapa* (Universal God) (Meetei 1961: 16). Therefore the nomenclature of the eye when animated for manifestation is *mi* (image) in *Inunglol*[21] and in *Khununglol*[22] it is *Mit*, meaning eye.

228

CENTRALITY OF BODY POLITICS

Pa: Nomenclature *Pa* means 'eyelash'. In *Inunglol* it has been described as *Pi* (tear) and in *Khununglol* as *Pa* (Meetei 1961: 17–8). Figure is taken and drawn from the front view of eyelash as the letter being at the middle.

Na: Nomenclature *Na* means ear. In *Inunglol* it has been described as *Malang nung* (Interior air) and in *Khununglol* it has been described as *Na* (ear) (Meetei 1961: 18–9). The figure is taken and drawn from the right view of an ear.

Chil: Nomenclature *Chil* means mouth. In *Inunglol* it has been described as *Ching* (hill) and in *Khununglol* it is *Chil* (mouth) (Meetei 1961: 19). The figure is taken and drawn from the right view of the mouth.

Til: Nomenclature *Til* means saliva. In *Inunglol* it has been described as *Tillang* (animated saliva secreted in the salivary glands) and in *Khununglol* it is *Til* (saliva) (Meetei 1961: 21). The figure is taken and drawn from the alphabetic form appearance of human mouth while discharging saliva fluid at the tongue tip out of an open human mouth.

Khou: Nomenclature *Khou* means vocal cords. In *Inunglol* it has been described as animated vocal cords and in *Khununglol* it is *Khoutang* (Meetei 1961: 22). The figure is taken and drawn from the right view of the open vocal cords and its trunk, tongue, showing the main articulators in itself.

Ngou: Nomenclature in *Inunglol* is *Ngou*, meaning animated hard palate and in *Khununglol* it is *Ngak* (Meetei 1961: 23). The figure is taken and drawn from the open right view of the open hard palate area.

Thou: Nomenclature in *Inunglol* is *Ithoukhom*, meaning animated breast, and in *Khununglol* it is *Thoupak*, meaning chest supported by ribs (Meetei 1961: 24). The figure is taken from the open front view of the ribs.

Wai: Nomenclature in *Khununglol* is *Wai*, meaning animated soul, and in *Inunglol* it is *Wa* (pure consciousness in which the omniscient Being pervades and reflects). Soul or self is unseen and when it enters the human embryo and foetus, it sets the heart centre beating for the first time and continues till the human existence. Therefore the middle ribs of human anatomy in the chest area point to the first abode of the unseen soul at the heart centre (Meetei 1961: 25–6). The figure is taken from the front view of the human chest area when the face of the man in observation turns rightward.

Yang: Nomenclature *Yang* means spinal column. In *Inunglol* it has been described as *Iyek* (animated spinal cord) through which astral soul passes up and down in governing both body and mind (Meetei 1961: 27–8). This figure is taken from the right view of the neck area where the spinal column starts running down from.

Huk: Nomenclature in *Inunglol* is *Huk*, meaning pelvis bone, and in *Khununglol* it is *Haksang* (main bones supporting the weight of the body)

(Meetei 1961: 29–30). The figure is taken and drawn from the front view of the open left pelvis bone.

Un: Nomenclature in *Inunglol* is *Un* meaning skin and in *Khununglol* it is *Unsa* meaning surface of the skin (Meetei 1961: 30–1). Drawn from the presume sweat gland and its associate serpentine canal up to its pore taken together within the layers of human skin.

Ee: Nomenclature in *Inunglol* is *Ee*, meaning blood, and in *Khununglol*, it is *Eesing*, i.e. purifying blood. Drawn and winded from human heart through which toxic blood returns, runs towards lungs for purification, returns through the left and moves up for circulation (Meetei 1961: 32–3).

Pham: Nomenclature in *Inunglol* is *Pham*, meaning seminal fluid consisting of spermatozoa, and in *Khununglol*, it is *Phampi*, i.e. seminal fluid discharged for purposive use (Meetei 1961: 34–5). The figure is taken from the front view of the lower abdomen area below the naval centre wherein the seminal fluid is secreted.

Atia: Nomenclature in *Khununglol* is *Atia*, meaning space or ether, and in *Inunglol* it is *Ama*, i.e. primordial figure of 'One' that manifests 'Oneself' in the physical counterpart, spermatozoa, which takes the physical form of the astral form of *Ama*. The alphabetical figure of *Atia* is taken from the roomy spaces caused by the presence of womb and bladder in the female body. The human bodies are formed in the roomy space covered by mother's womb (Meetei 1961: 35–6). This is the 18th and the last original *Kanglei* alphabet.

Similarly the Kanglei numerals and *phoon* (zero) and their original figures are coined from the embryonic developments of a human foetus during the period of nine months within a mother's womb and its deliberation in the tenth month leaving the uterus of the mother forming a vacant 'O' or a *phoon* (zero). According to Thokachanba Meetei, *Eepung Loinaba* (the 'One' without a second) takes the astral form of the *Thouwaimichak Apakpa* (North Pole Star) and *Chayol Talep* (Great Bear) taken together at the time of creation of the *Tengpanpa* (Cosmos). The male spermatozoon, again, takes the physical form of the aforesaid astral one at the time of being and entrant within a mother's uterus (*naopipham*) and approaching towards a female egg (*eelik*). When a *Leekla* (spermatozoon) penetrates a female *eelik* (egg) and pierces it, the *leekla* develops into *naowa* (foetus) of the first month of pregnancy. The *naowa* develops itself from the original figure of *Leekla* having its head, body and tail. Therefore the *cheisingeeyek* (numerical figures) represents the pristine form of *Leekla* and thus tells the story of origination of this numerical figure in its embryonic birth. Similarly in the tenth month

CENTRALITY OF BODY POLITICS

of impregnation the *angang* (child) completes its course and it is, as time enforces, liberated from its mother's uterus. When it is delivered the born child leaves its mother's *naoyom* (womb) vacant and apart, forming 'O' or*phoon* (zero) (Meetei 1961: 49–60). This is the very allegory of the birth of the alphabet form 'O' or *phoon* in the history of the Kanglei arithmetic (*cheishinglon*). Thus this plain and vacant circlet called *phoon* (zero) meaning 'fullness' has its own history, cosmology, metaphysics, and science so to say. He explains the whole philosophical concept of evolution of *Cheishinglon* (arithmetic) by linking to the organic evolution of the numerical figures.

Thus, in order to contest or resist the colonial socio-cultural hegemony, Brahmin dominance and monopoly by invoking the concept of *mangba–sengba*, which revolves around the human body in the visible form in the day-to-day life of the people, Thokachanba Meetei makes use of the very human body itself. And he provides the essence of the body to the Manipur identity and national imaging.

The *Kangla* has been considered as the capital of the Manipuri kingdom even since *Nongda Lairen Pakhangba*, the first historical king recorded in the *Cheitharolkumbaba,* came into being in AD 33 (Singh and Singh 1989: 1). When Manipur became independent from the British rule in 1947, Maharaja Bodhachandra celebrated Independence Day by hoisting *Pakhangba's* flag in front of the council hall and with ceremony of ritual in the old *Kangla* capital. In the second half of the 20th century the *Kangla* became an epicentre of political and religious issues amongst the Manipuris. Various rallies were organised, memorandum submitted and pamphlets circulated demanding the removal of the Indian army who were occupying it. The Government of India on 20 November 2004 completely handed over the *Kangla* to the Government of Manipur.

The *Kangla* was connected to the Manipuri consciousness of the 'sovereignty'. Based on legends and *puwaris* (history) popularised by the *puyanic* historiography, Manipuris consider that *Kangla* is the first dry land that emerged from the great deluge and then it became the epicentre for Manipuri civilisation. In other words, it is considered as the cosmic centre of the universe of the land and its people, a centre of the dignity and pride of the Manipuris. Spiritual and temporal liberation were interlinked and many perceived that the Manipuris would never be spiritually and intellectually liberated to become prosperous and progress unless the site was liberated for free access to perform the rites in right rites. In fact, for every auspicious day, people visit the *Kangla* to seek the blessings of the deities there. Thokachanba Meetei produces the *Kanglei Paphal*[23] and provides the organic link between the more than 108 sacred

231

sites inside the *Kangla*, which symbolically represent the spiritual domain to the temporal domain, i.e. the erstwhile sovereign political authority started with the ascendance of *Nongda Lairen Pakhangba* in 33 AD. His endeavours for revelation of issues connecting to *Kangla* and emphasis on *Kangleipak* as the name of 'their' land instead of Manipur revived the sentiment or territorial consciousness of 'their' land, thereby, an attempt was made for the unification and integration of the various communities of Manipur inhabiting in valley and hills, who were created schism, fixture by the colonial forces. In other words his efforts are an integral part of what Sumit Guha has described that the tribes were in fact deeply integrated into the political economy of the state (Guha 1999: 121). And moreover, the annual cycles of the festival and ceremonies such as the annual *Heikru Hitongba* (boat race) festival and annual *Mera Hao Chongba* (gathering of the hill tribes) were organised in or around *Kangla*. Such celebrations continuously nourished and sensitised the *Kangla* issue and perceived the occupation of *Kangla* as a symbol of subjugation. Revivalist interlinked *Kangla* and community identity by establishing a continuity of domination of the Manipuris by the British who destroyed the *Kangla* and continued by the Indian state by stationing its army. The independence in 1947 did not result in the return of *Kangla* to the Manipuris. As the British left, Indian troops moved in. The Defence Ministry of India took over and sent in Assam Rifles. In 1996 an area of 36 acres was handed over to the Manipur government and the state handed over it to the Indian Reserve Battalion, a central paramilitary force[24]. Therefore, people registered their resentment against the perceived state violation of their fundamental right, freedom of the religion and worshipping and charged the government of Manipur as not representing the people of Manipur but serving the interests of New Delhi. The *Kangla* issue thus aroused patriotism and contributed to the production of prejudices against the physical presence of *Mayangs* (outsiders) in Manipur and the construction of the subjugation Manipuri identity. The revivalists establish that liberation of *Kangla* from Indian Army's occupation, i.e. the control of which lay at the root of all political and religious power, would establish the liberation in the spiritual domain and bring unity and integrity in Manipur ('*Kangla* Question' 2005).

Simultaneously Thokachanba Meetei worked for the revival of the traditional cultural practices through his various organisations like *Thougal Langal Marup, Kangleipak Lamjing Thoushikon* etc. As an integral part of his endeavours to reform the internal structure of the society and liberate the spiritual domain from the clutches of Hinduism and *Bamon* hegemony, he critiques the social evils that were perceived associated

CENTRALITY OF BODY POLITICS

with Hinduism. And further to strengthen and revive the traditional cultural practices relating to ritual ceremonies such as *pokpa* (birth), *shiba* (death), *luhongba* (marriage) etc., he elaborately explains the rules and regulations required for chanting of religious hymns in these ceremonies. Thus his language, script and cultural revivalist activities were meant for creating an 'organic' imagined Manipuri community or Manipuri identity. However my understanding is that the revivalists like Thokachanba Meetei in their efforts for opposing Hindu cultural elements and call for replacing by Sanamahi elements necessarily resulted in the invention and reinterpretation of cultural elements in the 20th century. They discovered a Meetei era called Maliyapham Palcha era, the beginning of which is traced in time, i.e. earlier than 1398 BC, and compared it with those of Hindus. Ritual festivals such as *Cheiraoba* were reinterpreted and people were asked to celebrate it differently on a different date from the sanskritised festivals. The application of *tilak* or mark on the forehead was no longer the yellowish *chandan* but mud drawn from the abode of the Sanamahi. Many hymns or ritual songs were composed, new professional cooks are called *puhouba* vis-à-vis Hindu *Bamon chakthongba* (Brahmin cooks), many Meetei brides are wearing *phanek*[25] instead of *potloi*[26] or traditional Hindu marriage costume during marriage ceremony. They choose to replace the suffix title as Meetei instead of 'Singh' in case of man, a *Chanu* or *Leima* instead of *Devi* in case of woman. During the last two decades of the 20th century there were campaigns asking Manipuri woman to wear *Phanek* and *Inaphi* (indigenous upper clothing) instead of *sari, salwar* and other Western dresses, and by the beginning of the 21st century almost all the higher secondary schools and colleges in the valley prescribed *Phaneks* as the uniform for female students.

The revivalism of cultural heritage of Manipuri people, their language and script, worshiping and chanting religious hymns in their mother tongue etc., developed around the notion of defending their religion and culture from the outside cultural hegemony of colonial forces. Since the very operations of the Indian state in the post-merger Manipur destructed the local traditions, culture or identity in the name of 'Indian' national culture, the revivalists do not merely claim their autonomy in the spiritual domain or private domain but make use of this domain to perpetuate the consciousness of difference and popularised the dichotomy of identity politics or depicted a subjugated Manipur within a colonial paradigm. The revivalist movement is in fact an organised assertion in the attempt of the formation of imagined community and identity through the socio-cultural expression.

Notes

1 *Sanamahism* is the traditional religion of the Meeteis and some other communities in Manipur.

2 Interviews with Kangjia, ex-MaichouPurel (Head Scholar and Priest) SKRC, Expert Member of Meetei Mayek Expert Committee Government of Manipur, and daughters of Thokachanba Meetei, Ibemhal and Shilleima on 2 and 3 July 2008.

3 It is the process by which a 'low' Hindu caste or other tribal groups change their custom, ritual, ideology and way of life in the direction of a high and frequently 'twice born' caste (Srinivas 2000).

4 Manipuri called 'their' land as *Poirei Leipak* (land of *Poirei*), *Meetreibak* (land of *Meetei*), *Kangleipak* (land of *Kangla*), *Sanaleibak* (golden land), etc. Naoriya Phulo called *Meeteileibak* (land of Meeteis) and Thokachanba Meetei emphasised *Kangleipak* (land of *Kangla*). And in the last decades of the 20th century many scholars consider *Kangleipak* as more appropriate. But the point is that they might have different opinions but were unanimous in rejecting the term 'Manipur'.

5 Traditional deities were identified as Hindu deities, such as *Pakhangba* as 'Anant' of Hinduism, *Soraren* as Indra, *Marjing* as Kuber, *Wangbrel* as Yamraj, *Eerum ningthou* as Agni, *Nongpokningthou* as Mahadeva, *Khoireephaba* as Baruni, *Loiyarakpa* as Wayudeva, *Panthoibi* the goddess of prosperity and of war became Durga, *Imoinu* became Lakshmi, *Hiyangthang lairembi* was personified as Kamakhya Devi, *Thangjing* as Vishnu and so on.

6 *Heibok* hill became BhageshwarGiri, *Hiyangthang* hill became Shiharachalgiri, *Nongmaijing* hill became Neelkanthagiri, *Koubru* hill became Komarparwat, *Moirang* hill became MahirGangapur and so on.

7 River *Kongba Meirobi* became Ganga, *Nungjing Eeyokkom* became Bindu Shwarawar, *Chinggoiturel* became Baruni Nadi, *Sekmai turel* became Sobhadranadi and so on.

8 *Loktak* lake became Lakshmi Jhil. Thus the indigenous deities, mountains, rivers, and lakes which were considered *laipham* (worshipping place) were sanskritised with the coming of Vaishnavism.

9 On 22 March 1979, Association to Serve *Hiyangthang Ireima* organised to worship the traditional goddess, which was identified by the Hindus as Kamakhya Devi.

10 On 22 March 1979, Executive Committee of *Kongba Maru Laipham* took over the management of the *Laipham*, which had been identified as place of Shiva by Hinduism.

11 On 6 June 1979, Association for Saving *Mongba Hanba Umang* was formed and struggled for controlling the *Laipham* for the worshipping of traditional deity, which had been identified as Hanuman since 1729 during Maharaja Garibniwaz's period.

12 In 1978 the devotees of the traditional religion took over the *Laipham* and resisted the management of the Govind Temple Board. The *Ching Tam Lai Marup* (Association of deities of hills and valley) performed the rituals in the traditional way.

CENTRALITY OF BODY POLITICS

13 *Panthoibi* was identified as Durga and was worshipped for five days in September – October. But since 1960s, there had been an increase in the number of centres for the worshipping of *Pangthoibi* in place of Durga. In many villages and *Leikais* (locality), the place usurped by Durga, had been restored to *Panthoibi*.

14 The history of Brahman migration could be traced from 15th century during the reign of King Kiyaamba (1467–1508). Charairongba (1697–1709) was initiated into 'Nimandi' (corrupt Manipuri word for Nimbarka) in 1703, and Shantidas Gosai, a Brahman, converted King Mayaamba (1709–48) in 1717 into the Ramanandi cult against stiff opposition from the local *Maichou* (Pandits) like Lourembam Khongnangthaba and Moirang Lalhaba but Vaishnavism became a 'state' religion in his time. During Bhagyachandra's (1759–98) rule, the Chaitanyaite Vaishnavism found its supreme expression and flowering. See E. Nilakanta Singh, *Vaishnavism in Manipuri Literature*, and H. Ranbir Singh, *Vaishnavism in Manipur: Its Advance*, papers presented in the regional seminar 1985, held under the joint auspices of the Sahitya Academy, Delhi, and the Manipur Sahitya Parishad, Imphal.

15 During the reign of Maharaja Churachand (1891–1941), the Brahma Sabha took up a number of hegemonic and oppressive measures through the *mangba–sengba* (pure – impure) and declared many people as unclean such as *Chingmee* (Hillman), *Pangals* (Manipuri Muslims) and *Lois* (Scheduled caste).

16 The revivalists charged Garibniwaz and his Guru Shantidas Gosai for their unforgivable acts of burning more than 120 *Puyas* on 17 October 1732, destroying temples of *Sanamahi, Nongshaba, Yumtheilai, Panthoibi*, and *UmangLais,* banning of singing religious songs in Meetei vernacular and converting people forcibly to Hinduism. See, Nilabir 2002, 101–09.

17 Kangjia Mangang, resource person on *Meetei Mayek* or *Kanglei* script, argues that the *Kanglei* script is more than 4,000 years old (Mangang 2003, 11).

18 Governor of Manipur Order No. 1/2/78-SS/E dated 16 April 1980, vide *Manipur Gazette* No. 33 Imphal, Tuesday, 22 April 1980.

19 *Wakoklon Thilel Salai Amailon Pukok Puya* is considered by the people and Government of Manipur as the source of *Kanglei Eeyek* (Kanglei script).

20 Brian Keith Axel elaborates how the colonial state transformed and translated the masculinised body of *amritdhari* into representative or representatives for the Sikh identity and reconstituted the relation between the Sikh body to the Sikh homeland.

21 *Inunglol* is the revelational language, sacred language revealed through supernatural inspiration(*Inung* means subconscious mind and *Lol* means language).

22 *Khununglol* is the social language (*Khunung* means inhabited land or society and *Lol* means language).

23 *Kangleipak Meetei Impham Kanglei Paphal*, a topographical map of *Kangla* produced by Thokachanba Meetei, showed the ancient shrines of *Sanamahi* religion, sacred canals, tanks, sacred places, sites of different structures of royal palace and several departments and other important demarcations made by able philosopher and minister *Poileiton* in the reign of *Nongda Lairen Pakhangba* (AD 33–154).

24 The entire *Kangla* Fort area of 236.84 acres was supposed to be kept protected since 1992 under the provision of the Manipur Ancient and Historical Monuments and Archaeological Sites and Remains Act, 1976 (Rajesh 2000).

25 It is a sarong-type cloth wrapped around the body, in most instances below the breast.

26 It is a colourful costume worn below the chest introduced by King Chingthangkhomba (1763–98) when he invented *rasa dance*, one of the four most popular classical dances of India.

References

Administrative Report of the Manipur Political Agency, 1927–28. Imphal: Manipur State Archives.

Alter, Joseph S. 1997. *The Wrestler's Body: Identity and Ideology in North India.* Delhi: Munshiram Manoharlal Publishers.

Anderson, Benedict. 1983. *Imagined Communities: Reflections on the Origin and Spread of Nationalism.* London: Verso.

Arnold, David. 1987. 'Touching the Body: Perspectives on the Indian Plague, 1896–1900', in Ranajit Guha (ed.), *Subaltern Studies V.* New Delhi: Oxford University Press.

Axel, Brian Keith. 2001. *The Nation's Tortured Body Violence, Representation, and the Formation of a Sikh Diaspora.* Durham and London: Duke University Press.

Bahadur, Mutua and Paonam Gunindro. 1988. 'Cultural Evolution in Manipur (1500–1900 AD)', in N. Sanajaoba (ed.), *Manipur, Past and Present, Vol. II.* Delhi: Mittal Publications.

Burke, Peter and Roy Porter (eds). 1995. *Languages and Jargons: Contributions to a Social History of Language.* Cambridge: Cambridge University Press.

Chatterjee, Partha. 1993. *The Nation and Its Fragments: Colonial and Postcolonial Histories.* Princeton, New Jersey: Princeton University Press.

Chingtamlen, W. 2007. *A Short History of Kangleipak (Manipur) Part II.* Imphal: KHCRC.

Dun, E. W. 1975 [1886]. *Gazetteer of Manipur.* Delhi: Vivek Publishing.

Guha, Sumit. 1999. *Environment and Ethnicity in India, 1200–1991.* Cambridge: Cambridge University Press.

Hasting, Adrian. 1997. *The Construction of Nationhood, Ethnicity, Religion and Nationalism.* New York: Cambridge University Press.

Hobsbawm, Eric and Terence Ranger (eds). 1983. *The Invention of Tradition.* Cambridge: Cambridge University Press.

Hudson, T. C. 1984 [1911]. *The Meitheis.* Delhi: Low Price Publications.

Johnstone, Sir James. 2002. *Manipur and the Naga Hills.* Delhi: Manas Publications.

Kabui, Gangmumei. 1991. 'Socio-religious Reform Movement and Christian Proselytism', in Lal Dena (ed.), *History of Modern Manipur.* New Delhi: Orbit Publishers.

Kamei, Gangmumei. 1988. 'Glimpses of Land and People of Ancient Manipur', in N. Sanajaoba (ed.), *Manipur, Past and Present, Vol I.* Delhi: Mittal Publications.

'*Kangla* Question', Pamphlet circulated by Eramdam Manipur Mother's Association, Imphal, 5 August 2000.

CENTRALITY OF BODY POLITICS

Langford, Jean M. 2002. *Fluent Bodies: Ayurvedic Remedies for Postcolonial Imbalance.* Durham, NC: Duke University Press.

Malemnganba, Ng. 2004. *Meetei Resurgence and Nationalism (c.1900–2000): A Study of the Role of the Meetei in the Formation of 20th Century Manipur,* M.Phil. thesis, Delhi University.

Mangang, Kangjia. 2003. *Revival of a Closed Account a Brief History of Kanglei Script and the Birth of Phoon (Zero) in the World of Arithmetic and Astrology.* Imphal: Salai Punsipham.

'Manipur Constitution Act 1947 document', reproduced in N. Sanajaoba (ed.) *Manipur, Past and Present, Vol. I.* Delhi: Mittal Publications.

Meetei, Thokachanba. 1961. *Wakoklonthilelsalaiamailonpukokpuya.* Imphal.

Nilabir, Sairem. 1991. 'The Revivalist Movement of Sanamahism', in N. Sanajaoba (ed.), *Manipur, Past and Present, Vol. II.* Delhi: Mittal Publications.

———. 2002. *LaiyingthouSanamahiamasungSanamahiLainingHinggatEehou.* Imphal.

Parratt, John. 2005. *Wounded Land: Politics and Identity in Modern Manipur.* Delhi: Mittal Publications.

Parratt, S. Nalini. 1980. *The Religion of Manipur Beliefs, Rituals and Historical Development.* Calcutta: Firma KLM.

Rajesh, Salam. 2000. 'Kangla Impasse', *Manipur Update,* 1, IV.

Report of *Meeteimayek Expert Committee* 1958, 1969, 1976, 1978. Imphal: Manipur State Archives.

Singh, LairenmayumIbungohal and Ng. Khelchandra Singh (eds). 1989. *Cheitharol-Kumbaba,* Imphal: Manipur Sahitya Parishad.

Smith, Anthony D. 1988 [1986]. *The Ethnic Origins of Nations.* Oxford: Blackwell Publishers.

Srinivas, M. N. 2000. *Social Change in Modern India.* New Delhi: Orient Longman.

16

RECASTING SPACE

Politics of frontier-making

Thingnam Sanjeev

The making of frontier as a colonial project in 19th-century British India was shaped and conditioned by the anxieties and exigencies of empire-building. Starting out with some theoretical conceptualisations of the frontier in different contexts, the chapter focuses on how the North East Frontier region of India, with specific reference to Manipur, has been produced and administered as a geographical place within the Empire. The chapter attempts to trace the trajectory of the consolidation of the British Empire in the North East Frontier and, thereby, show how a series of treaties and alliances and the production of 'accurate' maps in the 19th century constantly recast the boundaries of the frontier region and transformed 'amorphous frontiers' into modern boundaries. Thus, I intend to put forth that the strategies and politics of frontier-making in Manipur are integral to the formation and emergence of a 'modern' Manipur within the Indian Union.

With the advent of the British Empire, indigenous spatial imagination competed with and was superseded by a new system of modern geographical measurement based on mathematical accuracy and scientific objectivity. However, the process of 'practising' frontier in the region has never been smooth. After Independence, the Indian State retained the region within the logic of strengthening the core and creating a sphere of influence in the eastern region. However, any attempt to homogenise the states of the North East, like the proposed formation of 'Purvanchal Pradesh', has been deeply fraught with tensions and contestations. The resistance against such geographical restructuring, from the earlier democratic movement to the present-day violence of the insurgency movement, indicates the possibility of an alternative geographical/regional imagining.

Delineating frontier: the problem of practising frontier in the North East region

Frontier is a multi-layered idea that has been conceptualised in different ways. Many historians see frontier as a political division between states, whereas others think of it as the margin of settled land in a wilderness, or as a cultural division between peoples. Thus, 'frontier' has been used to signify a state's boundary as well as a liminal zone of transition. Political geographers like C. B. Fawcett define frontier as both an area and a boundary line. Occasionally, it has also signified border lands, that is, territories much larger than a transitional zone, away from the recognised centre of state power; and included whole provinces, protectorates and even territories not part of the state in question, such as buffer states, sphere of influence, etc (Murthy 1978: 14). Taking the example of the Roman Empire, Daniel Power and Naomi Staden (1999: 4) point out how the making of frontier can also be guided by an expansionist ideology rather than being a defensive mechanism. We, thus, see that frontier as a concept and in practice is formed in conjunction with many co-existing institutions, practices and ideologies.

There have been insightful studies on how the 19th-century cartographic practices of the British colonial rule shaped, strengthened and rigidified the formation and consolidation of India's boundaries as a nation-state. If mapping and surveying were 'important aspects of the technologies of state formation' in early modern Europe, the consolidation of the British Empire in 19th-century India was marked by a series of surveys and mapping enterprises that pictorially represented the idea of British India (Kalpagam 1995: 87). By deploying scientific and mathematical forms of measurement, territories were demarcated and boundaries were fixed. As most of the lands under the British rule had been trigonometrically mapped by the end of the 19th century, the idea of frontier was 'abstracted and thought of as a permanent, natural fixture of the landscape' (Barrow 1994: 4). In such a conceptualisation, frontier becomes synonymous with the boundary line. Ainslee Embree argues that the transformation of 'amorphous frontiers' into modern boundaries predicate the formation of nation-states. The East India Company, through its engagement in and search for 'permanent and viable' frontiers, sought to transform and strengthen 'the company' into a state. The evolution of the pre-modern to modern nation-state also reflects the transformation of 'zonal frontiers' to 'linear boundaries' (Embree 1989: 80). Further, Ian J. Barrow, in his 'Moving Frontier: Changing Colonial Notions of Indian Frontiers', explains that the logic of subduing peripheral areas to secure the core domains not only sought to 'naturalise the Company's conquest and make it appear that expansion was teleologically legitimate', but 'suggests that India only became a modern nation when its natural boundaries were secured' (Barrow 1994: 1). Barrow argues that till late 18th century Indian frontiers were quite porous and 'undelimited' but in the first half of the 19th century advanced cartographic practices like route survey and trigonometric survey facilitated to extend the base line through a frontier and consolidated the natural boundaries of India to become a modern nation-state.

Barrow claims that 'the history of colonial maps of India is a history of possession' (Barrow 2003: 1) and explains how colonial cartographic practices underline an 'epistemological strategy' that legitimise the colonial possession of territory. Colonial cartographers and surveyors employed various strategies to embed a past into their narratives, and maps were used both to demonstrate a history of territory and, importantly, to justify the possession of land. Thus, maps become a powerful medium in formulating ideas, manipulating opinion and reinforcing perspectives.

The effectiveness of colonial cartography is based, in part, on the power of maps to shape understanding and influence policy. That power, in the colonial Indian context, was derived from specific conceptions of territory that were formulated as a way both to include India within an empire and to justify that inclusion (Barrow 2003: 3). David Zou, quoting Erik de Maaker and Vibha Joshi in his essay 'Mapping Frontier History', identifies the North East as a 'culture area' which is at the margin of the three firmly located geographical region as well as an academic 'study area' covering South Asia, South East Asia and East Asia (Zou 2009: 1). In her study of Goalpara district during the colonial period, Sanghamitra Misra talks about the confrontation of the native and the colonial conceptions of political space wherein the British 'had to contend with the conditions of *overlapping territoriality and sovereignty*, which characterised the indigenous polity of this region' (2005: 222, emphasis added).

In the case of Manipur, too, the problem of practising frontier makes it imperative to see how it has been variably imagined to overlap with the South East Asian region. Hill and Hitchcock (1996: 12) argue that in terms of ethnographic mapping, parts of North East India, along with Southern China and Taiwan, belong to South East Asia. This 'social space' of the South East Asian region constituted by 'shared ideas, related life ways, and long-standing cultural ties' (cited in van Schendel 2002: 649), contests and problematises the geographical imagining of a concrete and bounded northeast within the South Asian region. Variably located between South Asia and South East Asia, the northeast of India can thus be seen, in the words of Willem van Schendel (2002: 651), as 'a liminal space'. Even as some colonial ethnographic writings have surmised a South East Asian lineage of the people of the North East, with Captain Pemberton claiming that the Manipuris are 'the descendants of a Tartar colony, which is believed to have emigrated from the north-west borders of China' during the sanguinary conflicts for supremacy (Pemberton 1979: 17), the cartographic regimentation of the colonial rule sought to contain and limit the liminal space of the North East Frontier region and recast it into a geographical entity.

The North East Frontier could not be collectively imagined as a homogenous entity where colonial rule penetrated evenly in all the areas of the region. Rather, different areas had, and continue to have, in postcolonial India specific and varying significance. This is clearly outlined in George Nathaniel Curzon's conceptualisation of the 'threefold' frontier, which consists of an 'administrative' border, a frontier of 'active protection', and an outer or advanced 'strategic' frontier. While the 'administrative' border covers much of the present-day state of Assam, the 'Tribal Areas', marked by 'the Inner Line', which cordoned off areas that were under direct British governance, came under the frontier of 'active protection'. Even as these Tribal Areas, like the Naga Hills, were claimed as British territories, the British were more interested in subjugating the tribes through occasional military raids rather than directly ruling them under modern governmental institutions (cited in Baruah 2009: 3). Moreover, there was stiff resistance from the native tribes and the colonial government chose to adopt a policy of non-interference in the hills. The advanced 'strategic' frontier comprised of territories beyond the Tribal Areas, which were technically independent but served as a buffer zone for the British Empire. It is seen as an area or a boundary through and with which the mainland could be saved from impending threats or could be used as a gateway for consolidating the Empire. The then kingdom of Manipur, sandwiched between two belligerent Empires, the Burmese and the British, became a theatre of advancing strategic frontier. The Burmese aggressively followed an expansionist policy up to 1824, subduing most of the northeastern region and even reaching as far as Cachar and Sylhet, which were within British protection. The then British Imperial frontier was extended up to the farthest limits of Chittagong, Sylhet and Goalpara district.

The formation and consolidation of the advancing colonial frontier in Manipur show how the acquisition of territories in the northeastern frontier by the East India Company 'can be seen as a search for a permanent and viable frontier' (cited in Barrow 1994). The British Empire, once it subdued and brought territories under its rule and Protectorate, followed a process of pacification that involved reconfiguring power relations through the language of treaties and alliances. Thus, through the Offensive and Defensive Alliance of 1762, both England and Manipur sought to manage both the rapidly expanding Burmese Empire and the rising French influence in the region. Around the time of the signing of the treaty, the British were engaged with France in the Seven Years' War (1756–63). This Anglo-French rivalry for colonial expansion had a serious repercussion in India. During that time, France had a strong hold in Burma and it managed to instigate the king of Ava, Alaung-paya (1752–59), to destroy the English settlement at Negrais. As a result, about 10 Englishmen and 100 Indians were killed (Dena 1991: 3).

In such a situation, by establishing an alliance with Manipur, the East India Company could demand reparation from the Burmese for the humiliation at Negrais. Internal conflict among the princes for the throne and the incessant raids from the Burmese army also created a frontier crisis in the region, which gave the Company authority an opportunity to intervene in the matter and thereby facilitate the creation of an advancing frontier in Manipur. Apart from its political significance, the treaty gave the provision for ensuring that 'every facility for the prosecution of the trade with China' be made (Pemberton 1979: 41). The treaty ensured the expansionist policy of the British Empire in South East Asia, and Manipur served as a buffer zone.

Internal feud among the ruling class elite ultimately led the Burmese to strangle the sovereignty of Manipur. It was during this period, from 1819 to 1826 that Manipur was doomed to devastation, popularly known as the Seven Years' Devastation (*Chahi-Taret Khuntakpa*) in history. It was more severe than the primary devastation or *koolthakahalba* of 1755 (Dun 1975:39). Subsequently, in 1823, Gambhir Singh, while forming the Manipur levy with 500 soldiers under his command, sought the protection of the British government. With co-operation from the British Army, Manipur was finally liberated from Burma and the Treaty of Yandaboo was signed in 1826. As a result, Assam was directly annexed and Manipur was reduced to a buffer state. Subsequently, the strength of the Manipur levy, which the British thought would be a 'match for an equal number of Burmese', was increased up to 2,000 men and placed under the command of Captain Grant with whom the expulsion of the Burmese from the Kabaw Valley as far south as Kalle was made possible (Mackenzie 2003: 151).

On 18 April 1833, the Jiri Treaty, a trade and defensive treaty, was signed between Gambhir Singh and the British Government. It represented an instrument for exchange through which Jiribam was handed over to Manipur and the latter had to give up the *thana* (police station) at Cachar (Sanajouba 1988: 102). The British took over the task of defending Cachar from the weak ruler of Manipur. Thus, they decided to annex the Cachar plains in 1832 and formed a district of the British Empire. As per the agreement, the hilly tract in the eastern part of Cachar was given to Gambhir Singh. However, the boundary between the new Cachar and Manipur was not well defined.

After the Jiri Treaty, the British government followed a policy of pacification by giving up the Kabaw valley and paid a compensation of 500 *sicca*s for the alienated territory to the Manipur government. By transferring the Kabaw Valley to the Burmese under the treaty of 1834, the British government sought to contain the rising French influence and thereby secure its Eastern frontier. With the establishment of the office of the British political agent in 1835, British control over Manipur was on the ascendant. All these alliances, engagement, treaties and sanads (written agreements) reflected, as Karam Manimohan Singh puts it, 'an acknowledgement of concessions, authority and privileges, generally coupled with conditions proceeding from the paramount power'. They generally provided for 'internal sovereignty' and 'protection of the State'; prohibition of mutual aggression; payment of tribute; and lastly, the right of the British government to advise on certain circumstances (Singh 1989: 20–21). But the rights that the paramount power laid claim to in executing the duties of the Crown in relation to the Manipur State covered both internal and external matters.

Thus, from the Offensive and Defensive Alliance of 1762, which was more of a *quid pro quo* nature, to the Treaty of the Kabaw Valley in 1834, through the Treaty of Yandaboo in 1826 and the Jiri Treaty of 1833, the Empire gradually consolidated its hold by transforming and recasting the relation in terms of a subsidiary alliance. After the Jiri Treaty, considering the rising French influence in the region, the British government sought to negotiate the Anglo-Burmese relation and thereby secure its Eastern frontier by handing over the Kabaw valley of Manipur to Burma and a payment of compensation to the Manipur government.

In post-colonial India, the Kabaw Valley was permanently gifted to Burma and the payment of compensation to Manipur discontinued. The controversy and discontent that were engineered during the colonial rule thus continue to resonate in contemporary politics as the proverbial 'bone of contention'. From the earlier democratic resistance against the proposed formation of a 'Purvanchal Pradesh', which sought to subsume Tripura, Cachar and Manipur under one administrative

Contestations at the margin

As also mentioned before, the process of colonial mapping had to negotiate with the idea of 'overlapping territoriality' and required the transformation of liminal spaces to concrete boundaries. The controversy over the transfer of the Kabaw Valley to the Court of Ava in 1833 best brings out how the colonial and the native negotiate and confront issues of territoriality. The Kabaw Valley was a 'semi-independent' territory lying between the Yoma range, which bound the eastern side of the Manipur valley, and the Ningthee River. For long it remained a contested terrain between Ava and Manipur. 'It was in the possession of Burma on the outbreak of the first Burmese War, and had been so for twelve years before. For about the same period preceding these twelve years it had been in the possession of Manipur' (Mackenzie 2003: 176). However, just before the 1826 Treaty of Yandaboo was signed, 'the whole extent of the Kubo Valley . . . were held by Manipuri Thannahdars on the part of the Manipuri Raja Churjeet Sing' (ibid.: 180). Following the rounds of negotiations with the Court of Ava, the British government finally conceded the Kabaw Valley to Burma in 1833 in 'the spirit of amity and good-will' (Mackenzie 2003: 182) and provided the Manipuri King, Gambhir Singh with a compensation of a monthly stipend of 500 *sicca* rupees.

Van Schendel explains that kingdoms in present-day South East Asia have clearly 'defined' and 'powerful' centres but 'vague' and 'contested' peripheries (2002: 650). Thongchai Winichakul (1994) remarkably brings this out in his study of the confrontation between Siamese and British conceptions of space. During 1834–36, British missions were constantly sent to Chiangmai and Siam to settle boundaries demarcating British and Siam territories. As against the colonial obsession with 'clear' boundary lines and jurisdiction, the Siamese expressed remarkable flexibility with regard to territories at the edges. According to the Siamese court, areas at the border were under the jurisdiction of different local authorities. In addition to this, the forests on the borders were like a 'liminal space' where people of both Burma and Siam could earn their living by collecting honey, sappan wood and teak. The court complained that the arrival of the British had disrupted this system (Winichakul 1994: 75–76). Similarly, the 'contested' and turbulent terrain of the Kabaw Valley at the fringes of the Manipur kingdom was stabilised through the transfer and eventual demarcation of boundary. Subsequently, to secure peace in the frontier region, a British political agent was stationed in Manipur.

In post-independent India, contestations have ranged from asserting the idea of a bounded autonomous state to the imagining of an intra-regional front. On 8 September 1948, after the formation of the Manipur Interim Government, the Working Committee of the Indian National Congress under the chairmanship of Sardar Vallabhbhai Patel proposed the formation of Purvanchal Pradesh, which would group together the states of Tripura, Cachar and Manipur on linguistic lines. Though the proposal was accepted by a faction of the Manipur State Congress, it was strongly resented by the other faction led by Tompok and Manipuri nationalists like Hijam Irabot. It was argued that Manipur should be maintained as an autonomous unit of India since it was racially, ethnically, culturally and linguistically distinct from the rest of India.

Consequently, on 21 September 1948, the Manipur Krishak Sangha and the Manipur Praja Sangha organised a meeting to protest against the Purvanchal Pradesh proposal. However, the meeting turned violent when the police started *lathi*-charging a group of delegates from Lamlai who decided to march till the meeting place in Imphal in apparent violation of the ban on processions. When the news reached the venue of the meeting, Irabot realised that he could be arrested on the pretext of the incident, so he cancelled the meeting and went into hiding, finally being compelled to go underground.

This resistance against the incorporation of Manipur in the proposed Purvanchal Pradesh is reflective of a distinct territorial imagination, which could not be contained within a larger, concentric framework. Arjun Appadurai (2000: 7) talks about something similar to this when he refers to how 'regions imagine their own worlds' in the context of globalisation (cited in van Schendel 2002: 659). Even as Appadurai is writing about an altogether different context, the idea of recovering agency in the regions' tendency and ability to 'imagine their own worlds', in opposition to what is imposed by global paradigm, remains relevant for our understanding of the shifting notions of region formation in the North East. These contestations show the possibility of postulating an alternative regional imagination.

Similar to this possibility of a transnational imagining, but also differently, on 18 May 1947, *The Hindustan Standard* reported that General Aung San of Burma had been invited to Manipur. Later on, another report in the same newspaper quoted the Information Minister of Burma as stating that Manipur was a part of Burma and that it had seceded 100 years ago. These news reports generated a series of speculations. Members of the ruling Manipur Congress surmised that the idea of forming a communist front in collaboration with the Burmese was in progress. As Singh explains, the attempt to incorporate Manipur within the Burmese territory was not a recent concern. When the Burmese territory was first segregated from India, the General Burma Council Association demanded in 1937 that if the territory had to be segregated at all, Manipur should be incorporated within their boundary. This political demand had been printed in the Burmese daily *Turiya* (The Sun) published from Rangoon (Singh 1989: 203). When the same is read in conjunction with Irabot's attempts to establish links with Mandalay, we get a vague sense of a transnational imagining.

Of late, different forms of geo-spatial imagining within the region has also been manifest, such as the movement for Greater Mizoram in the 1980s and the continuing struggle for Greater Nagalim since the late 1990s on ethnic lines. The legacy of geo-strategic concerns still persists in 'independent' India's administration. Nathaniel Curzon's threefold conceptualisation of the frontier has an afterlife in the present-day legislation as the Inner Line Permit, Protected Area Permit and Restricted Area Permit. The policy thrust has been more on border rationalisation with Burma and China to make the region militarily secure from India's position. Even as the colonial frontier has overtly been transformed into a boundary in the official lexicon, the idea of a zone of intervention and control still persists. Whether the region will serve the purpose as a defence line for the Indian State or a space for expanding their sphere of influence beyond the sub-continent is a case in point.

References

Appadurai, A. 2000. *Globalisation and Area Studies: The Future of a False Opposition*. Amsterdam: Centre for Asian Studies Amsterdam.

Barrow, Ian J. 1994. 'Moving Frontiers: Changing Colonial Notions of the Indian Frontiers', http://www.inic.utexas.edu/asnic/sagar/fall.1994/ian.barrow.art.html. Accessed 2007.

Barrow, Ian J. 2003. *Making History, Drawing Territory: British Mapping in India, c. 1756–1905*. New Delhi: Oxford University Press.

Baruah, S. 2009. 'Northwest by Northeast: A Tale of Two Frontiers', *Imphal Free Press*, 19 July. Also available at: https://www.opendemocracy.net/author/sanjib-baruah, accessed 17 July 2009.

Dena, Lal (ed.). 1991. *History of Modern Manipur, 1826–1949*. New Delhi: Orbit Publishers.

Dun, E. W. 1975. *Gazetteer of Manipur*. Delhi: Vivek Publishing House.

Embree, Ainslie T. 1989. *Imagining India: Essays on Indian History.* New Delhi: Oxford University Press.

Hill L., and Hitchcock M, 1996, "Anthropology", in M Halib, T Huxley (Eds) *An Introduction to Southeast Asian Studies.* London: IB Tauris.

Kalpagam, U. 'Cartography in Colonial India', *Economic and Political Weekly* 30(30) (29 July 1995): 87. Also available at: http://www.jstor.org/stable/4403049. Accessed on: 16/11/2009.

Mackenzie, Alexander. 2003. *The North-East Frontier of India.* New Delhi: Mittal Publications.

Misra, Sanghamitra. 2005. 'Changing Frontiers and Spaces: The Colonial State in Nineteenth-century Goalpara', *Studies in History,* 21(2): 215–46.

Murthy, T. S. 1978. *Frontiers: A Changing Concept.* New Delhi: Palit & Palit Publishers.

Pemberton, Robert B. 1979. *The Eastern Frontier of India.* New Delhi: Mittal Publications.

Power, Daniel and Staden, Naomi (eds). 1999. *Frontiers in Question: Eurasian Borderlands, 700–1700.* Great Britain: Macmillan Press Ltd.

Sanajouba, Naorem, ed. 1988. *Manipur: Past and Present, Vol. I.* New Delhi: Mittal Publications.

Singh, Karam Manimohan. 1989. *Hijam Irabot Singh and Political Movements in Manipur.* Delhi: B.R. Publishing Corporation.

Van Schendel, Willem. 2002. 'Geographies of Knowing, Geographies of Ignorance: Jumping Scale in Southeast Asia', *Environment and Planning D: Society and Space* 20(6): 647–68.

Winichakul, Thongchai. 1998. *Siam Mapped: A History of the Geo-Body of a Nation.* Chiang Mai, Thailand: Silkworm Books.

Zou, David. 2009. 'Mapping Frontier history: The "Geo-Body" and Enclavement of Colonial Northeast India', Paper presented at the seminar 'Writing Northeast India: A New Perspective', Jawaharlal Nehru University, New Delhi.

GLOSSARY

abhinay	character in a play
achanba	favoured
Ama	one
amangba/mangba	impure;
amin chakthak	free feeding of state officials by villagers
Angang	child
Apokpa Marup	association of ancestors
asengba/sengba	pure/ purity
Bamon	Brahmin
Bamon Chakthongba	Brahmin cook
Baruni	a Hindu festival celebrated on the thirteenth day of the dark half of Phairen (Jan-Feb). It is devoted to the worship of Lord Shiva. It is introduced by Chandrakirti in the nineteenth century.
Bhadralok	educated class
Bor Saheb	higher ranked colonial English officials
Brahmasabha	Hindu religious organisation
Brindaban	holy place situated in Uttar Pradesh state of India
Chabok Wangol	a kind of tax collected from the people on the eve of the birth of the king's child
Chahi-Taret Khuntakpa	Seven Years' Devastation
Chayol Talep	Great Bear
chandan	the mud used to apply on the forehead by Hindus
chandan senkhai	tax for wearing the *tilak*
Chanu	title conferred to unmarried Meetei lady
Cheiraoba	New Year of the Meeteis
Chingoi Eruppa	Holy Bath
Cheishing Eeyek	numerical
Cheisinglon	Manipuri numerical
Cheitharol Kumbaba	Royal Chronicle of Manipur
Cheiraoba	Meetei New Year's Day

GLOSSARY

chin kangjei	verbal repartee
Ching	hill
chira	flattened rice
darbar/durbar	royal administrative court
dewani	authority to collect revenue
dolai	Palanquin
dolaireng	carrying of government peons on the *dolai* by villagers during monsoon
Eepung Loinaba	the one without a second
Eelik	female egg
gaddi	throne
gopi	female companions of Hindu goddess Radha
Gostha Asthmi	the eighth lunar day of Hiyangei or November
Goura Lilad	drama enacting the childhood of Gouranga Chatyanya Mahaprabhu
Hakchang	human body
Heikhru Hitongba	boat race
Iyek	script
Inaphi	indigenous upper clothing
jagir	land holding pattern in feudal society in south Asia
jagoi	dance
Jatra	a generic term referring to 20th-century theatrical plays in
Bengal *Jatrawali*	performers in Jatra
jawan	soldier
Kabul Lila	play enacting characters from Kabul
kang thouri	rope used in pulling chariot
kangchingba	pulling chariot
Kanglei	Manipuri
Kanglei eeyek lamyanba	pioneer of the Manipuri (Meetei) script
Kangleicha	Manipuri
khillut	robe of honour sanctified by being touched to the body of the patron and then presented to a client
khillut	honour conferred by the British government
Khubak Eshei	community singing
khudei	a casual lower garment; a shorter version of the dhoti
khul	village
Koolthakhalba	devastation
Kwaktanba	a festival observed by Meeteis
kunja sen	attire taxation
Laininghanba Ehau	revivalist movement
Lam	land
lambu	village chief
Laipham	abode of gods

250

GLOSSARY

Lai Haraoba	a ritual observed by Meeteis implicating the creation of mankind
Laininghanba Eehou	revivalist movement
Lais	gods
lallup	a form of forced labour enforced by the Monarch in Manipur
Lathi	stick
Leekla	spermatozon
leikai	locality
Leima	title conferred to married Meetei women
Lom Eyek, Lonsum, Cheitap, Khudam, Cheising	allied script
Luhongba	marriage
lugun senkhai	sacred thread tax (tax for wearing sacred thread)
lukun	sacred thread
madrasa	Islamic educational centre
mahal	hall
maiba	priest
maibi	priestess
mal	acrobatics
Malangnung	interior space
Mapu	the creator
Mapu's Ting	absoluteness of the creator
Mami	image
mangba–sengba	impurity and purity
maulvi	Muslim religious heads
Mayangs	outsiders
Meetei/Meitei	one of the communities in Manipuri
Meetei Mayek	Meetei script
Meeteilon	Manipuri language
meeyan	foreigner
Meiraching	peak of flames
Meira Paibi	torch-bearing women activist
Mera Haochongba	gf interface with the hill tribes
Mi	image
mithun	cattle of Hilly Region
Mitlis	visual nerves
Mitnaha	eyelash
mora	a type of stool
Naopipham	uterus
Naowa	foetus
Naoyom	womb
napet senkhai	barber tax
natak	drama

GLOSSARY

nayika	lead woman actor
Nupi Lan	Women's War
pandit loishang	board of pandits
Pangal	Manipuri Muslim
parvana	permission
patta	land ownership status
pebet	a small mythological bird
Phadibi Lila	play of tattered rags
Phagee Lila	comic play
Phampak Lila	Proscenium theatre
phanek	sarong-like wraparound
pheijom	Dhoti
Phoon	zero
phunganai	domestic slavery
Pokpa	birth
pothang	free carriage tendered to kings and his officials
pothang senkhai	tax associated with free carriage tendered to kings and his officials
potlois	female costume worn in Rasa Lila, and also by the bride during the marriage ceremony
Pi	tear
Piba	male sibling
pung yeiba	*Mridanga* (a musical instrument) player
Puyas	ancient Manipuri texts
Puwari	history
Puhonba	professional cooks
purdah Veil	
Ras Mandal	dancing hall
Rasa Lila	dance depicting the celestial and eternal love of Radha and Krishna
rath	Chariot
Ratha Jatra	Cart Festival
Salai	clan
Salailel; Sitapa	the creator
sanad	a deed granted to the native princely state rulers confirming them in their states, in return for their allegiance
Sanamahi (Movement)	a religious movement
sankirtan	a chanting process for achieving love of God in Vaisnavism
Sanjenba	a drama/play depicting an episode from Krishna's childhood when he reveals his true self and plays mischief with the Gopis while grazing cows in the Vrindavan

252

GLOSSARY

Sap riangvaia	the poor whites
senapati	head of army
senkhai	a type of taxation
sengtokpa	purification; a purification rite
Shajam Iha	a ritual practiced by the Kukis
Shiba	death
shumang	courtyard
Shumang Lila	courtyard theatre
Sitapa	immortal
Sradha	ritual performed for deaths
subedar	police official
Taipangpanpa Mapu	the creator
Taipangpan	World of Beings
tala	rhythm
Tamanglang	timeless state
Tangkhul shaba	Tangkhul character
Tengpanpa	cosmos
thana	police station
thengu	a kind of wooden hammer
Thengu Lila	a humorous play
Thawaimichak Chayom Talep	Great Bear
Thawaimichak Apokpa	the north pole star
Thok Lila	contrick play
Khudei	traditional casual lower clothing
Thoupok	chest
tilak	a Hindu religious marks on forehead
Tillang	saliva
Ting	power
Tingpanpa	ultimate source of cosmos
tulsi	holy basil
Udukhol	play enacting episodes of Krishna childhood
Ulema	Muslims religious scholar
Upham	occipital lobe
urik	sacred necklace of *tulsi* beads
Wakoklon Thilen Salai Amailon Pukok Puya	ancient scriptural code of the Meeteis
wakhei sel	settlement fee
Wakon	reservoir
(lord) Wangbren	in Meitei belief, a deity or guardian of the south, and one among eight guardian deities of the eight directions
yairek sentry	guarding of the official revenue (at night)
vakil	lawyer
Singli	nerves

253

INDEX

Anglo–Burmese War of 1885–86 36, 57, 79, 140, 149, 156
Anglo–French Entente Cordial of 1904 137
Anglo–Manipuri Mutual Defence Treaty 8, 147–9
Anglo–Manipuri Treaty of 1833 150–1
Anglo–Manipuri War 2, 36–7, 76, 79, 99, 104, 140, 154, 160, 163, 178, 188, 193; defeat in 58, 161; relations 57–8
Anglo–Russian Accord of 1907 137
Apokpa Marup (association of ancestors) 218
appropriation, ethnicisation in Manipur: acquaintance of British with Nagas 32; appointment of *lambus* 33; civilizing mission 34; clans and sections 36; cultures, treatment of 34; directives, Lushais and Naga Hills 33; genesis of ethnicisation 34–5; Kuki Rebellion of 1917, repression of 32–3; Kukis, definition 34; Meeteis 35; nature of 'tribal divisions' 35–6; negative use of power 31; notion of brethrens of hills 34
Armed Forces (Special Powers) Act, 1958 (AFSPA) 26, 53–4
Article 52 of the Vienna Convention on the Law of Treaties, 1969 210
Asiatic power in alliance: defeat in Anglo–Manipuri War of 1891 161; subordinate and protected state 160–3; treaties, boundary of Manipur and Kabaw Valley 161; Treaty of

Yandaboo, 1826 160; treaty or 'compact of allegiance' due 162
Ayuk Anganba (Dawn) 98
Ayurveda, 'reinvention' of 224

battle of Imphal 143–5; Allied offensive 143; Battle of Sangshak and Tank Battle 143–4; capturing of Tamu – Imphal and Tiddim – Imphal roads 143; Operation 'U-Go' 143; widening of Imphal 143
Battle of Java Sea 142–3
Battle of Sangshak 143–4
Bengali education 93
Bhadralok culture 120
Bor Saheb Ongbi Sanatombi 104–14
Brahma Sabha 59–60, 62, 85, 218–19, 226
Brahminical domination 81–2, 87
Brahmins of Brahmasabha 85–6
'brethrens' of hills, notion of 34
British colonialism in Manipur 79–82; crafts of colonial rule 79–81; socio-cultural changes in Manipur 81–2; Treaty of Yandaboo 79
British colonisers 81–2, 84, 183
British Empire 8–12, 24, 47, 57, 64, 92, 109, 116, 139–40, 143, 151, 178, 183, 195, 238–43
British India 20, 24–5, 57, 63, 66, 94, 117, 140, 143–4, 160, 163, 175–6, 184, 193, 198, 217, 238–9
British India's 1920 notification 193
British 'indirect rule' in Manipur: activities of Political Agents 153;

255

INDEX

Minute of 25 March 1833 152;
office of British Political Agency,
establishment of 152; recognition to
gaddi 152; Treaty of Yandaboo in
1826 154
British Political Agent, establishment
of 243
British self-governance 22
Burmese devastation (*Chahi
TaretKhuntakpa*) 57, 139
Burmese expedition in 1825 57, 140
Burmese invasion of Manipur 139
Burmese occupation and socio-religious
life 77–9; Brahmin representatives
78; Islamic revivalism 78–9; Manipur,
independence and sovereignty 77;
Manipuri *Pangals* 78; orthodoxies or
communalism 79; reconsolidation of
Hinduism 78; socio-cultural aspect
of people 78; socio-religious and
political life of people 77–8

capitalist exploitation 18
Cart-tax Monopoly 64
cast of colonialism: Armed Forces Act,
1958 26; colonialism and resistance
23–4; consolidation of political
hegemony 18–23; contextualising
North East 17–18; despotism of
Orientalism 16; Eurocentrism
17; 'frenzy of liberalism' 16;
hegemonisation 16; hierarchisation
of races 16; idea of geo-militarism
26; LEP 26; politics and economy
16; poor human rights record 25;
post-Renaissance fabrication 17;
representative democracy 25; wages of
plantation labour, Africa and India 16
Chahi Taret Khuntakpa (Seven Years'
Devastation) 57, 76, 149, 242
chandan senkhai 59, 83, 92, 118, 194
Chassad Rebellion 188
Chengba Phagee 124
Chhatra Federation 198
Chinga session 62–3, 197–8
Ching-nga Declaration 98
Christianisation 9, 187, 189
Christian missionaries: Chassad
Rebellion 188; civilising mission

183–5; cultures of natives 185–8;
dialects, customs of natives 181–2;
ethnic classification 182; identity
formation 182, 188; imposition
of tax 188; Kuki Rebellion 188;
Lushais, trouble from 183–4; mission
for Christ 184; modernity through
Western education 187; natives of
hills of Manipur 181–2; NEIGM
187; primordial beliefs and values
187; response of natives 188–9; *sap
riangvaia* 184–5; science and medicine
186–7; social welfare schemes 187
Christian religious beliefs 42, 93–4
'civilising mission' 42, 65, 183–5, 194
CMC *see* Constitution Making
Committee (CMC)
colonial cartography 240
colonial intervention 116–19; British
Empire 116; concept of 'divine
kingship' 117; Constitution Drafting
Committee 118; elite culture 117;
Manipur Merger Agreement 118–19;
Manipur under British Management
117; practice of *mangba-sengba* 118
Colonialism and its Form of Knowledge 44
colonial rule 43, 79–81; Anglo–Manipuri
War of 1891 104; anti-colonial
movement 46; *Bor Saheb Ongbi
Sanatombi* 104–14; colonised
otherness and colonial racialisation
104–5; colonisers, resources by
79–80; definition of 'conversion'
80–1; desire, intimacy and disgrace
106–7; domination and exploitation
45; intimating colonial desire 106–10;
Orientalism 109; question of disgrace
110–13; religious and cultural beliefs
80; and sexuality 106; 'socio-cultural
industry' 79; 'white' identity 109
Constituent Assembly 176–7; contestation
177; 1st July Agreement 177; Manipur,
joining of 176; representation of
Manipur by Guha 177
Constitutional amendment 214
constitutional transition 164–6; CMC
164; Manipur State Durbar, change
of 165; MSCA 165–6; Rules for
Administration 165

256

INDEX

Constitution Drafting Committee 118
Constitution Making Committee (CMC) 68, 164, 200–2
Contestations at margin: confrontation, Siamese and British 244; formation of Manipur Interim Government 244; incorporating within Burmese territory 245; Kabaw Valley 244; protest against Purvanchal Pradesh proposal 245; struggle for Greater Nagalim 246
conversion, definition 80–1
Creed of Islam 97
cultural supremacy, deployment of 21
cultural ties, notion of 30–1

Day of Judgment 97
decolonisation 1, 54, 103
desanskritisation 220
despotism of Orientalism 16
direct and distanced engagement 19–20
'divide and rule' policy 5, 37, 64, 194
'divine kingship,' concept of 117
dog tax, cycle tax, conscription (*pothang senkhai*) 83
Dominion Agent, role of 207–8
Dominion Government 209
'double allegiances,' principle of 155
double allegiances and ritual representations: feudal institutions, re-enforcement 155; power transfer 154–6; recognition and honour 156
Durga Puja festival 122

Eikhoigi Tada (My Brother) 101–2
electioneering and alliances 202–3
elite culture 117, 123
elite theatre and genres 7, 116, 119–20
Empire's education system 93–4
English education 93, 194, 197
Enlightenment movement in Europe 15
epistemological strategy 240
ethnicisation 5, 12, 28–9, 31, 34–9, 92; administration of hill and 'plain' areas 37; Anglo–Manipuri War of 1891 36; construction of image of King 38; divide and rule 37; divided administration 39; Kuki Rebellion 37–8; Manipur State Durbar 38;

Meeteis 38; militant form of resistance 37; oppression of *lam-subedars* 39
Eurocentrism 17
Europe, inter-war geopolitics 138
evangelism and colonial education 93

feudal institutions, re-enforcement 155
feudalism 6–7, 64, 91, 101, 116, 121–2, 193, 201
feudal rights of kings 22
First Anglo–Burmese War 149, 797
First Labour Corps 47
First World War of 1914 49, 99
forced labour system (*pothang*) 83
Franco–Russian treaty of 1894 137
'frenzy of liberalism' 16
frontier in North East region: British Political Agent, establishment of 243; colonial cartography 240; epistemological strategy 240; internal conflict among princes 242; Jiri Treaty 242–3; Offensive and Defensive Alliance of 1762, 242–3; overlapping territoriality and sovereignty 240; Seven Years' Devastation 242; social space 240–1; threefold frontier, conceptualisation 241; transformation of zonal frontiers to linear boundaries 239; 'Tribal Areas' 241

geo-militarism, idea of 26
geopolitics: Anglo–French Entente Cordial of 1904 137; Anglo–Russian Accord of 1907 137; bipolar system 136; developed in Europe 134; Franco–Russian treaty of 1894 136; geopolitics, definition 137; *Institute fur Geopolitik* 136; inter-war geopolitics in Europe 138; *Lebensraum* or expanded imperial space 136; military revolution 136; Nazi *geopolitik* 136; race for overseas expansion 135; roots in territorial states 134
Gosth Lila 122
Gouralila (drama) 119
Gour Dharma Pracharini Sabha 84
Government of India Act, 1935 168, 173, 176

257

INDEX

Great Depression of 1929 99
Greater East Asia Co-Prosperity Sphere 141

hegemonisation 16, 18–23; British self-governance 22; capitalist exploitation 18; deployment of cultural supremacy 21; direct and distanced engagement 19–20; feudal rights of kings 22; Inner Line Regulation system in 1873 19–20; missionaries and education 22; peoples resistance 19; policy of conciliation 20–1; policy of defence and conciliation 19; policy of direct and distanced interference 19; politics of engagement and disengagement 19; tea cultivation, resistance to 19; violation of Inner Line 21
hierarchisation of races 16
Hijam Irabot, leadership of 3, 52, 62, 95, 97, 197, 199, 203, 245
Hinduisation, factors of 76, 81, 86, 88, 219
Hmar Association in 1945 65

identity formation 76, 182, 188, 222
Imagi Puja (Worship of Mother) 98
imperialism: British 7, 9, 18, 145, 159; informal 43; motivating forces behind 43
Imperialism: The Highest Stage of Capitalism 43
INC *see* Indian National Congress (INC)
Indian Independence Act, 1947 166–8; and merger issue 215–16; sections 170–1
Indian National Congress (INC) 66, 202–3
Inner Line Permit system 20, 22
Inner Line Regulation system in 1873 19–20
Institute fur Geopolitik 136
Instrument of Accession, 1947 167–76; amendments, Government of India Act, 1935 173–4; Indian Dominion on three subjects 167–8; Indian Independence Act, 1947 167–8,

170–1; Maharaja of Manipur 169, 172; Manipur State Constitution Act, 1947 172; Merger Agreement 171; signing of 172; transfer of Manipur's sovereignty to Dominion of India 169–70
Islamic revivalism 78–9, 94

jagoi, dances 82, 119
Jahera 100–1
Jamiat-ul-Ulema-e-Hind 97
Japan Association of Geopolitics 140
Japanese geopolitics and South East Asia: Battle of Java Sea 142–3; economic blockade 142; geopolitical school of Imperial University of Kyoto 140; Greater East Asia Co-Prosperity Sphere 141; growth of militarism in Japanese society 141; Japan Association of Geopolitics 140; 'New Order in East Asia' 141; policy of expansionism 141
Jatra of Bengal 127
jester and grotesque realism 121–7; *Chengba Phagee* 124; cultural and political forces 125–6; Durga Puja festival 122; employment of improvisation 121; feudalism 121–2; *Jatra* of Bengal 127; *Kabul Lila* (Kabul play) 125; *Phadibi Lila* (play of tattered rags) 125; Phagee Lila tradition 123–4; *phunganai* (domestic slavery) 122; reign of Maharaja Chandrakirti 122; Shumang Lila 121; *Thengu Lila* 126; *Thok Lila* (con-trick play) 126–7
jesters of popular genres: colonial intervention 116–19; cultural performances 115; cultural production 115; elite theatre 116, 119; jester and grotesque realism 121–7; Manipuri performative genres 119–21; performative reflexivity 116; reflexive politic 115; *Shumang Lila* 116, 127–8
Jiri Treaty 242–3

Kabaw Valley 149–51, 156, 161, 242–4
Kabui Samiti of Ruongmei in 1934 65
Kabul Lila (Kabul play) 125, 127

258

INDEX

Kangla 54, 147; importance 231–2; issue, impacts 232
Kangleipak Lamjing Thoushikon (Association of Pioneers of Kangleipak) 218
Kanglei script, state-level conference 11, 222–8
Kansha Vadh (1945) 97
Khamba Thoibi 97
Krishak Sabha 199–200
Krishi Sanmelani 66–7, 199
Kuki National Assembly (KNA) in 1947 65, 69, 203
Kuki Rebellion, 1917–19 37–8, 60, 92, 188, 195; accommodation of natives 47; anti-colonial movement 52; colonial explanation 49; demand for labourers for Manipur Labour Corps 47; enforcement of house tax and forced labour (*pothang*) 49–50; feature of *Sajam Ihah* 47; features 46; First Labour Corps 47–8; pride in being warrior 46; Punitive action by British 51; recruitment, suspension of 48; repression of 32–3; resistance to colonial domination and oppression 49–50; revolt of Thadou Kukis, causes 48–9; suppression of Rebellion 51; Thadou Kukis 48; Thado warfare 46
Kukis, definition 34

Lai Haraoba, festival 119
Laininghanba Eehou see revivalist movement
Lairaba (Poverty) 98
Lalit Manjuri Patrika (1933) 97
lallup system 58–9, 82–3, 194–5
Laman 100–1
lam-subedars, oppression of 39
lapse of British suzerainty 166–7; independence of native states 167; Indian Independence Act, 1947 166; Memorandum on States Treaties 167
Lebensraum or expanded imperial space 136
literary conceptions: genre and subject matter 93–9; Bengali script 94–5; *Ching-nga* Declaration 98; Christian religious texts 93–4; Empire's administration and education 94;

evangelism and colonial education 93; *Imagi Puja* (Worship of Mother) 98; *Lairaba* (Poverty) 98; *Madhavi,* contemporary theme and style 96; *Mahabharata,* epic 97; Manipuri *maulvis* 94; *Nar Singh,* Manipuri historical novels 99; official opening 102; *Pangals* (Manipuri Muslim) 94, 97; recovery of 'Mother Manipur' 95; richness of *Meeteilon* (Manipuri language) 95–6; *Seidam Seireng,* collection of poems 98; writings for school textbooks 94
literature 92–3; Empire's education system 93; English and Bengali education 93; Manipuri literature 92; modern education 92; *pothang* system and *yairek sentri* 92; taxation systems 92
Lom Eeyek 223
Look East Policy (LEP) 26
Lushais, trouble from 183–4

McMahon Line 24
Madhavi 96–7
Mahabharata 97, 219
Maharaja Chandrakirti, reign of 122
Maharaja of Manipur 10, 148, 168–9, 172, 200, 206–8, 212–14
maiba – maibi and Brahmins 75
Maliyapham Palcha era 233
mangba–sengba, concept 231; Brahmins of Brahmasabha 85–6; consolidation of socio-religious institutions 82; distribution of Brahmin settlements 85; dog tax, cycle tax, conscription (*pothang senkhai*) 83; establishment and consolidation of *Brahmasabha* 83–5; forced labour system (*pothang*) 83; Gour Dharma Pracharini Sabha 84; new system of land holding 82; Nikhil Hindu Manipuri Mahasabha 82–3; odd taxes 83; patta system in land ownership 83; religious subjects 84; scandals 62; *sengtokpa* (a purification rite) 83; system of *mangba* and *sengba* politics 84; taxation on socio-religious grounds 84
Manipur and British imperial interest 138–40; Anglo–Manipur defence

INDEX

treaty in 1762 139; Anglo–Manipuri War of 1891 140; Burmese expedition in 1825 140; Burmese invasion of Manipur 139; French and Portuguese, support of 139; Naga Hills expedition of 1879 140; Third Anglo–Burmese War of 1885–86 140; Treaty of Yandaboo 1826 139; wars between Manipur and Burma 138

Manipur Constitution Act 1947 69, 202, 212, 222–3

Manipuri *maulvis* 94

Manipur Interim Government, formation of 244

Manipuri *Pangals* 78

Manipuri performative genres 119–21; Bhadralok culture 120; elite theatre and genres 119–20; Nara Singh, historical play 121; period of sanskritization 120; religious/ritualistic and non-religious forms 119; Stage Lila 120–1, 127; Tikendrajit, play 121

Manipur Krishak Sabha (MKS) 65–6, 198

Manipur Labour Corps 47–8

Manipur Merger Agreement, 1949 118–19, 213–15; allegations 210–11; Article 52 of Vienna Convention on Law of Treaties, 1969 210; Indian Independence Act, 1947 and merger issue 215–16; and Manipur State Constitution Act 212–15; Shillong conspiracy 207–8

Manipur Praja Sangha (MPS) 65–6, 198

Manipur State Congress (MSC) 65–6, 68, 200–3

Manipur State Constitution Act (MSCA) 68, 165–6, 172, 212–15; absence of ratification 214; Article 1 212; Constitutional amendment 214; controversial nature 215; procedural lapses 213

Manipur State Durbar (MSD) members 38, 63, 165

Manipur State Meetei Marup (Manipur State Meetei Association) 218

Manipur under British Management 117

Manipur Zeliangrong Union in 1947 65

Meeteilon, richness of (Manipuri language) 95–6

Meeteis 30, 34–5, 38–9, 46, 63, 218–21

Meira Paibi movement 53

Meitei Chanu 97–8

Memorandum on States Treaties and Paramountcy 167, 175

Mera Haochongba (festival) 30–1

mercantilism and industrial capitalism 23

Merger Agreement 171, 208

Message of Islam 97

militarism in Japanese society 141

military revolution 136

Minute of 25 March 1833 152

MKS *see* Manipur Krishak Sabha (MKS)

modernisation, process of 88

Modern Manipur, politics, society and literature: advent of British imperialism 91; colonialism, responses and literature 92–3; literary conceptions: genre and subject matter 93–9; modern literary texts 91; post-World War II times and literature 99–102

modern 'secular State' 89

monolithic and extraterritorial power 147–51; agreement, Kabaw Valley 151; Anglo–Manipuri Mutual Defence Treaty 148–9; Anglo–Manipuri Treaty of 1833 150; *Chahi Taret Khuntakpa* (Seven Years' Devastation) 149; First Anglo–Burmese War 149; indirect rule in India 148; multiple reasons 148; Political Agent in Manipur in 1894 151; treaty system 148; use of term 'protected state' 150

'Mother Manipur,' recovery of 95

MPS *see* Manipur Praja Sangha (MPS)

MSC *see* Manipur State Congress (MSC)

MSCA *see* Manipur State Constitution Act (MSCA)

MSD *see* Manipur State Durbar (MSD) members

Musalman-i-Manipuri (1934–36) 97

Naga Hills expedition of 1879 57, 140

Naga National Council 69

'Nara Singh,' historical play 121, 139

INDEX

Nar Singh, Manipuri historical novels 99, 153–4
nativism 58–60, 76–7, 81–2, 88; abolition of exploitative systems 58–60; *Brahma Sabha* 60; controlling by coloniser 44; defeat in Anglo–Manipuri War of 1891 58; revivalism 87–8; society stratification 59; status of 43; system of *pothang* 59
Nazi *geopolitik* 136
negation, ethnicisation in Manipur 29; authority from folklore and myth 30; *Mera Haochongba* (festival) 30–1; notion of cultural ties 30–1; tradition based on legends and myths 30
'new imperialism' 42
'New Order in East Asia' 141
NHMM *see Nikhil Hindu Manipuri Mahasabha* (NHMM)
Nikhil Hindu Manipuri Mahasabha (NHMM) 61, 82–3, 98, 196–7
North East, contextualising: prospect of tea cultivation 17; subsistence farming, discouraged 18; Treaty of Yandaboo, 1826 18
North East India General Mission (NEIGM) 187
Nupi Lan (1939) 52–4, 97; AFSPA 53; famines of 1920 53; food scarcity and starvation 53; leadership of Manipuri women 52; *Meira Paibi* movement 53; nude protest 54; struggle for emancipation from all oppression 53; struggle of Irom Chanu Sharmila 54
Nupi Lan (Women's War) of 1904 92, 194–5

Offensive and Defensive Alliance of 1762 242–3
office of British Political Agency, establishment of 152
Operation 'U-Go' 143
organisational politics: abolition of temple allowances and Monarch's allowances 198; British India's 1920 notification 193; Chhatra Federation 198; Chinga session 197; 'divide and rule' policy 194; electioneering and alliances 202–3; English education

194; Kuki Rebellion of 1917 195; Lallup 195; Manipur Constitution Act 1947, 202; MKS 198; NHMM 196–7; organisations 203; penetration of INC 202; PMSD 200–1; Praja Sangha and Krishak Sabha 199–201; Sheikh Abdullah Divas Pallan 198; socio-political programme 199; tax structures 194
Orientalism 23, 44
orthodoxies or communalism 79

Palace Rebellion of 1891 57, 155
Pangals (Manipuri Muslim) 94, 97, 102
patta system in land ownership 58, 83
performative reflexivity 116
period of sanskritization 120
Phadibi Lila 125
Phagee Lila 119, 123–5, 127
phunganai (domestic slavery) 122
PMSD *see* President of the Manipur State Darbar (PMSD)
policy of conciliation 20–1
policy of defence and conciliation 19
policy of direct and distanced interference 19
policy of expansionism 141
Political Agents: activities of 153; in Manipur in 1894 151
political conditions: Anglo–Manipur relations 57–8; Burmese devastation (*Chahi TaretKhuntakpa*) 57; monopoly to Marvari traders 58; Palace Rebellion of 1891 57; Third Anglo–Burmese War 1885–86 57
political consciousness 60–5; Cart-tax Monopoly 64; Chinga Session 63; civilising mission 65; growth of organisations 65; Kuki Rebellion of 1917 60; *mangba* and *sengba* scandals 62; MSD members 63; NHMM 61; 1913 protest against taxation 60; publications and journalistic activities 61; refusal to perform *pothang* services 60; resolution number 11 63; Second Women's War 65; suppression of radical political formation 64; Women's War or *Nupi Lan* of 1939 64; Zeliangrong Movement 60–1

261

INDEX

political parties and movement 65–9; CMC 68; INC 66; Krishi Sanmelani 67; Manipur Constitution Act of 1947 69; MCA 68; MKS 65; MPS 65; MSC 66; Naga National Council 69; Praja Sangha, meetings 67; process of formation of MSC 68; PSP 69

positivism, strength of 99

post-Renaissance fabrication 17

post-World War II times and literature 99–102; cultural practices 101; *Eikhoigi Tada* (My Brother) 101–2; *Jahera* and *Laman*, novels 100–1; strength of positivism 99

pothang services 60, 92

power transfer 154–6

Praja Sangha 67, 199–201

Praja Shanti Party (PSP) 69, 203

Pravas Milan 119

President of the Manipur State Darbar (PMSD) 64, 68, 165, 200–1

print media houses 196

PSP *see* Praja Shanti Party (PSP)

Pulsiratki Pambei 97

*Puma*s (sacred texts), 218–19

Purvanchal Pradesh proposal 245

Rasa Lalas 78, 119

Rather Jatra 78

religious revivalism and colonial rule 76; Anglo–Manipuri War of 1891 76; British colonialism in Manipur 79–82; Burmese occupation and socio-religious life 77–9; Chahi Taret Khuntakpa 76; as cultural and religious reaction 76; dual government and politics of *mangba–sengba* 83–6; forms of resistance 77; maiba – maibi and Brahmins 75; Meitei faith and Hinduism 75; method of controlling people 75; nativism 76–7; revivalist resistance to religious hegemony 86–7; salai (clan) in Manipur 76; Sanamahi Movement 76; Sanskritization 76; socio-political context 76

resistance and colonialism 23–4; corrupt practices and extensive tax systems 24; employment for youth 24; encroachments upon habitations 23;

McMahon Line 24; mercantilism and industrial capitalism 23; refraining of Jaintias from eating potato 23

'resolution number 11' 63

revivalist movement: activities of Thokachanba Meetei 222; alternative imagined community 221–2; Brahmin hegemony 221; *Lom Eeyek* 223; movement for Manipuri language and *Kanglei* script 222–3; state-level conference on *Kanglei* script 223; transformation, society 221

revivalist resistance to religious hegemony 86–7; factors of Hinduisation 86; Sanamahi Movement 86; socio-political status 87; socio-religious movement 86–7

Revolt of 1857 in India 155

Revolutionary People's Front (RPF) 206, 210, 213

RPF *see* Revolutionary People's Front (RPF)

Rules for Administration 165

Rules for Management 164

Sajam Ihah, feature of 47

salai (clan) in Manipur 76

'Sanad State,' political status of Manipur: administration, British officers 163; British/GoI 163; political agent, executive and legislative powers 164; Rules for Management 164

Sanamahi Movement 76, 86; functional role 88–9; modern 'secular State' 89; native revivalism 87–8; process of Hinduisation and modernisation 88; religious revivalism and colonial rule 76; revivalist resistance to religious hegemony 86; socio-religious movement 87

Sanamahi 'revivalism,' process of 81

Sanamahism 11, 81, 88, 218, 222

Sanjenba 119

'Sanskritization' 76, 120

sap riangvaia 184–5

science and medicine 186–7

'Second Women's War' 65

Second World War 65–6, 97, 198; *see also* World War II

262

INDEX

Seidam Seireng, collection of poems 95, 98
sengtokpa (a purification rite) 83
Sheikh Abdullah Divas Pallan 198
Shillong conspiracy 207–8; appointment of Dewan 208; Dominion Agent, role of 207–8; Dominion Government 209; Merger Agreement, signing of 208; Standstill Agreement and Instrument of Accession 207
Shumang Lila 116, 121, 127–8
social welfare schemes 187
society stratification 59
socio-cultural aspect of people 78, 81–2; Brahminical domination 81–2; British colonisers 81; Hinduism and Meiteism 81; modernism, Hinduism and nativism 82; process of Hinduisation 81; process of Sanamahi 'revivalism' 81; revival of 218–20; rise of orthodoxy 81
socio-political programme 77–8, 199
socio-religious movement 86–7
Stage Lila 120–1, 127
Standstill Agreement 204; Memorandum on States' Treaties and Paramountcy 175; signing of 174; transfer of paramountcy 175
Standstill Agreement and Instrument of Accession 207
subsistence farming, discouraged 18

talangmalang, explanation 226
Tangkhul Long (Tangkhul Assembly) in 1919 65
Tangkhul New Testament in 1926 93
Tank battle 143–4
taxation systems 92; imposition of 188; on socio-religious grounds 84; structures 194
tea cultivation: prospect of 17; resistance to 19
Thadou Kukis 48; revolt of, causes 48–9; translation in 1928 93
Thengu Lila 126–7

Third Anglo–Burmese War of 1885–86 57, 139
Thokachanba's script and body politics: concept of *mangba–sengba* 231; enchantment of absolute humiliation 225; identity and ideology 225–6; incarnations of *Ama* 226–30; *Kangla,* importance 231; *Kangla* issue, impacts 232; language and scripts in revivalist movement 224; Maliyapham Palcha era 233; reinvention of Ayurveda 224; revivalism of cultural heritage 233; revival of traditional cultural practices 232–3; spiritual and temporal liberation 231–2; *talangmalang,* explanation 226
Thok Lila (con-trick play) 126–7
Thoubal Resistance of 1909 92, 195
Thougal Langal Marup (1954) 218
Tikendrajit, play 121
Tonu Laijing Lembi 97
Traditions of the Prophet 97
Treaty of Versailles 141
Treaty of Yandaboo 1826 8, 18, 79, 139, 149–50, 154, 160, 178, 242–3
tribal divisions, nature of 35–6

Udukhol 119
United National Liberation Front (UNLF) 206, 210

Vaipei National Organisation in 1944 65
violation of 'Inner Line' 21

Women's War or *Nupi Lan* of 1939 *see* Nupi Lan (1939)
World War II 100, 143–5; *see also* Second World War

Yakairol (1930) 61, 97, 165

Zeliangrong Council in 1947 65
Zeliangrong Movement 60–1, 70